The Lion Has Roared

The Lion Has Roared

Theological Themes in the Prophetic Literature of the Old Testament

EDITED BY
H. G. L. Peels and S. D. Snyman

☙PICKWICK *Publications* · Eugene, Oregon

THE LION HAS ROARED
Theological Themes in the Prophetic Literature of the Old Testament

Copyright © 2012 Wipf and Stock Publishers. All rights reserved. Except for brief quotations in critical publications or reviews, no part of this book may be reproduced in any manner without prior written permission from the publisher. Write: Permissions, Wipf and Stock Publishers, 199 W. 8th Ave., Suite 3, Eugene, OR 97401.

Pickwick Publications
An Imprint of Wipf and Stock Publishers
199 W. 8th Ave., Suite 3
Eugene, OR 97401

www.wipfandstock.com

ISBN 13: 978-1-61097-659-6

Cataloging-in-Publication data:

The lion has roared : theological themes in the prophetic literature of the Old Testament / edited by H. G. L. Peels and S. D. Snyman

xiv + 242 p. ; 23 cm. Includes bibliographical references and index.

ISBN 13: 978-1-61097-659-6

1. Bible. O.T. Prophets—Criticism and interpretations. 2. Bible. O.T.—Theology. 3. I. Peels, H. G. L. (Hendrik George Laurens), 1956– II. Snyman, S. D. III. Title.

BS1505.52 P43 2012

Manufactured in the U.S.A.

Contents

Preface | vii
—Eric Peels and Fanie Snyman
Introduction | ix
—Eric Peels and Fanie Snyman

Chapter 1: Prophets and Prophetic Literature | 1
—Gert Kwakkel

Eighth-Century Prophets

Chapter 2: Amos, Prophet of God's Justice | 17
—Fanie Snyman

Chapter 3: Hosea, Prophet of God's Love | 27
—Gert Kwakkel

Chapter 4: Isaiah, Prophet in the Service of the Holy One of Israel (Isa 1–39) | 40
—Jaap Dekker

Chapter 5: Micah, Prophet of Hope through Judgment | 65
—Gunnar Begerau

Seventh-Century Prophets

Chapter 6: Nahum, Prophet of the God Who Avenges Injustice | 79
—Dan Timmer

Chapter 7: Zephaniah, Prophet of the Day of Yhwh | 87
—Mart-Jan Paul

Chapter 8: Jeremiah, Prophet of Ultimate Ruin and New Hope | 96
—Eric Peels

Chapter 9: Habakkuk, Prophet of Comfort in God Alone | 119
—Michael Williams

Sixth-Century Prophets

Chapter 10: Ezekiel, Prophet of the Glory of the Lord | 127
—Herrie van Rooy

Chapter 11: Obadiah, Prophet of Retribution and Restoration | 149
—Douglas Green

Chapter 12: Isaiah, Prophet of the Lord Who Heals His People and Restores Their Land (Isa 40–66) | 156
—Hennie Kruger

Chapter 13: Haggai, Prophet of the New Temple | 175
—Herbert Klement

Chapter 14: Zachariah, Prophet of the King of Jerusalem and All the Earth | 183
—Wolter Rose

Fifth- to Second-Century (?) Prophets

Chapter 15: Malachi, Prophet Proclaiming the Lord in the Present, Past and Future | 197
—Fanie Snyman

Chapter 16: Jonah, Prophet Struggling with Yhwh's Mercy | 205
—Ron Bergey

Chapter 17: Joel, Prophet Proclaiming God's Future Judgment | 212
—Jin Soo Kim

Chapter 18: Daniel, Prophet of Divine Presence in Absence | 221
—Hans van Deventer

List of Contributors | 235
Scripture Index | 237

Preface

ONE OF THE MOST fascinating features of the Bible is the prophetic teaching and preaching about the ardent love and fierce wrath of Yhwh, the God of Israel, with regard to his chosen people and towards the nations of this world. In close touch with the religious developments and the socio-political circumstances of their day, the prophets proclaimed the word of Yhwh, sometimes even to the risk of their own life. Refusing to be God's instrument in his communication with the covenant people is not an option: "If I say, 'I will not mention him or speak any more in his name,' his word is in my heart like a fire, a fire shut up in my bones. I am weary of holding it in; indeed, I cannot" (Jer 20:9). In the course of six centuries, roughly speaking, the so-called Latter Prophets passed on the messages of their God to their people, in a wide spectrum of oracles of doom and salvation, using a variety of literary forms and stylistic devices. Their prophecies were collected, adapted, reinterpreted and later on edited in a way that can only be partially traced. Their message still stands out as a vibrant witness to the living word of God, applicable to our current time as well. Old Testament prophecy is an inexhaustible source of religious and theological inspiration that never runs dry, both for the academy, the church, and the practice of personal piety.

With pleasure we present this new volume on the prophetic theology of the Old Testament that reflects recent research on the Old Testament prophetic literature. The book aims to provide an overview of the core message and most important theological themes in each of the so-called Writing Prophets, including the book of Daniel. The prophetic books are arranged according to their respective time of origin as far as possible. Each chapter on a specific book covers the following topics and displays an overall structure consisting of: a) the historical setting of the book, b) the content and literary structure of the book, c) the core message and theological themes of the book, and d) a selected bibliography. The third part (c) constitutes the main body of each chapter. What is to be considered here is the important question of how God is revealed in the particular book. In other words, how is God presented in this prophetic book? What are the claims God made to his people or the nations in general? How does that fit the historical conditions of the time when the book came into being? Do the theological themes explored have any bearing on our current time?

These are important and exciting questions that can only be dealt with adequately in a "communion of saints". It was a challenge and a privilege to get together scholars from a wide range of evangelical and reformed institutes, and to invite them to contribute to this international project. They are attached to fourteen universities and theological training institutes in eight different countries far apart in four different continents (Africa, Asia, America, and Europe): Belgium, France, Germany, the Netherlands, South-Africa, South-Korea, Switzerland, and the United States of America. This global approach is what we believe makes this project unique. We hope this book will serve as a textbook for many who want to deepen and expand their understanding of the prophetic preaching of the Old Testament, both academics, students, pastors and lay people who have an interest in this part of Scripture, to the benefit of the theological academy and ecclesiastical life.

We wish to express our gratitude to Wipf & Stock Publishers for the cordial willingness to accept this manuscript in their Pickwick Publications imprint. We are also greatly indebted to Wouter Beinema and Henk de Waard, both attached to the Apeldoorn Theological University, for their technical skills in formatting and their endeavor in proofreading the text of this book. They deserve our heartfelt appreciation for the effort they put into the final stages of the publication of this book.

Eric Peels
Fanie Snyman
May 1st, 2012

Introduction

READING THE PROPHETIC BOOKS of the Old Testament is a fascinating experience. From the side of the academic study of the prophetic books, the interest never ceases. A constant flow of research papers and monographs published on the books that make up the prophetic literature of the Old Testament demonstrates the lasting theological and religious importance of this literary corpus. The way in which the prophetic books are appreciated in the church and believing community is always there and the way the prophetic literature is appropriated within public theology is seen again and again in public discourses.

In the garden of the United Nations headquarters in New York City stands a bronze statue called *Let Us Beat Swords into Plowshares*, representing the figure of a man hammering a sword into the shape of a plowshare. This impressive work of art portrays the human wish to end all wars by converting the weapons of death and destruction into peaceful and productive tools that are more beneficial to humankind. It was sculpted by Evgeniy Vuchetich, and donated by the Soviet Union to the United Nations in 1959. This sculpture was inspired by the well-known biblical text: "They will beat their swords into ploughshares and their spears into pruning hooks. Nation will not take up sword against nation, nor will they train for war any more" (Isa 2:4; Mic 4:3). That a text from the prophetic literature serves as a motto to inspire the United Nations to promote and establish world peace is a testimony in itself for the enduring value of this part of the canon of the Bible.

This book deals with the main theological themes of the Old Testament Writing or Latter Prophets. They are called "Writing Prophets" in distinction to their precursors (e.g., Samuel, Nathan, Elijah, and Elisha), who didn't leave us any written testimonies. They are also called "Latter Prophets," in distinction to the so-called Former Prophets in the Old

Introduction

Testament canon (the historiographical books of Joshua, Judges, 1 and 2 Samuel, and 1 and 2 Kings). The prophetical books are dealt with in separate chapters: Isaiah (1–39 and 40–66), Jeremiah, Ezekiel, and the twelve books of the Minor Prophets. Although strictly speaking the book of Daniel is not among the Latter Prophets—it belongs to the *ketuvim* ("Writings," the third part of the Jewish canon, whereas the *neviim* ("Prophets") form the second part of this canon)—we included a chapter on this book for the very reason that Daniel is considered a prophetic book *par excellence* by many, not the least by the authors of the New Testament. Starting with a general introduction in chapter 1 "Prophets and Prophetic Literature," the other chapters are arranged in a rough historical order, according to the supposed time of first appearance of the prophet at stake, or the putative date of the book itself. It goes without saying that this order is debatable, since historical precision is in most cases unattainable.

The title of this study is taken from Amos 1:2 (but cf. also Joel 3:16), where at the very beginning of the book the speaking of Yhwh is likened to a lion that roars. Amos is the first of the writing prophets proclaiming the word of Yhwh, and therefore we thought the phrase apt as a title for a book on the prophetic literature—to make one realize whose words are spoken. To hear a lion roar in the African wild is an awesome experience. When a lion roars the thundering sound can be heard within a radius of five to eight kilometers, and when it happens the rest of the wild simply falls to silence. The presence of the lion is felt long after the roaring ceased. A lion roars mainly to claim his territory and to establish his power to reign in that particular part of the wild beyond questioning. Every one (including possible intruding lions from elsewhere!) must realize the power and control the dominant lion has in that specific area. The image of a lion roaring is thus very appropriate to make people aware who is actually speaking in the book of Amos.

The prophetic message of the Old Testament is first and foremost a theological message revealing God and proclaiming his will. The very word "prophet" in Greek has the notion of someone delivering a message from the gods to human beings. Prophets were seen as messengers from God. The only responsibility they have is to deliver a message received from God. The so-called messenger formula ("This is what Yhwh says . . .") so often found in these books is another indication of how serious the theological message of the prophets should be taken. Although not every prophetic book mentions the calling of the prophet to proclaim

Introduction

Yhwh's message to his people, the calling narratives we do have also show that the message of the prophets is first and foremost understood as a theological message and not just the personal opinion of a particular individual.

The prophetic literature is marked by unity and diversity. On the one hand there is an undeniable unity to be detected when reading through the prophets. They speak of the same history, the great acts of judgment and redemption in this history, they testify to the same God, Yhwh, who is time and again willing to enter yet again in a conversation with his people Israel via the prophets. It is remarkable that in the course of so many years there was a certain measure of consistency in speaking the word of Yhwh.

On the other hand there is a huge diversity to be seen in the prophetic books. Every prophetic book bears its own identity, none is simply copying or repeating the message of another prophetic book. Also the fact that the different prophetic books bear the name of individuals is a testimony to the uniqueness and individuality of each prophetic book. Although little can be gained from the prophetic books pertaining to the respective personalities displayed by the different prophets, it is clear that each prophetic book has its own and unique characteristics. A variety of metaphors, language styles, poetic devices and images were employed to proclaim the prophetic words they have to utter. A rich variety of literary forms was used to bring home their messages. These known literary forms were used in new and creative ways. There is also huge diversity in the way in which prophets received the message they have to proclaim. In fact, little can be said with confidence on how the messages of the prophet have exactly been communicated to them by God.

Even more important than these unique characteristics of the prophetic books are the audiences they addressed and the time at which they delivered their prophecies. Some of the prophecies were directed to Israel, others to Judah, or even to foreign nations. The prophets cover the years between roughly speaking 750–150 BCE (including the book of Daniel). For a period of almost 600 years the prophetic word guided the people of God through times of tribulation. Within that period of time major historical events took place. The Northern Kingdom Israel ceased to exist, the Southern Kingdom Judah went into exile but returned to the land. Political and military power switched from the Assyrian to the Babylonian to the Persian empires and even beyond in the case of the book of Daniel. The kingdom of David, supposed to be an everlasting kingdom, was no more after the Babylonian exile and consequently the priests were in a position of becoming more and more important in the Persian province Yehud.

The message of the prophets is concrete, actual and very much life related. It addresses the life situation of everyday people. This life-relatedness of the prophetic message can be seen in especially three areas. Firstly, the prophets addressed the moral conduct of people. Where there is a disregard for fellow human beings that is apparent in the maltreatment of especially the weak and vulnerable in society, the prophets did not hesitate to speak out against such malpractices. Secondly, the prophets also addressed the cultic worship of the people. Yhwh demands to be worshipped in the correct way and especially he demands to be worshipped as the one and only God. When that did not happen the prophets were obliged to unmask superficial religious practices that do not really honor Yhwh. Cultic worship without true devotion and dedication of daily life to Yhwh is worthless and to be condemned. Thirdly, the message of the prophets has also social-political and international implications, as is apparent in the oracles against the foreign nations. Yhwh is not a local god interested only in his people living in the land he granted to them. He is the universal God to whom the practices and wrongdoings of foreign nations do not go by unnoticed. Therefore, the prophets on numerous occasions addressed foreign nations.

The prophetic literature reveals a perspective from the past to the present and eventually to the future. The past served as a rich deposit of God's great acts in the history of his people. The prophets are firmly rooted in the Torah and in covenant theology. Because of what God did in the past, one can expect new acts of salvation in the present and future. Traditions from the past were appropriated and applied in new ways, illustrating the enduring value of these traditions in contemporary times. Concerning the present the people are reminded that they live *coram Deo*, in the presence of the Lord who entered into a covenant relationship with them and that therefore they should live an ethically sound life rooted in the revealed will of Yhwh, the covenant God. Concerning the future the prophetical message is that either salvation or doom awaits the people. The doom and destruction predicted, with sometimes terrifying and even horrible images, must be understood as a final call for repentance before the destruction becomes inevitable. On the other hand, the people may look forward to salvation in future where the injustices and suffering of the present time will be surpassed by eschatological blessings

Introduction

of a future time. Past, present, and future are comprehended in the ultimate prophetic witness about and from Y<small>HWH</small> who seeks his people who doesn't seek him.

Given the prominence of the prophetic literature and the prophets in the Old Testament it is no surprise that in New Testament times Jesus Christ was also thought of as a prophet, a bearer of the word of God. He was acclaimed as a prophet by many who witnessed his miracles and listened to his teaching. People recognized him as Elijah, Jeremiah or one of the prophets (Mark 6:15; 8:28; John 9:17). In Luke 4:24 it seems as if Jesus accepts the role of a prophet after he read a part from the book of Isaiah (61:1–2) in the synagogue in the town of Nazareth: "No prophet is accepted in his home town." John the Baptist was identified by Jesus as the expected Elijah (Matt 11:7–15) to serve as a forerunner to his own ministry where he proclaimed the coming of the kingdom. When Jesus entered Jerusalem and the people enquired about who this man was, the crowds answered, "This is Jesus, the prophet from Nazareth in Galilee" (Matt 21:11). According to Luke 24:19 it seems clear that the disciples of Jesus regarded him as a prophet. The way in which Jesus called upon people to repent, coupled with his words on deliverance and judgment, serves as a vivid reminder of the prophets in Old Testament times. Both the apostle Peter and Stephen pointed at Jesus as *the* Prophet who was to come (Acts 3:22; 7:37; cf. Deut 18). At the same time, Jesus by far surpasses the Old Testament prophets (Matt 12:41), fulfilling their prophecies (Luke 24:44; 2 Cor 1:20). The exalted Christ is the source and essence of all true prophecy (Rev 19:10).

The prophetic literature is part of the canon of Scriptures. This means that the prophetic literature is at the same time inspired and inspiring literature to read and to ponder. Being part of the canon of Scriptures the church regards it as authoritative word of God inspired by the Spirit. At the same time it is also inspiring literature to read about what a world may look like when God's will is adhered to and realized in the real world of ordinary human beings.

Chapter 1

Prophets and Prophetic Literature

Evidently, the prophets are among the most enigmatic characters in the Old Testament. This chapter intends to shed light on their identity and activities. The topics that will be discussed are the Hebrew terms used to denote the prophets, the tasks performed by the prophets, the contents and the reception of their messages, and their relationship to other persons who claimed the gift of prophecy. The chapter concludes with a short discussion of the process that led to the production of the prophetic books, which can now be found in the Old Testament canon.

Hebrew Terms

The English word "prophet" is a loan word from Greek. In Greek προφήτης denotes, roughly speaking, a person who passes or declares the will of the gods to humans. The Septuagint uses the word to translate the Hebrew נָבִיא, which occurs more than 300 times in the Old Testament. Thus, προφήτης found its way to the New Testament and to the vocabulary of the Christian church and theology.

According to 1 Samuel 9:9, the נביא was formerly called רֹאֶה "seer." Most occurrences of this term are found in Chronicles, where it refers to Samuel (see, e.g., 1 Chr 9:22) and to Hanani (2 Chr 16:7, 10). In Isaiah 30:10 it is paralleled by חֹזֶה. חזה is used somewhat more frequently than ראה, also mostly in Chronicles. As a synonym to ראה it is likewise commonly translated as "seer" in English. Another term, which is used for, among others, Elijah, Elisha, and the anonymous prophet from Judah in 1 Kings 13, is אִישׁ הָאֱלֹהִים "man of God."

Both "seer" and "man of God" reveal some aspects of the prophetic office. Obviously, "seer" refers to the prophets as persons who had the gift of seeing things that the average Israelite was not able to see, such as visions. "Man of God" makes it clear that they had a special relationship to God or represented him to others. Unlike these terms, נביא is opaque. Since its etymology is disputed this does not reveal anything certain about the meaning of the noun or the function of those it denotes. Consequently, the identity and task of the persons called נְבִיאִים "prophets" must be inferred from contextual data.

Commission

The Hebrew word נביא "prophet" occurs for the first time in Genesis 20:7. In this text God orders King Abimelech to return Sarah to Abraham. He goes on to say: "for he is a prophet, and he will pray for you and you will live." The fact that God calls Abraham a prophet may be related to his being God's intimate, for whom God did not want to hide his plans (cf. Gen 18:17–19). As such, Abraham was under God's special protection. However, the expression "for he is a prophet" may also be connected with what follows in Genesis 20:7; that is, Abraham's intercession on behalf of Abimelech. Well-known prophets such as Samuel, Elisha, Isaiah, and Jeremiah likewise prayed for other people (see 1 Sam 12:19, 23; 2 Kgs 4:33; 19:2–4; Jer 42:2–4). Accordingly, intercession was part of the prophetic ministry.

The next text in which נביא "prophet" is found is Exodus 7:1: "Then the Lord said to Moses, 'See, I have made you like God to Pharaoh, and your brother Aaron will be your prophet.'" This statement relates to Moses' complaint in Exodus 4:10 that he was not a good speaker. God had solved this problem by designating Moses' eloquent brother Aaron as his spokesman. Aaron would serve as Moses' mouth and Moses would be as God to his brother (Exod 4:11–16). These texts show that the relationship between God and a prophet is analogous to the relationship between a person and his spokesman. A prophet served as God's mouthpiece.

This function is also reflected in the formula by which several prophets introduced their words to the people: "This is what the Lord says." A similar formula was used by messengers sent by kings to another king or to their subjects (see 1 Kgs 20:1–5; 22:27; 2 Kgs 1:11). In short, prophets were messengers, who brought the words of God to their fellow men.

According to Deuteronomy 18:15-18, the people of Israel themselves had wished that God would not continue to speak to them directly, as he had done at Horeb. They preferred that he would address them by means of a person from among them, like Moses. God granted this request by appointing Moses as his prophet. In the future, he would act in the same vein by sending prophets, who were able to speak his words, because God himself put them in their mouths (cf. also Jer 1:9).

The first female prophet mentioned in the Bible is Miriam, Moses' sister (Exod 15:20). In Numbers 12:2 she and her brother Aaron assert that the Lord has spoken through them, just as through Moses. This may be the reason why she is called a prophetess. Exodus 15:20-21, however, says that "Miriam the prophetess" led the women of Israel in playing the tambourine, dancing, and singing in honor of God. Similarly, Chronicles describes how prophets or seers were involved in singing, playing musical instruments, and organizing temple worship (see, e.g., 1 Chr 16:41-42; 25:1; 2 Chr 29:30; cf. also the band of prophets in 1 Sam 10:5). Besides, Chronicles says that some prophets wrote the records of the kingdom (cf., e.g., 1 Chr 29:29; 2 Chr 9:29; 12:15; 26:22).

This overview shows that the prophets fulfilled a variety of functions. Yet it is beyond doubt that their main task was to pass the word of God to the people. In this respect, the picture evoked by the historical books fully agrees with what is found in the books of Isaiah up to Malachi.

In a number of cases, prophets seem to have enjoyed an official status as servants of the king. This applies especially to Gad, "David's seer," and Heman, "the king's seer" (2 Sam 24:11; 1 Chr 25:5). According to 1 Kings 22:6, 22-23, King Ahab had no less than four hundred prophets. In addition, prophets may also have been members of the temple staff, but this is less certain.

A special element in the stories about Elijah and Elisha in the books of Kings is that they frequently refer to "the sons of the prophets" (KJV) or "the company of the prophets" (NIV). Perhaps the Hebrew expression, which is translated more literally in the KJV, relates to students instructed and trained by Elijah and Elisha. In any case, these men shared Elijah's and Elisha's conviction that the Israelites should worship YHWH and no other god. The books of Kings describe twice how a member of the company of the prophets passed the word of God to other people (1 Kgs 20:35-42; 2 Kgs 9:1-10). Apart from that, however, the stories do not present clear indications as to their functions.

Except from Kings, the term "son of a prophet" only occurs in Amos 7:14. In this text, Amos remarkably denies that he is a prophet or a prophet's son. The point that he wanted to make was that for him acting as a prophet was not a kind of job by which he earned his living, as Amaziah the priest had suggested (see Amos 7:12). He preached his prophetic words only because Yhwh had called him to do so (Amos 7:15; cf. also Smith, 1995: 139–40). Obviously, Amos here formulates a principle that was on the heart of all true prophets. Although some of them may have performed the prophetic ministry as if it were their profession, all of them were convinced that Yhwh's calling was the only decisive factor that made them prophets. This calling, moreover, enabled them to act as independent persons. They did not say what the kings wanted them to say, but dared to confront them with unpleasing messages (see, e.g., 1 Kgs 14:6–16; 18:16–18; 2 Kgs 20:14–18; 2 Chr 12:5; Jer 21; 38:14–23).

Prophecy and Foretelling

The most essential function of the prophets was to transmit messages from God to the people. Popular usage of the terms "prophet" and "prophetic" connotes the idea that prophetic messages mainly concern the future. Does this also hold for the prophets of Old Testament times?

At first sight, the idea that prophets were foretellers seems to be confirmed by Deuteronomy 18:9–22, for this pericope presents the activity of a prophet as the alternative that God would give instead of the Canaanite practice of consulting diviners, interpreters of omens, mediums, and spiritists. The Israelites did not need to have recourse to sorcery or divination, because Yhwh would raise up a prophet for them.

In the subsequent historical books, prophets sometimes transmit oracles similar to those the Canaanites tried to obtain through their diviners (see 1 Sam 9:6–10; 22:5). Yet it seems doubtful that this aspect of the prophetic task was at the heart of Moses' intention in Deuteronomy 18. In this text Moses presents the prophets as his own successors in the ministry of speaking God's word to the people. Moses, however, only rarely foretold future events (see, e.g., Deut 31:29; 32). Ever since God had accepted Israel's wish that he would not speak to them directly any more and appointed Moses as intermediary, Moses' prophetic words mainly consisted of divine commandments and instructions.

The Old Testament does not present much information about the activities of prophets in the first centuries after Moses' death. Therefore it is hard to say whether prophetic words of those days mainly were divine commandments and instructions or not. The state of affairs changes in the era of the divided monarchy. From the appearance of Elijah and Elisha in the ninth century BCE onward, prophets played an important part in Israelite society. All collections of prophetic words such as the books of Isaiah and Jeremiah date from the eighth century or later. At the same time, prophecy got a sharper profile in regard to its content. Incidentally, former prophets had already charged the people with unfaithfulness vis-à-vis YHWH (see esp. Judg 6:7–10; cf. also 1 Sam 2:27–36; 2 Sam 12:1–12), but beginning with Elijah that became the most conspicuous element of their messages.

Accordingly, the prophets did not just reveal what would happen in the future. To be sure, announcing the interventions by which God would respond to his people's unfaithfulness was an important aspect of their preaching. Yet this was always closely connected to an analysis of the people's behavior in the present and a reminder of all the blessings God had given in the past (see, e.g., Ezek 20). Furthermore, the prophets gave concrete instructions as to the way of life required by God (see, e.g., Amos 5:14–15). Particularly in this part of their work the prophets show similarity to Moses' prophetic ministry. This does not mean, however, that all of them frequently quote from or refer to Mosaic revelation. References to the laws of the Pentateuch or the Sinaitic covenant can often be found in later prophets; for example, in Jeremiah and Ezekiel. In the books of Amos, Hosea, and Isaiah the relationship with Moses' laws mainly pertains to allusions and similarity in substance.

In short, the prophets spoke about the future, but no less about the past and the present. It is true, the New Testament highlights the foretelling elements of Old Testament prophecy, but this is because Jesus and the apostles wanted to point out the fulfillment of the words of the prophets in their own days. Therefore it is only natural that they concentrated on prophetic announcements for the future, and not on words about the past or the present.

A final comment is in order regarding the nature of prophetic announcements about future acts of God. According to Deuteronomy 18:21–22, the hallmark of a prophetic message that really comes from YHWH is that it takes place or comes true. Nevertheless, this does not imply that prophetic announcements are a sort of blueprints of things to come, which will always be realized in a way that corresponds exactly to the wording. The story of Jonah nicely illustrates this point. Jonah's prophetic message evidently was an announcement about the near future. It even mentioned a fixed date: "Forty more days and Nineveh will be overturned" (Jonah 3:4). The story does not tell that the prophet added: ". . . unless you be converted to the Lord." Jonah longed for the city's destruction and therefore it seems very improbable that he ever referred to the possibility that God's judgment would be revoked. Unexpectedly, however, the Ninevites were converted and the city was saved.

Although Jonah's announcement was a prophecy that really came from Yhwh, it did not come true. Yet the aim of the prophecy was reached, because the Ninevites responded to the prophetic words in a way that fully agreed with God's intentions. This reveals an important feature of prophetic announcements; namely, that God used them to appeal to the hearts of those who heard them. In other words, they functioned in the context of lively communication. Accordingly, the way in which they came true may have depended on the response of those addressed (cf. also Jer 18:7–10). In this respect they share the nature of God's covenantal promises. The fulfillment of God's promises was also related to the reaction of those that received them. Nevertheless, this did not alter the fact that they were perfectly reliable.

Reception of Prophetic Messages

As God's spokesmen to human beings, the prophets depended on God for receiving their messages. This can be seen very clearly in the story of God's promise to David in 2 Samuel 7. When David informed Nathan that in his view the ark of God should not remain in a tent, the prophet spontaneously responded that David could do what he had in mind. Some hours later, God spoke to Nathan, corrected the prophet's initial support for David's plans, and sent him back to the king with an opposite message.

Another case in point is the confrontation between Jeremiah and the false prophet Hananiah in Jeremiah 28. After Hananiah had denied the trustworthiness of Jeremiah's prophecies, Jeremiah had to wait shortly before he received the word of God that could be addressed to Hananiah. Another time, he had to wait even ten days before the word of Yhwh came to him (Jer 42:7). Yet such waiting did not always imply total passivity, as can be gathered from, for example, 2 Kings 3:11-19. When the kings of Israel, Judah, and Edom came to Elisha in order to get a prophetic message, Elisha asked for a harpist. This was effective, for the hand of Yhwh indeed came upon Elisha while the harpist was playing.

The Old Testament does not present much information about the various ways in which God transmitted his words to the prophets. In Numbers 12:6 God says that normally he revealed himself to the prophets through visions and dreams. He distinguishes these usual means of revelation from the special way in which he communicated with his intimate servant Moses: "With him I speak face to face, clearly and not in riddles; he sees the form of the Lord" (Num 12:8; cf. also Deut 34:10).

Several prophetic texts describe how God indeed made use of visions to communicate his revelation to the prophets (see, e.g., Amos 7:1-9; 8:1-3; Zech 1-6). As for dreams, God uses them in some well-known stories such as those of Jacob's dream in Bethel (Gen 28:10-19), Solomon's dream in Gibeon (1 Kgs 3:5-15), and the dreams of King Nebuchadnezzar in Daniel 2 and 4. These dreams, however, were not received by prophets. Actually, apart from Numbers 12:6, Joel 2:28[3:1] is the only other text that explicitly refers to dreams as a means of prophetic revelation. Some other texts relate that God spoke to a prophet at night, but they do not specify that he did so in a dream (viz. 1 Sam 3; 15:10-11; 2 Sam 7:4). Furthermore, Daniel had a dream according to Daniel 7:1, but Daniel is never called a prophet in the Old Testament.

Jeremiah 23:25-32 may even suggest that appealing to dreams was characteristic of false prophets and that Yhwh dissociated himself from this practice. Be that as it may, in spite of their dreams the false prophets certainly could not pretend that they had stood in God's council. This statement (found in Jer 23:18, 22) suggests that admittance to God's council was the privilege of the true prophets. God allowed them to be involved in his heavenly deliberations and let them into his secrets. This agrees with Amos 3:7, where God says: "Surely the Sovereign Lord does nothing without revealing his plan to his servants the prophets" (note that "plan" is the translation of Hebrew סוד, which is translated by "council" in Jer 23:18, 22).

These passages in Jeremiah 23 and Amos 3 show that the Old Testament is much more explicit about the *effect* of prophetic revelation than about its *means*. Apart from dreams and visions, God may have used several other vehicles of revelation, including the prophets' personal thinking about God's intentions and former revelations. The personal involvement of the prophets in the process of revelation could account for their own specific style and interests, which can be detected in the prophetic books. It may also explain why one sometimes gets the impression that they quote the words of other prophets, a phenomenon that can be noticed in the prophecies to foreign nations in particular (see, e.g., Isa 16:6 and Jer 48:29; Jer 49:16 and Obad 4). Nevertheless, what counts is not the form of revelation, but the fact. However the prophets were involved in shaping their messages, they were totally convinced that they did not pronounce their own words and ideas, but only those of God himself (see, e.g., 1 Kgs 22:14).

Other Prophets

A true prophet is sent by God and only preaches the message that God has put in his mouth. However, other persons also claimed a divine commission to speak to the people. The previous section has already made mention of false prophets, who had not received a revelation from Yhwh and had not been sent by him. Apart from them, there were also prophets who spoke in the name of other gods. In 1 Kings 18:19, for example, Elijah refers to four hundred and fifty prophets of Baal and four hundred prophets of Asherah, who apparently were employed by King Ahab and his wife Jezebel (cf. also Deut 13:2–3; 2 Kgs 10:19).

Prophets were active not only in Israel, but also in other countries of the Ancient Near East. In Jeremiah 27, Yhwh orders Jeremiah to send word to the kings of Edom, Moab, Ammon, Tyre, and Sidon. Among other things, Jeremiah must exhort the kings not to listen to their prophets, diviners, interpreters of dreams, mediums, or sorcerers (Jer 27:9). In addition to the presence of prophets in those countries, this text points to the fact that prophets could be bracketed with other persons that predicted the future, such as diviners and mediums. This ties in with Deuteronomy 18:9–15, where Moses describes the prophetic office as the alternative that God gave to his people instead of diviners, interpreters of omens and the like (cf. also Jer 29:8).

Old texts recovered by archaeological research reveal that the prediction of future events was a widely spread phenomenon in the ancient Near East. There were several categories of foretellers, who got their information through different means. The main distinction that must be made relates to technical versus intuitive divination. Those making use of technical divination took their insights from the observation of spontaneous or organized events, for example, miscarriage or consulting the liver of a sheep. Intuitive diviners received their predictions in a more direct way, through dreams, visions or inspiration.

Obviously, prophets belonged to the category of intuitive diviners. Apart from that, distinguishing prophets from other persons who foretold the future is not an easy task. Etymological similarity between the Hebrew word נביא "prophet" and its cognates in other Semitic languages does not yield a clue. Consequently, the only way to identify the colleagues of the Israelite prophets is to define as sharply as possible which activities can be considered prophecy. Huffmon has presented a helpful definition. He understands prophecy as "inspired speech at the initiative of a divine power, speech which is clear in itself and commonly directed to a third party" (Huffmon, 1995: 477).

If this definition is applied to the texts, the most important evidence for prophetic actions is found in letters from Mari (situated on the Middle Euphrates) dating to the eighteenth century BCE and in the so-called Neo-Assyrian prophecies from the seventh century BCE. Another famous example is the Egyptian story of the journey of Wen-Amon to Byblos (eleventh century BCE), which refers to an ecstatic delivering an oracle. All these prophecies occurred in the context of the royal court. In this respect, they differ from the prophecies recorded in the Old Testament, which often had a wider audience. The difference, however, may be related to the coincidences of the rediscovery of ancient texts.

This short overview of the evidence from the ancient Near East may suffice to show that the true prophets of Yhwh had many competitors. For the Israelites, it was far from self-evident that they would listen to them and not to others. When they had made the choice of faith to dissociate themselves from men or women prophesying in the name of other gods, they still had to find out which prophets among those that spoke in the name of Yhwh were really sent by him. According to Deuteronomy 18:22, a false prophet betrays himself in that his words do not come true, but this criterion did not help much so long as the imaginary moment of fulfillment had not yet arrived. In the meantime, the only thing the Israelites could do was to compare new prophecies with former authenticated revelation (for some examples, see Deut. 13:1–3; Jer. 28:7–9). This surely required the gift of spiritual discernment.

Prophetic Books

Many of the revelations received by the true prophets of YHWH have been kept in the books of Isaiah, Jeremiah, Ezekiel, and the Twelve Minor Prophets (one could add Daniel, although it does not belong to the prophetic books in the Hebrew Bible). How did these books come into being? Did the prophets compose them themselves?

Some prophets were certainly active as writers. As has already been mentioned, Chronicles tells that prophets kept the records of the kingdom. In Jewish tradition, the books of Joshua, Judges, Samuel, and Kings are called the Former Prophets, which reflects the idea that they have been written by prophets. Furthermore, just as Moses wrote down the precepts YHWH had given him on Mount Sinai, Ezekiel recorded the design, laws, and regulations of the new temple (see Exod 24:4; Ezek 43:11).

For the prophets, however, writing was not the usual way to communicate their messages. Instead, they used to pass on their revelations orally. They were speakers rather than writers (see, e.g., 1 Kgs 17:1; 21:17–27; Isa 7:3–9; Jer 7:1–15; 26:2–7; Ezek 24:18; Amos 7:10–17; Jonah 3:1–4; Hag 2:1–9; Zech 7:4–7). When they made use of writing, it mostly had a special purpose. Habakkuk had, for example, to write a prophetic message on a tablet, so that many people could read it (Hab 2:2; cf. also Isa 8:1). Occasionally, prophets wrote letters, because this was probably the only way in which they could contact the addressed. Thus King Jehoram of Judah received a letter from Elijah (2 Chr 21:12) and Jeremiah sent letters to the exiled in Babylon (Jer 29; cf. also Jer 51:60–64).

These examples do not shed light on the question how and why the books of the prophets were written. Most information about this issue comes from Jeremiah 36. In this chapter, YHWH orders Jeremiah to write on a scroll all the words he has spoken to him since the beginning of Jeremiah's ministry until that time (i.e. the fourth year of King Jehoiakim). Jeremiah then dictates the words of YHWH to Baruch the scribe. After King Jehoiakim has burned the scroll, Baruch prepares another scroll, on which he writes the same words. Jeremiah 36 closes with the comment that "many similar words were added to them."

It is hard to be sure about the exact relationship between the present book of Jeremiah and Baruch's scroll. Nevertheless, Baruch's ever growing collection of Jeremiah's words most probably laid the foundation of the book. As for the reason for writing down the prophetic words, Jeremiah 36:3 reveals that according to YHWH's expectation this might help the people to turn from their wicked way, so that he could forgive their sins. The collection of so many words spoken over the years would perhaps bring about their conversion, which Jeremiah's separate speeches had failed to bring about.

Isaiah 30:8 mentions another reason for writing down prophetic words, namely, that thus they might become an everlasting witness for the days to come. The people, who refused to listen at that time, could be convinced of the trustworthiness of Isaiah's prophecies in later days, when his words had come true. Jeremiah 31:1–3 likewise suggests future verification as the reason why prophecy had to be kept in writing (cf. also Dan 12:4). If, however, the scrolls could be used to show that the prophets were right, people could also appeal to them in order to remind God of prophecies that still had to be fulfilled. This is precisely what Daniel did with the written words of Jeremiah according to Daniel 9.

Evidently, remembrance and the possibility of later use were the main purposes for which the words of the prophets were collected in books. It is often assumed that the process of collecting and writing down was greatly stimulated by the Babylonian exile, because then the true prophets of Yhwh, who had often met with obstinacy in their own days, were finally vindicated by the facts. If that is correct, the books were not composed by the prophets themselves, but by later editors. In this connection, one could also point to the headings of the books, which refer to the prophets in the third person singular (the only exception is Ezekiel, which is in the first person singular right from the beginning).

As texts resulting from a process of collecting and editing, the books of the prophets give evidence of much variety. Some of them only hold collections of prophetic words (e.g., Obadiah, Micah, Zephaniah), while others combine sets of oracles with stories about events that happened in the lives of the prophets (e.g., Isaiah, Jeremiah, Hosea, Amos). Jonah is exceptional in that the whole book is a story about the prophet and his experiences.

The structure of the books and the order in which the prophetic words are presented are also diverse. Ezekiel has a clear structure and mainly follows a chronological order. In this respect Jeremiah is different. Neither the stories about the prophet nor the records of his prophetic messages reflect the chronology of his life. In several prophetic books oracles are provided with dates, which help the reader to connect them with a specific phase of the history of Israel. Conversely, Joel, Obadiah, Jonah, Nahum, Habakkuk, and Malachi do not give any explicit information about the time in which the prophet received his revelations. In Hosea the only indication can be found in 1:1-2, whereas the rest of the book never mentions the date of a prophecy.

The editors certainly felt free to add headings and similar useful information to the books. Many scholars assume that they also took the opportunity to bring the prophecies up to date, but the extent to which they may have done so is disputed.

A final comment must be made with respect to the canonical order of the books of the prophets. The order followed in most modern Bible translations roughly corresponds to the Hebrew manuscripts. In the Septuagint, however, the Twelve Minor Prophets precede Isaiah, Jeremiah, Ezekiel, and Daniel. Furthermore, the Minor Prophets, which are treated as one book in the Jewish tradition, are presented in a different order. The canonical shaping and ordering of the books is a field of research which has only recently been opened. It will probably yield interesting insights in the future.

This chapter has certainly not resolved all enigmas around the prophets of the Old Testament. In several respects, these people seem to come from another world. This, however, was related to their main function: they were enabled to bring God's heavenly word to people on earth. Thus their presence and work foreshadowed the greatest miracle of all times: the word of God's love incarnate in his Son Jesus Christ.

Bibliography

Day, John, editor. *Prophecy and Prophets in Ancient Israel: Proceedings of the Oxford Old Testament Seminar*. Library of Hebrew Bible / Old Testament Studies 531. New York: Clark, 2010.

Gordon, Robert P., editor. *"The Place Is Too Small for Us": The Israelite Prophets in Recent Scholarship*. Sources for Biblical and Theological Study 5. Winona Lake, IN: Eisenbrauns, 1995.

Huffmon, H. B., et al. "Prophecy." In *The Anchor Bible Dictionary*, edited by David Noel Freedman, 5:477–502. New York: Doubleday, 1992.

Kaltner, John, and Louis Stulman, editors. *Inspired Speech: Prophecy in the Ancient Near East: Essays in Honor of Herbert B. Huffmon*. Journal for the Study of the Old Testament Supplement Series 378. London: T. & T. Clark, 2004.

Koch, Klaus. *Die Profeten*. Volume 1: Assyrische Zeit. Urban-Taschenbücher 280. 3rd ed. Stuttgart: Kohlhammer, 1995. Volume 2: Babylonisch-persische Zeit. Urban-Taschenbücher 281. 2nd ed. Stuttgart: Kohlhammer, 1988. English Translation: *The Prophets*. Two volumes. Philadelphia: Fortress, 1983–84.

Kwakkel, G., editor. *Wonderlijk gewoon: Profeten en profetie in het Oude Testament*. TU-Bezinningsreeks 3. Barneveld, the Netherlands: De Vuurbaak, 2003.

Meier, Samuel A. *Themes and Transformations in Old Testament Prophecy*. Downers Grove, IL: InterVarsity, 2009.

Parpola, Simo. *Assyrian Prophecies*. State Archives of Assyria 9. Helsinki: Helsinki University Press, 1997.

Seitz, Christopher R. *Prophecy and Hermeneutics: Toward a New Introduction to the Prophets*. Studies in Theological Interpretation. Grand Rapids: Baker Academic, 2007.

Smith, Billy K., and Frank S. Page. *Amos Obadiah Jonah*. The New American Commentary 19B. Nashville, TN: Broadman & Holman, 1995.

VanGemeren, Willem A. *Interpreting the Prophetic Word: An Introduction to the Prophetic Literature of the Old Testament*. Grand Rapids: Zondervan, 1990.

Watts, James W., and Paul R. House, editors. *Forming Prophetic Literature: Essays on Isaiah and the Twelve in Honor of John D. W. Watts*. Journal for the Study of the Old Testament Supplement Series 235. Sheffield, UK: Sheffield Academic Press, 1996.

Westermann, Claus. *Grundformen prophetischer Rede*. Beiträge zur evangelischen Theologie 31. Munich: Kaiser, 1960. English translation: *Basic Forms of Prophetic Speech*. London: Lutterworth, 1967.

Eighth-Century Prophets

Chapter 2

Amos, Prophet of God's Justice

Historical Setting of the Book

According to Amos 1:1 the prophet Amos delivered his prophecies when Jerobeam II, son of Joash, was king of Israel (787/6–747/6). It was a time when there was little threat from neighboring and foreign powers. The Aramean kingdom that launched several attacks on Israel during the last years of the ninth century was subdued by Assyria. Assyria itself was kept occupied by the kingdom of Urartu and had to suffer a period of internal weakness. The Northern Kingdom of Israel and the Southern Kingdom of Judah enjoyed a period of peaceful relations. All this opened the door for Israel to expand its borders. Territories east of the Jordan were annexed and the northern border reached as far as Lebo-Hamath (2 Kgs 14:25; Amos 6:13–14). Major trade routes passing up and down Transjordan and into northern Arabia through Israelite territory paved the way for an economical revival in Israel. Commerce and trade flourished, houses were build on a grand scale with some Israelites owning both a summer and winter house (Amos 3:15). These houses were luxuriously furnished and decorated with ivory. In the houses they were feasting on the finest quality of food available—in short it was a time of peace and prosperity. One should also keep in mind that to have a home as a physical place of shelter was part of the Israelite view of the close ties between a person and his share of the promised and inherited land (Koch, 1983: 47).

On the basis of the dates associated with the reigns of Uzziah (788–736) in Judah and Jerobeam II (787/6–747/6) of Israel, the prophetic activity is most likely to be dated at the end of Jeroboam's reign, around 750 BCE. This makes him a contemporary of other prophets like Hosea who also delivered his prophecies in the Northern Kingdom of Israel, and Isaiah and Micah who delivered their respective prophecies in the Southern Kingdom of Judah.

Although the historical setting of the book suggests a mid-eighth century BCE date there are some indications of an exilic or post-exilic redaction. For instance, in 1:2 it is said that the Lord roars from Zion and thunders from Jerusalem and also in 6:1 Zion is mentioned, while in 1:1 it is explicitly said that the words of Amos are directed at Israel. In the closing verses of the book (9:11–15) the restoration of the fallen tent of David is foreseen, suggesting a return from exile and the rebuilding of ruins of the city and the land. Hence, Amos' prophecies, which proved to be true when the Northern Kingdom of Israel came to a fall in 722/721, appear to have been reapplied to the Southern Kingdom of Judah when this kingdom had suffered a similar fate in 587/586 BCE.

Content and Structure of the Book

The structure of the book of Amos can be outlined in the following way:

A	1:1-2	Heading: The Lord roars like a lion from Zion
B	1:3—2:16	Oracles against seven nations including Judah and culminating in Israel
C	3:1-8	The calling of the prophet Amos
D	3:9—6:14	Various prophecies against Israel and Samaria
E	7:1—9:10	Five visions of the prophet interrupted by a dispute between Amos and the priest Amaziah (7:10-17)
F	9:11-15	A prophecy on the restoration of the fallen house of David

From this overview it is clear that the book can be divided into two major parts. The first part consists of Amos 1:3—2:16 as a major prophecy pronounced upon six foreign countries followed by two prophecies on Judah and Israel. The second part (3:9—9:15) consists of a series of prophecies and visions directed at the Northern Kingdom of Israel, followed by a prophecy of restoration addressed to the Southern Kingdom of Judah. Amos 3:1-8 functions as a hinge that connects these two parts together and authorizes the prophecies uttered in both of them. Indeed, "The Lord YHWH does nothing without revealing his plan to his servants the prophets" (Amos 3:7). It is also clear that the book follows the same line of progress that can be detected in other prophetic books of the Old Testament, moving from doom and devastation to deliverance and restoration.

Theology of the Book

1. The importance of the Word of God

Amos 1:1 states quite clearly that what follows are the words of Amos, one of the shepherds of Tekoa. It is also clear that Amos speaks what he saw, that is, the words he utters were revealed to him. Therefore it is not Amos but Yhwh who roars from Zion and thunders from Jerusalem (1:2). The last verse of what can be seen as the calling narrative of Amos (3:1-8) uses the metaphor of a roaring lion once again, stressing the inevitable cause and effect pattern of Yhwh who has spoken and the prophet who has to prophesy the very words Yhwh has spoken. Later on when a dispute between Amos and the priest Amaziah is reported (7:10-17), the same emphasis on the interconnectedness of a calling to prophesy to the people and the inevitable obedience to that call came to the fore once again. In these glimpses of what happened between God and the prophet, one senses the mysterious and inexplicable coming together of God's word in human speech.

2. Social justice is theologically important

The book of Amos is perhaps best known for its message of social justice. In 5:24 the emphasis on social justice is formulated in a striking way: "Let justice roll on like a river, righteousness like a never failing stream." From the book it is clear that Yhwh is concerned about social justice not only as far as it pertains to Israel or Judah but indeed beyond the borders of the land. It is remarkable that the accusations against the foreign nations made in chapters 1-2 have the maltreatment of human beings at stake. Where prisoners of war who are already in a precarious situation are treated like grain that is threshed with iron implements, it amounts to a degrading of human beings in violation of the will of Yhwh (1:3). When prisoners of war are taken captive and treated in a harsh way and when they are even handed to a third party, it amounts to a situation where human beings are viewed as objects deprived of any human dignity (1:6). The treatment of powerless pregnant women who are violently killed by ripping them open, is also criticized (1:13). Social justice does not only concern powerless pregnant women and their unborn children, even the dead should be treated with respect. To burn the corpses of captives and thereby denying them a proper burial, is to be guilty of the crime of social injustice (2:1). Even within the inhumane conditions of warfare, there are ways in which people should be treated in a humane manner.

Social injustices within the community of the people of God are also brought to light. Whereas with regard to the foreign nations the focus was on a war time situation, with regard to the Israelites themselves the focus is more on the ordinary life within a community. To be sold into debt-slavery was an almost unthinkable option for an Israelite who might share in the land and therefore enjoy freedom. It is especially the plight of the poor that is underlined (2:6).

It is remarkable to see how social injustices committed in society are equaled to violence. To acquire wealth without taking general codes of proper conduct into account is regarded as nothing else but violence (3:10). Instead of acquiring wealth, what actually happened was an acquiring of violence. The result of such practices is described as utter confusion and devastation in society. Society is made up of people, human beings that interact with one another. The prophecy is therefore directed to the people in society because it is people who acquired wealth, it is people who do not act according to general accepted codes of conduct and it is people who are affected by the results of violence. To make matters even worse, Israel has no regard for a general code of conduct observed by foreign nations (3:10). It is also clear that injustices committed to fellow human beings do not leave the relationship with YHWH untouched. Reconciliation with YHWH will prove to be impossible while the people remain guilty of social injustices (3:13–15). In another passage (4:1–3) even the women are accused of social injustices by oppressing the poor; they crush the needy but do not seem to be bothered by their behavior.

The same applies to 6:1–7. When people of Zion and Samaria regard themselves as important and stretch themselves out upon beds inlaid with ivory, stretch themselves upon their couches, eat lambs (mutton) and calves (veal), sing and improvise songs as David did and drink from bowls of wine while they anoint themselves with the finest of oil without any regard for the plight of Joseph (Israel, the Northern Kingdom), it is regarded as nothing but violence in 6:1–7. An attitude of indifference coupled with a luxuriant lifestyle is what is unmasked as a grave form of social injustice.

This emphasis on social justice is not something new that Amos brought to the people. The way in which people should behave toward one another is part and parcel of the stipulations of the covenant between Yhwh and his people. In 3:2 the people are reminded that they are "chosen of all the families of the earth." In Hebrew the word translated as "chosen" is the verb "to know," expressing the close covenantal relationship between Yhwh and the people. Paul (1991: 102) translated this verse as follows: "Only you have I selected as my covenant partner." The emphasis on social justice is nothing else but a lived covenant with God (Zenger, 2008: 543) which means that being part of the covenant does not only pertains to a relationship with Yhwh but also in the way in which people of the covenant interact with one another.

3. Yhwh demands to be worshipped in the right way

As is the case in other prophetic books (in fact the whole of the Old Testament) the prophet has to warn the people against malpractices in their worship of Yhwh. In the community addressed by Amos, there was a constant urge to go astray and worship other gods (2:4). More specifically, Amos speaks out against a kind of religion that is insincere and more concerned about the people's self-interest rather than the true worship of Yhwh (4:4–5; 5:4–6; 5:21–27). Religious rituals performed for the sake of only the ritual itself is no religion at all. Therefore, Amos says, it is of little use to make the journey to places like Bethel and Gilgal and to practice all kinds of religious acts like sacrifices and music but without sincerity, while social injustices go rampant in society (4:4–5).

4. The Lord of Israel is not a local but a universal God

It is quite remarkable that the book commences with a series of prophecies directed not to Israel or Judah in the first place but to foreign nations. The common theme of all these prophecies is that of social injustices committed by foreign people. Yhwh, the God of Israel, is thus not only concerned about the sins and trespasses of his own people, but also the social injustices of foreign people matter to him. In 3:9 the Philistines and Egyptians are called to witness the unjust conditions in the capital of Samaria and in 6:2 the people of Israel are compared to the foreign peoples of Calne, Hamath, and Gath in Philistia.

Even in spite of several nations mentioned by name (Damascus, Gaza, Tyre, Edom, Ammon, Moab) no mention is even made once of a foreign god or gods worshipped by these nations. What the other nations worship as gods is not worth mentioning. It is therefore simply a matter of fact that YHWH is concerned about the ethical malpractices of foreign nations. Amos never enters into an extended polemic with Israelites who dare to worship the gods of foreign nations. Only once there is a brief remark on the issue of idolatry (Amos 5:26). This is remarkable because his contemporary—the prophet Hosea—has to point out in almost graphic detail the futility of worshipping the Baal of Canaan.

That YHWH is the universal God is further emphasized in Amos 9:7 when YHWH's greatest act of salvation in the history of his people (the deliverance from the bondage of Egypt), is put on par with other migrations of nations like the Philistines from Caphtor and the Arameans from Kir.

5. The Lord of Israel is the Creator God

Closely connected to the theme of YHWH as the only universal God, is the notion of God as Creator. The book is characterized by a number of doxologies (4:13; 5:8–9; 9:5–6) each of which proclaim the Lord as Creator. He is the Lord who created the mountains and the winds (4:13); he is one who made the Pleiades and Orion (Amos 5:8); he is the Lord almighty who touches the earth and it melts and who builds lofty palaces in the heavens and sets its foundation on the earth (Amos 9:5–6). In the very first verse of the book an earthquake is mentioned serving as a pointer to the forces of nature created by God.

6. The Day of the Lord

The term "Day of the Lord" (יום יהוה) is a term unique to the prophetic literature but is found for the first time in the book of Amos (5:18–20). This does not mean, however, that the prophet Amos invented the term. The origin of the term is still clouded in mystery but it seems that the coming Day of the Lord was a known concept and perceived by the people as something to be looked forward to as the time of YHWH's wrath upon the foreign peoples threatening the people of God and his glorious deliverance of his people. Now, Amos brought a shocking and disturbing message to the people which turned the positive expectations of the coming day upside down. The Day of the Lord is painted in dark colors; it will be a time of darkness "without a ray of brightness" (5:20) *for Israel*. Nobody will escape the day even though one may try to do so. The attempt to escape the day is like a man who fled from a lion only to encounter a bear or like someone who may think he arrived in the safety of his home and then is bitten by a snake (5:19). The intention of the metaphor is clear: an attempt to escape is futile and the end result is nothing else but death. Likewise the Day of Lord is an event that will bring death to Israel with no chance of escaping this fateful time.

7. The land promised, granted, lost, and regained

There is general agreement that the theme of the land in the Old Testament is an extremely important one. According to Brueggemann (1977: 3) the issue of the land is "a central, if not the central theme of Biblical faith." Von Rad (1975: 297) views the promise of the land as the distinguishing *Leitmotiv* of the Hexateuch.

The tradition of the land is also a *Leitmotiv* in the book of Amos. The land is promised and granted to Israel (2:9–10; 3:2; 3:9), but because of the people's disobedience to the covenant the land itself will turn against them (1:2; 4:6–13; 7:2–4; 8:8–11). Moreover, there is the constant threat of losing the land because Israel does not live according to the covenant stipulations of Deuteronomy (3:11; 4:2–3; 5:2, 5, 27; 6:7; 7:10–17; 9:8–9). Eventually they will regain the land and enjoy its abundance once more (9:13–15).

In the light of the prominent role of the tradition of the land in the book, the earthquake mentioned in Amos 1:1 should perhaps be reconsidered. The reference to the earthquake is interpreted as a historical indication of the time of Amos' appearance as prophet. It serves also as an indication of the length of Amos' preaching activity, probably not more than a year. In the light of the importance of the land in the book and the looming threat of a coming exile due to the conditions in the land, is it not possible that the reference to the land may take on another, additional metaphorical meaning? The reference to the earthquake is perhaps a premonition of what may be expected: turmoil and upheaval in the land and even expulsion from the land, instead of peace and stability. Mentioning the earthquake right at the beginning may be a subtle reminder that the land is at stake in the prophecies that will follow in the rest of the book.

8. The Lord of Israel is a loving God ready to forgive

Israel is a people who came into being by the grace of God. It was Yhwh who heard the cry of the people in Egypt and delivered them from the bondage of slavery. Yhwh led them through the desert before granting them the land to live in, so that the people are clearly the chosen people of God (2:10; 3:1–2). Amos is thus well aware of the long history of Yhwh's deeds of deliverance toward his people. The people have experienced Yhwh's grace in what happened to them in the course of history.

The very notion of an announcement of judgment is born out of God's passionate heart for human beings that suffer at the hands of others. It is because God is a God of love that he is concerned about the plight of human beings and consequently judgment is proclaimed upon those with little or no regard for their fellow human beings. Even when judgment is pronounced there is a slight possibility that the announced judgment may be averted by seeking the Lord (5:6) and to seek what is good and not evil (5:14), thereby opening a divine "perhaps" where Yhwh's mercy may prevail. Amos 4:6–11 gives a vivid description of Yhwh's untiring measures to call his people back to him. In Amos the judgment is imminent and to a certain extent even unavoidable, but when it happens the people will know that this is God's ultimate action when all else failed.

The fact that the prophecy of judgment is called upon the people is also a sign of his love for his people. The prophecies of doom are not yet fulfilled, they are only announced and therefore there is still time for repentance. When the Lord commissioned his prophets with a message of judgment it serves as a call to repent and turn away from their evil ways. Thus it is nothing else but God's love in action on behalf of his people. It is remarkable that God is time and again willing not to judge his people because of the prophet asking God to reconsider his plans of destruction (Amos 7:3, 6).

However, it is equally true that judgment is pronounced in no uncertain terms and that utter doom and destruction await the people (3:12). This very real possibility is brought home by a telling metaphor of

Israel as a virgin who has fallen "never to rise again with no one to lift her up" (5:2). This prophecy came into fulfillment when Israel came to a fall in 722/721 and indeed as 5:2 said "never to rise again."

The book comes to a conclusion with a glorious prophecy of restoration. Even when God's judgment comes to fruition it is still not the final word. After the judgment he restores his people in what only can be described as a miracle.

From this very brief overview it is clear that this book is rich in theological insights speaking to modern day readers as well. Current societies still suffer from social injustices, the plight of the poor, exploiting some so that other may benefit from it and an attitude of indifference to that what is wrong. The book of Amos addresses these issues from a theological point of view. The issues raised in this book are echoed in the ministry of Jesus in many ways, both in what Jesus did (Mark 6:35-44; 7:24-30) and in the words he spoke (Luke 6:24-26; 12:13-21). Present day Christians are reminded by the book of Amos that to be a Christian is not only a spiritual matter but that it involves the realities of present day events just as much.

Bibliography

Barton, J. "The Theology of Amos." In *Prophecy and Prophets in Ancient Israel: Proceedings of the Oxford Old Testament Seminar*, edited by J. Day, 188-201. LHBOTS 531. London: T. & T. Clark, 2010.

Jeremias, J. *Amos*. ATD. Göttingen: Vandenhoeck & Ruprecht, 1995.

Koch, K. *The Prophets. Volume One. The Assyrian Period*. London: SCM, 1982.

Paul, S. M. *Amos. A Commentary on the Book of Amos*. Hermeneia. Minneapolis: Fortress, 1991.

Schart, A. *Die Entstehung des Zwölfprophetenbuch. Neubearbeitungen von Amos im Rahmen Schriftenübergreifender Redaktionsprozesse*. BZAW 260. Berlin: De Gruyter, 1998.

Snyman, S. D. "Eretz and Adama in the book of Amos." In *Stimulation from Leiden. Collected communications of the XVIth Congress of the International Organization for the Study of the Old Testament*, edited by H. M. Niemann and M. Augustin, 137-46. Frankfurt am Main: Lang, 2006.

———. "Towards a Theological Interpretation of HMS in Amos 6:1-7." In *"Dort ziehen Schiffe dahin . . ." Collected Communications to the XIVth Congress of the Organization for the Study of Old Testament, Paris, 1992*, edited by M. Augustin and K.-D. Schunck, 201-10. Frankfurt am Main: Lang, 1996.

Van Leeuwen, C. *Amos. De Prediking van het Oude Testament*. Nijkerk: Callenbach, 1985.

Wolff, H. W. *Joel and Amos*. Hermeneia. Philadelphia: Fortress, 1977.

The Lion Has Roared

Zenger, E. *Einleitung in das Alte Testament. Siebte, durchgesehende und erweiterte Auflage*. Stuttgart: Kohlhammer, 2008.

Chapter 3

Hosea, Prophet of God's Love

Historical Setting of the Book

ACCORDING TO HOSEA 1:1, Hosea served as a prophet during the reigns of Uzziah, Jotham, Ahaz, and Hezekiah, kings of Judah, and during the reign of Jeroboam son of Joash (= Jeroboam II), king of Israel. Thus, Hosea's prophetic career is dated in the eighth century BCE, more particularly, in the second half of that century. In those years, however, Jeroboam was not the only king of the Northern Kingdom, Israel. Second Kings 15–18 informs us that the reigns of the Judean kings mentioned in Hosea 1:1 also overlapped those of Jeroboam's successors, Zechariah, Shallum, Menahem, Pekahiah, Pekah, and Hoshea. The fact that their names are left out is remarkable, because the prophet Hosea ministered in Israel rather than Judah. To be sure, Hosea mentions Judah several times (e.g., Hos 1:7; 4:15; 5:10–14; 6:11; 11:12[12:1]), but references to Ephraim and Israel figure much more frequently in his book. The name of the northern capital, Samaria, can be found six times (*viz.* in Hos 7:1; 8:5–6; 10:5, 7; 13:16), whereas Jerusalem does not occur at all.

During the reigns of Jeroboam II and Uzziah, Israel and Judah were hardly troubled by foreign powers. The prosperity of that period may be reflected in Hosea 2:5, 8[7, 10]. After Jeroboam's death in about 750 BCE, the situation rapidly changed, especially when Tiglath-Pileser III became king of Assyria in 745. In his days and those of his successors Shalmaneser V (727–722) and Sargon II (722–705) the Assyrian empire dominated the scene everywhere in the Near East. Israel and Judah tried to save as much of their independence as possible, sometimes by joining anti-Assyrian coalitions and seeking support from Egypt, sometimes by accepting the position of an Assyrian vassal state (cf. 2 Kgs 15–18).

Apparently, disagreement about the course to be followed in foreign policy played a major part in the coups and regicides that destabilized the Northern Kingdom after 750 BCE (Hos 7:4–7; 8:4 refer to these events; maybe also 13:10–11). King Menahem sided with the Assyrians. Second Kings 15:19 records that he paid tribute to Tiglath-Pileser (called Pul, in this text) "to gain his support and strengthen his own hold on the kingdom." King Pekah, who assassinated king Pekahiah, Menahem's son, was an ally of Rezin of Aram-Damascus against the Assyrians. In the Syro-Ephraimite war (ca. 733) they jointly attacked Ahaz of Judah and tried to replace him by the son of Tabeel, who, as a puppet king, would be more willing to support their policy (see Isa 7:1–6; in the view of many scholars, Hos 5:8 alludes to these events; cf. Macintosh, 1997: 194–98). When Tiglath-Pileser intervened, he annexed a huge part of Pekah's territory and exiled the inhabitants (cf. 2 Kgs 15:29). He also conquered Damascus and had Rezin killed (732 BCE). Hoshea conspired against Pekah, murdered him and was enthroned as Israel's last king. In fact, his domain did not comprise much more than the former territory of the tribe of Ephraim (which may have furthered the use of Ephraim as a synonym of Israel in the book of Hosea; cf. Alt, 1953: 176). Initially, Hoshea accepted the Assyrian supremacy, but soon he rebelled and sought support from Egypt. Shalmaneser V reacted by imprisoning Hoshea and laying siege to Samaria. The city fell shortly before or after Shalmaneser's death and the ascension of his successor, Sargon II (ca. 722; for more details, see Becking, 1992). The event marked the end of Israel as an independent state and thus fulfilled Hosea's prophecy in Hosea 1:4.

It is uncertain whether the prophet Hosea was still active or alive at that time. In the last text in which Samaria is mentioned (i.e., Hos 13:16[14:1]) the fall of the capital is still in the future. However, this does not preclude the possibility of later prophecies, especially in Hosea 14.

Content and Structure of the Book

Hosea 1 and 3 relate the story of Hosea's marriage with an adulterous wife. Since Hosea 2 is also about adultery, it is closely related to Hosea 1 and 3, but now the deceived husband is YHWH, while Israel is the adulterous woman. Both Hosea 1 and 2 open with judgment and end with oracles of salvation. Hosea 3 also comes to a close on a positive note.

Chapters 4–14 are a collection of prophecies, in which Hosea's marriage is not mentioned anymore (though the underlying idea is still present, see below). They mainly announce judgment on Israel. However, twice doom gives way to restoration, based on a relationship of renewed love between God and his people; namely, in Hosea 11:8–11 and 14:4-8[5-9]. Furthermore, 12:3 mirrors 4:1, as both verses refer to a charge (ריב) of Yhwh against Israel. Besides, Hosea 12–13 differ from 4–11 in that they refer more frequently to the early history of Israel and the patriarchs. Accordingly, the collection can be subdivided into two sections, namely Hosea 4:1—11:11 and 11:12[12:1]—14:9[10].

Hosea 1–3	Prophecies related to Hosea's marriage
Hosea 4:1—11:11	First cycle of oracles of judgment, giving way to salvation
Hosea 11:12[12:1]—14:9[10]	Second cycle of oracles of judgment, giving way to salvation

Theology of the Book

1. Exclusive love

At the beginning of Hosea's ministry, Yhwh ordered him to marry an adulterous wife, "because the land is guilty of the vilest adultery in departing from the Lord" (Hos 1:2). Later on, Yhwh instructed him once again to show his love to an adulterous woman. By doing so, Hosea was called to imitate what God himself was doing; that is, to love the Israelites in spite of the fact that they turned to other gods (Hos 3:1). According to both texts, the relationship between God and Israel is analogous to the relationship of a husband and wife. The same idea pervades Hosea 2:2-23[4-25]. In this pericope God accuses his wife, Israel, of unfaithfulness. Her unfaithfulness sharply contrasts with the loving care God has shown by providing her with grain, new wine, olive oil, silver and gold (Hos 2:8[10]).

In Hosea 4–14 Hosea makes use of several metaphors and expressions to describe the exclusive bond that binds the Israelites to their God. The metaphor of marriage, husband and wife, is not prominent in the prophecies in these chapters, but the idea is still present; for example, when Israel's unfaithfulness towards God is circumscribed as prostitution, as in Hosea 5:3-4 and 9:1. Hosea 8:14 presents God as the Maker of Israel, whom the people should not have forgotten. In Hosea 11:1 Yhwh is the father, while Israel is the son, whom he had called from Egypt. As a loving parent, Yhwh taught Ephraim to walk, "taking them by the arms" (Hos 11:3a). His tender care for his people is further described in terms of healing (11:3b) and feeding (11:4; cf. also 13:5-6). The Hebrew text of Hosea 11:1-4 is complicated and apparently makes use of diverse metaphors, such as father (or mother) vis-à-vis child, and farmer vis-à-vis beast of burden (cf. Macintosh, 1997: 436-50; Ben Zvi, 2005: 234). It is clear, however, that all these metaphors describe God's ardent love for Israel, to which the people should have responded by serving him as their only God (cf. 11:2). In Hosea 13:4 the same idea is expressed very briefly: "But I am the Lord your God, *who brought you* out of Egypt. You shall acknowledge no God but me, no Savior except me" (cf. also 9:1; 12:9[10]; 14:1[2]).

In view of all this, it is surprising that in texts which refer to Israel's relationship with God, Hosea hardly makes use of the Hebrew word usually translated as "covenant" (i.e., ברית). Apart from Hosea 6:7, which is an enigmatic text, he only does so in Hosea 8:1. Nevertheless, it is crystal clear that Hosea describes Yhwh as a God who had entered into a special relationship with Israel, which should be characterized by mutual and exclusive love, such as between husband and wife.

2. Loyalty and acknowledgment

Yhwh was Israel's faithful husband and the people had to respond to his love. According to Hosea 2:15(17), the people did so after they had left Egypt, when they trekked through the wilderness (NIV here reads "she will sing"; instead, one could also translate "she will respond"; cf. Andersen and Freedman, 1980: 276-77). Responding to Yhwh's love obviously implied that they would serve him as their only God. They had to invoke him for help (cf. Hos 7:7). They had to wait for him (Hos 12:6[7]) and should never forget him (Hos 2:13[15]; 8:14; 13:6). In other words, God expected that they would rely on him and respect his will in all aspects of life.

Yhwh loved the Israelites and they had to love him. This formulation certainly agrees with the purport of Hosea's prophecies. Nevertheless,

Hosea never uses the Hebrew verb אהב "to love" to describe the people's response, but reserves it for Yhwh's attitude towards Israel (Hos 3:1; 9:15; 11:1; 14:4[5]). For the people's response he prefers two other terms, namely חסד "steadfast love," "loyalty," or "mercy," and ידע "to know" or "to acknowledge." Both words occur in Hosea 4:1: "There is no faithfulness, no love, no acknowledgment of God in the land," and in Hosea 6:6: "For I desire mercy, not sacrifice, and acknowledgment of God rather than burnt offerings."

As for חסד, it is not clear from the outset whether it refers to love or loyalty towards God or towards one's neighbor. On the one hand, Hosea 4:2, which accuses the Israelites of sins that break precepts found in the second half of the ten commandments, pleads for the latter option. The same applies to Hosea 6:8–9, which is also about bloodshed, just like Hosea 4:2. Moreover, חסד parallels the social virtues צדקה "righteousness" and משפט "justice" in Hosea 10:12 and 12:6[7] respectively. On the other hand, Hosea 6:7 could be in favor of the former option, for this text accuses the people of unfaithfulness to Yhwh, just after Hosea 6:6 called them to חסד. Probably, it is wise not to press the issue. Apparently, love and faithfulness towards God and towards one's neighbor were so closely interrelated that for Hosea it was not necessary to distinguish the one from the other. Be this as it may, it is abundantly clear that Yhwh required from his people that they would show an attitude of constant love and faithfulness, not a חסד that dissipated as quickly as the morning mist and the early dew (Hos 6:4).

As for ידע, the scope of this verb comprises much more than intellectual knowledge. This is evident from, for example, Hosea 2:20[22], where "you will acknowledge the Lord" is the aim and climax of the new marriage that Yhwh will contract with his people. Accordingly, "to know [ידע] Yhwh" is to love him (cf. also Hos 5:4b: "A spirit of prostitution is in their heart; they do not acknowledge the Lord"). In addition, it entails recognizing his divine authority, which is at least one aspect of the meaning of the expression "acknowledgment of God" in Hosea 4:1 and 6:6 (note that these verses have אלהים "God," not Yhwh). Furthermore, Hosea 4:6 holds a priest responsible for the downfall of God's people as a result of their lack of knowledge, because the priest refused to instruct the people. Instruction, then, is at the basis of the knowledge required from his people. The relationship of love meant by "knowing Yhwh" evidently includes knowledge of his nature, his deeds and his will.

Other aspects of the response that God expected from his people can be inferred from the charges that Hosea brings against them. These will be presented in the next section.

3. Israel's adultery

The people of Israel did not respond to Yhwh's love in the proper way. Indeed, God immediately denounces their adultery, in the very first word he spoke to Hosea (Hos 1:2; for "the land" as the subject of adulterous behavior in this verse, see Kwakkel, 2009b: 168–69, 180–81). Subsequently, the topic of unfaithfulness, adultery or prostitution occurs several times (cf. Hos 2:2, 5[4, 7]; 3:1; 4:12; 5:3–4; 9:1). It is the central charge brought against Israel in the book of Hosea.

What exactly does Hosea mean by unfaithfulness or adultery? In Hosea 2 the accusation obviously relates to Baal worship. The lovers after whom Yhwh's wife (Israel) goes (2:5, 7, 13a[7, 9, 15a]) can be no others than the Baals mentioned in verses 13[15] and 17[19] (cf. also verse 8[10]). Israel was unfaithful because she expected food, drink, wool, linen not from Yhwh but from the Baals (2:5, 8, 12[7, 10, 14]; cf. also 9:1–2).

Adultery, then, is a metaphor, which describes the people's unfaithfulness in matters of religion and worship. It seems, however, that more was involved than adultery in the metaphorical sense of the word. In Hosea 4:13–14 God says to Israelite fathers that he will not punish their daughters or daughters-in-law for turning to prostitution, because they themselves consort with prostitutes. According to the most natural interpretation of this indictment, both fathers and daughters committed prostitution in the literal sense of the word.

At the same time, prostitution was related to the cult, as can be inferred from the sacrifices mentioned in Hosea 4:13a and perhaps also from the Hebrew קדשות ("shrine prostitutes" in NIV) figuring in verse 14. Based on these and related data, several scholars have developed the idea that cultic prostitution was an important element of Baal worship. In their view, prostitution at the shrines served as a kind of sympathetic magic, which stimulated Baal's procreative power (cf., e.g., Mays, 1969: 11, 25, 75; Wolff, 1976: 16, 42, 110). More recently, a number of scholars have argued that this idea rests on a shaky basis, since there is almost no evidence for the practice of cultic prostitution, neither in Canaan nor elsewhere in the Ancient Near East (see, e.g., Gruber, 1986; Frymer-Kensky,

1992: 199–203). It is wiser, then, to abandon the idea of prostitution as an official element of the Baal cult and to accept the more sober view that Hosea 4:13–14 alludes to sexual debauch, such as may easily have taken place in the context of exuberant religious festivals (cf. Macintosh, 1997: 158; Ben Zvi, 2005: 115).

In Hosea 4 the mention of Baal is strikingly absent. Moreover, Hosea 4:15 expresses the wish that Judah will not become as guilty as adulterous Israel and underscores this by warning against pilgrimages to Gilgal or Beth Aven (= Bethel) and oaths taken in the name of Yhwh. Accordingly, the corrupt cult denounced in Hosea 4 may have been a syncretistic form of Yhwh worship. Perhaps the people in Hosea's days thought that they served Yhwh, but there were so many elements relating to Baal in their religion that for the prophet it was tantamount to flat Baal worship. Hosea 2:16–17[18–19], where Yhwh says that he will make an end to Israel's habit to call him "my Baal," might be in favor of such a view (cf. Vriezen & Van der Woude, 2000: 285, 288).

Syncretism was certainly a characteristic of the cult of the calves of Beth Aven referred to in Hosea 10:5–6 (cf. also 8:5–6; 13:2). The same applies to the numerous altars paralleled by embellished sacred stones in Hosea 10:1–2. According to the Israelites the construction of these cultic implements had to keep up with agricultural production and the prosperity of the land. Hosea 10:2 typifies this attitude as deceit. Deceit recurs in Hosea 10:4, but here it figures as a vice that imbues social life, foreign policy, and the administration of justice (cf. also verse 13a; for an extensive discussion of 10:4b, see Macintosh, 1997: 395–98). The transportation of the calf (or part of it) to Assyria in Hosea 10:5–6 may have been enforced by the Assyrians, but it may also have been an element of Israel's deceitful and ever changing foreign policy (cf. also 5:13; 7:11; 8:9–10; 12:1[2]). Hosea 10:13b reveals the mentality that prompted the people to do all these things: "you have depended on your own strength and on your many warriors."

A similar interconnectedness of idolatry or syncretism, deceit and injustice, relying on human strength and on coalitions with Egypt or Assyria, can also be found in Hosea 5; 7; 8; 11:12—12:1[12:1–2]; 12:7–8[8–9]. The regicides alluded to in Hosea 7:4–7; 8:4 are another element of this complex, while the arrogance mentioned in 5:5; 7:10; 13:6 describes once again the underlying attitude. In conclusion, Israel's adultery manifested itself first of all in Baal worship or syncretism, but it was also intrinsically related to a whole complex of sinful behavior, by means of which the people tried to help themselves, instead of building on the loving care of Yhwh, their only God.

4. Israel's inevitable fall

In such a situation, one would expect the prophet Hosea to summon the people of Israel to mend their ways and to convert themselves to their God. He indeed does so in a number of texts (viz. 2:2b[4b]; 10:12; 12:6[7]; 13:4; 14:1–2[2–3]). Moreover a call to change their lives is implicit in every passage that denounces the people's sinful behavior.

Hosea 5:4a flatly denies, however, the possibility of a return to God: "Their deeds do not permit them to return to their God" (cf. Hos 8:5b; 11:5b, 7a; see also Yhwh's critical reaction to the people's plan to return to God in Hos 6:1–4). Hosea 5:4b relates this to a spirit of prostitution, which is in the people's heart. Apparently, they are no longer able to resist the power of that spirit. Similarly, other texts suggest Israel's incapability to renew their faithfulness to Yhwh by pointing to the deep historical roots of their bad behavior. According to Hosea 9:10, Israel's spiritual adultery began already at the end of the trek through the desert, as soon as they reached the borders of the cultivated land, which was supposed to be Baal's domain (cf. Macintosh, 1997: 361–63). Hosea 10:9 declares that Israel has sinned "since the days of Gibeah"; that is, since the era of the judges (see Judg 19; Macintosh, 1997: 412–13; cf. also Hos 9:9). Worse still, they have inherited the deceitful nature of their ancestor Jacob, who grasped his brother's heel in the womb (Hos 12:3[4]).

In view of this, one need not be surprised that Hosea announces time and again God's inevitably coming judgment over the people of the Northern Kingdom, Israel (see, e.g., Hos 5:9; 9:7a; 10:10; 13:12). Right from chapter 1, the names of Hosea's children communicate a message of doom. The first son is called Jezreel, because Yhwh will put an end to the kingdom of Israel by means of a devastating defeat in the Valley of Jezreel (Hos 1:4–5). The name of Hosea's daughter, Lo-Ruhamah, proclaims that Yhwh will no longer show love and mercy (רחם) to the house of Israel (1:6). The name of the second son, Lo-Ammi testifies to the climax of all disasters: Israel will no longer be Yhwh's people (עַם) and he will no longer be their God (1:9). In effect, this means that he cancels his covenant, which is expressed even more clearly if one translates "I will not be their

'I Am,'" instead of "I am not your God" (cf. Exod 3:14; Wolff, 1976: 24; Macintosh, 1997: 27–28).

In the rest of his book, Hosea mentions several elements of God's judgment. Yhwh will deprive the Israelites from the agricultural products they ascribe to their lovers, the Baals (Hos 2:9, 12[11, 14]; cf. also 8:7; 9:1–2). He will put an end to their festivals and syncretistic cult (2:11[13]; 9:4–5). Sacrifices will not help them to regain his favor and avert their downfall (5:6; 8:13). On the contrary, the altars will be demolished (10:2, 8). Likewise, Israel's defense policy will fail (7:11–12; 8:8–10). The fortresses will be devastated (8:14; 10:14) and "swords will flash in their cities" (11:6). The tribe of Ephraim was famous for its fertility, but Yhwh will bereave this tribe of its children (9:11–16). Israel will have to leave the promised land and return to Egypt, either literally, or figuratively by becoming slaves of the Assyrians (8:13; 9:3, 6; 11:5; cf. Kwakkel, 2009a).

In Hosea 9:15, God summarizes all this by declaring: "I will no longer love them." Instead, he will attack his people like a bear and devour them like a lion (13:7–8; cf. also 5:14). Thus they will feel the consequence of their decision to turn against Yhwh, their only helper: such stubbornness cannot but lead to their destruction (13:9).

5. New love

Judgment and destruction are inevitable, but they are not Yhwh's final word. In Hosea 11:8–9 he considers the possibility of completely destroying Israel, just as he once did with the cities of Admah and Zeboiim (cf. Deut 29:23[22]). At that very moment his heart turns within him, his compassion is aroused, and he decides not to devastate his people. If he were only a man, he would have had no other option. But he is the holy God. Therefore he can afford not to come in wrath, even when his people are determined to turn from him (cf. 11:7).

Thanks to Yhwh's divine nature and his holiness, Israel will not be destroyed forever. However, this does not imply that God's judgment will be cancelled. The next verses, Hosea 11:10–11, announce that the Israelites will come back from the west, Egypt, and Assyria. Evidently, this can only happen if they first have left their country. Moreover, they will recognize that their exile was justified, for they will come like birds, trembling at the roaring of the lion, Yhwh.

God's judgment will come to pass, but precisely in this way he will open the door to a new future. He will bring his people back to the desert. He will strip them of all things on which they built their lives. He will even withdraw from them and abandon them to their fate. But in the end, the result of all this will be that they realize that they fully depend on him. They will return to him and respond to his love (cf. Hos 2:6–7, 14–17[8–9, 16–19]; 3:4–5; 5:15).

In his divine and holy policy, Yhwh uses judgment and destruction to rekindle Israel's love. Next, he puts her again in possession of the promised land and restores to her all its gifts, such as fertility, prosperity, and security (1:10[2:1]; 2:15, 18, 21–22[17, 20, 23–24]; 14:5–8[6–9]). Doom will be reverted, for Yhwh will love those he did not love any more, Israel will be his people and they will call him "my God" (1:10[2:1]; 2:23[25]).

Yhwh will remarry his wife Israel, in spite of her adulterous behavior and after they have been divorced. Will this new marriage last? It will, for Yhwh himself will make it successful, by paying a very special bride price, consisting of righteousness, justice, love, compassion, and faithfulness (Hos 2:19–20[21–22]). Yhwh himself will heal his people's waywardness and love them freely (14:4[5]). In the end, Israel will be saved purely by virtue of Yhwh's sovereign love.

6. God's people reunited

The previous sections have focused almost exclusively on Hosea's prophecies to the Northern Kingdom Israel, but there are also a number of texts that mention Judah. Several interpreters have defended the idea that the Judean elements are the result of an editorial process, which was carried out in Judah after the prophet's death (for a detailed discussion, see Emmerson, 1984). In support of this theory, one can point to texts such as Hosea 1:7 and 6:11 (cf. also 11:12b[12:1b]). The form of these texts, which refer to Judah, deviates from their context. Moreover, one would not have missed them if they had not found a place in the book. In other passages, however, the words about Judah cannot be removed without destroying the text (see esp. Hos 1:11; 5:12–14; 6:4; 10:11). The latter observation justifies the conclusion that Hosea himself also had a message for Judah.

In some cases, Judah is distinguished from Israel and is dealt with less severely (Hos 1:7; 4:15; this may also apply to 11:12b[12:1b], but the

Hebrew text is very obscure). Other texts put Judah on a par with Israel. Since it is as guilty as its northern neighbor, it will also share its destiny (5:5, 10, 12–14; 6:4, 11; 8:14; 10:11; 12:2[3]). But ruin is not Hosea's final word for Judah, just as little as it is so for Israel. Hosea 1:11[2:2] says that when Yhwh will accept Israel once again as his people, Judah and Israel will be reunited. Accordingly, in the end Judah will be restored, no less than the rest of Israel.

Hosea 1:11[2:2] adds that in those days the peoples of Judah and Israel will appoint one leader. The text does not mention the name of the leader, but Hosea 3:5 does. After the Israelites have been deprived from all things on which they have built their existence (Hos 3:4), they will again seek Yhwh their God "and David their king." This is the only time that David is referred to in Hosea. Obviously, God's promises to his dynasty are not a prominent element in Hosea's prophecies. Nevertheless, they are alluded to in the text as it has been handed down through the ages.

7. God's right ways

A long time has passed since Hosea served as a prophet. Many of his prophecies have come true, as, for example, the fall of the Northern Kingdom of Israel. Others still wait for their fulfillment. Hosea expected the return of the northern tribes to the promised land. Will this still be realized? Hosea proclaimed that those who were not God's people will be God's people. According to the apostle Paul, God was realizing the fulfillment of this prophecy when Jews and Gentiles believed in Jesus Christ as their Savior (Rom 9:24–26; cf. also 1 Pet 2:9–10). Is this all that can be said about the fulfillment of the promises to Ephraim and the other northern tribes? Or can we expect more?

The book of Hosea ends with a postscript, which urges those who want to be wise to walk in the ways of Yhwh as revealed by the prophet. What is the essence of these right ways, which still wait for the righteous that they may walk in them, but also make the rebellious stumble (14:9[10])?

Of course, only a few aspects can be pointed out here. First of all, Hosea reveals that being God's people requires a response characterized by steadfast love towards God and neighbors and by acknowledgment of God. God's people always runs the risk of trusting in other means than

God's loving help, in order to secure their lives. For God this is nothing less than adultery.

Second, God's policy of love may imply that he bereaves his people of everything upon which they rely apart from him. In that way, he makes it clear to them what it means that he really is their only helper. If they prefer to seek help elsewhere or if he stops helping them, there will not be any help left for them at all.

Third, God's persevering love is the only hope of God's people. As for themselves, they can only head for their downfall. They must realize that the only way to be saved from God's judgment is to accept the fact that they will have to go through it. But exactly in that way God's love reveals itself most abundantly: when they can only face their final destruction, God's love still compels him to accept them again as his beloved people and to save them.

God can act as a ravenous lion. Yet his love is the only refuge of his people. The lion has roared. Who will not follow him in fear?

Bibliography

Alt, Albrecht. *Kleine Schriften zur Geschichte des Volkes Israel*. Vol. 2. Munich: Beck, 1953.

Andersen, Francis I., and David Noel Freedman. *Hosea*. The Anchor Bible 24. New York: Doubleday, 1980.

Becking, Bob. *The Fall of Samaria: An Historical and Archaeological Study*. Studies in the History of the Ancient Near East 2. Leiden: Brill, 1992.

Ben Zvi, Ehud. *Hosea*. The Forms of the Old Testament Literature XXIA/1. Grand Rapids: Eerdmans, 2005.

Emmerson, Grace I. *Hosea: An Israelite Prophet in Judean Perspective*. Journal for the Study of the Old Testament Supplement Series 28. Sheffield, UK: JSOT, 1984.

Frymer-Kensky, Tikva. *In the Wake of the Goddesses: Women, Culture, and the Biblical Transformation of Pagan Myth*. New York: Free, 1992.

Gruber, Mayer I. "Hebrew *qĕdēšāh* and Her Canaanite and Akkadian Cognates." *Ugarit-Forschungen* 18 (1986) 133–48.

Kwakkel, Gert. "Exile in Hosea 9:3–6: Where and for What Purpose?" In *Exile and Suffering: A Selection of Papers Read at the 50th Anniversary Meeting of the Old Testament Society of South Africa OTWSA/OTSSA Pretoria August 2007*, edited by Bob Becking and Dirk Human, 123–45. Oudtestamentische Studiën 50. Leiden: Brill, 2009a.

———. "The Land in the Book of Hosea." In *The Land of Israel in Bible, History, and Theology: Studies in Honour of Ed Noort*, edited by Jacques van Ruiten and J. Cornelis de Vos, 167–81. Supplements to Vetus Testamentum 124. Leiden: Brill, 2009b.

Macintosh, A. A. *A Critical and Exegetical Commentary on Hosea*. The International Critical Commentary. Edinburgh: Clark, 1997.
Mays, James L. *Hosea*. Old Testament Library. London: SCM, 1969.
Stuart, Douglas. *Hosea-Jonah*. Word Biblical Commentary 31. Waco, TX: Word, 1987.
Vriezen, Th. C., & A. S. van der Woude. *Oudisraëlitische en vroegjoodse literatuur*. 10th edition of *De Literatuur van Oud-Israël*. Kampen: Kok, 2000.
Wolff, Hans Walter. *Dodekapropheton 1: Hosea*. Biblischer Kommentar Alten Testament XIV/1. 3rd ed. Neukirchen-Vluyn: Neukirchener, 1976.

Chapter 4

Isaiah, Prophet in the Service of the Holy One of Israel (Isa 1–39)

THE BOOK OF ISAIAH has received more scientific attention than any other prophetic book of the Old Testament. This is probably due to the fact that it is also the prophetic book most referred to in the New Testament. In the early church Isaiah received the honorary title of the "fifth gospel." The ecclesiastical interest in the book of Isaiah focused primarily on its theological—and christological—message. The scientific interest in the book, however, concentrated on its historical references and characteristics. These two interests have often been two more or less distinct tracks of inquiry lacking any serious interaction. It is the challenge of present day biblical scholarship to come to a theological understanding of the book of Isaiah in which the fruits of historical research are seriously and critically incorporated.

Historical Setting of the Book

Unity

Though it has been common practice for many years to separate the treatment of the book of Isaiah into different chapters or even into different books, that practice is showing signs of strain. Since the end of the nineteenth century Isaiah has nearly always been divided into first Isaiah (1–39), second Isaiah (40–55), and third Isaiah (56–66), though there is only the one book of Isaiah, bound together by clearly recognizable lexemes and themes that recur throughout the entire book. It is of interest to note that in the past few years a new consensus has been growing in biblical scholarship, one that would have Isaiah read and studied as a unity, a complex one no doubt, but a unity nonetheless in both form and content. This poses difficulties for an Introduction, which attempts to deal with the prophetic books in a more or less historically consistent way. The historical setting of the book of Isaiah as a whole does not coincide with the historical setting in which the prophet Isaiah lived. Only in the first part of the book the prophet is mentioned by name and only there the historical circumstances of the Assyrian Period that dominated the second half of the eighth century BCE are shining through. This does not mean that all prophecies in Isaiah 1–39 originate from this Assyrian Period, but from Isaiah 40 onwards we definitely step into the Babylonian and Persian Periods of the sixth century, hearing about "new things" YHWH is planning to do (42:9; etc.). So, though linguistically and theologically the book of Isaiah should be treated as a coherent unity, this chapter limits itself to Isaiah 1–39, in order to better grasp the historical circumstances of the book's origins.

Prophet

The book introduces Isaiah as the son of Amoz. Though his private life remains hidden behind his message and though "his" book has been extensively reworked and elaborated over successive periods, we do know that he apparently was married and had become the father of at least two sons bearing prophetic names (7:3; 8:3). There is a Jewish tradition that links Isaiah to the royal court of Jerusalem and identifies his father as a brother of king Amaziah. Whether true or not, the prophecies Isaiah delivered and the narratives told about him, give a clear indication that he lived in Jerusalem during the second half of the eighth century. He was well educated, was politically well informed, and he had easy access to the royal court. Some scholars think that before becoming a prophet Isaiah must have been a royal counselor at the court, and others believe that he had been an official linked with some kind of temple service.

Approaching Assyrian threat

According to the superscription, the Judean kings Isaiah had to deal with were Uzziah, Jotham, Ahaz, and Hezekiah (1:1). If Isaiah 6 truly narrates the foundational vision and calling of the prophet and does not merely refer to an incidental commission account concerning a specific period of his preaching, then Isaiah's call took place in the year king Uzziah died. This would mean that he prophesied mainly from ca. 745 BCE onwards (according to the usual dating; there are, however, difficulties with dating Judah's kings). This coincides with the period in which the Assyrians expanded and consolidated their New Assyrian Empire. Already in 743 BCE king Tiglath-Pileser III (745-727 BCE) led a military campaign to the west, subduing several kingdoms of Syria. Because of continued rebellion the Assyrians once again campaigned to the west in 738 BCE. In spite of this approaching Assyrian threat they had not yet threatened the kingdom of Judah during the reign of Jotham (?-742 BCE). The preaching of Isaiah during this time most likely centered around the social injustice he detected in Judean society, although explicit references to historical circumstances are lacking (cf. 1:10—17; 3:1—4:1; 5:1—24).

Syro-Ephraimite War

The relative independence of Judah drastically changed during the reign of Ahaz (742-727 BCE). The Judean kings got involved in international politics. A new rebellion against the Assyrians was developed in the northern regions. King Rezin of Aram (Syria) initiated a coalition. King Pekah of Israel joined him, but king Ahaz of Judah declined. Rezin and Pekah campaigned against Jerusalem and tried to install a puppet king on the Davidic throne in order to force the Judeans to participate in the coalition. This campaign is known as the Syro-Ephraimite War (734-732 BCE). Against the advice of Isaiah, king Ahaz pinned his hopes on the Assyrians (Isa 7-8). According to the biblical narrative it was Ahaz who called Tiglath-Pileser III to help him (2 Kgs 16:7), but historians think the Assyrians themselves had already planned to subdue the kingdoms of Syria and Israel, as well as the kingdom of Judah. At any rate, the Assyrians frustrated the plans of Rezin, destroyed Damascus (732 BCE), turned Israel into an Assyrian province and made Judah their vassal state (cf. 17:1-6). In a few years continuous rebellions of the successive kings of Israel would lead to the destruction of Samaria (cf. 10:7-11; 28:1-4) as well as the deportation of its inhabitants (722 BCE) by the Assyrian kings Shalmaneser V (727-722 BCE) and Sargon II (722-705 BCE).

Assyrian crisis

When Ahaz died in 727 BCE (uncertain, cf. 14:28), Hezekiah formally became king (727-698 BCE), but in fact he was still too young to ascend the throne. After a period of temporary guardianship, during which probably one or more prominent court officials were in command, Hezekiah took power ca. 715 BCE (for the problems dating Hezekiah, see Dekker, 2007: 90-94). From the outset he was sensitive to any initiative that might lead to a break with Assyria. That is why he sympathized with the revolt of the Philistine city of Ashdod in 713-711 BCE. It is possibly due to Isaiah's preaching (Isa 18; 20) that Hezekiah withdrew his support just in time. Ashdod was severely punished by the Assyrians. When king Sargon II suddenly died in 705 BCE, Hezekiah became the driving force of a well planned revolt in the west, with Egyptian support. Assyria did not hesitate to act. The new appointed king Sennacherib initiated a campaign against Palestine, subdued all Hezekiah's coalition-partners, defeated the Egyptian helping-forces, destroyed many Judean cities, killed or deported numerous innocent people and threatened the city of Jerusalem (701 BCE). Unexpectedly, however, Jerusalem was spared. The Assyrian annals make no mention of the reason for this turn of events, while the biblical narrative tells of a miraculous liberation by the intervention of an angel of YHWH (37:36; 2 Kgs 19:35).

Content and Structure of the Book

The content of Isaiah 1-39 may be summarized as follows:

Isaiah 1	Prologue
Isaiah 2-12	First collection of judgment oracles and salvation oracles
Isaiah 13-23	Oracles against the nations
Isaiah 24-27	Isaiah apocalypse
Isaiah 28-33	Second collection of judgment oracles and salvation oracles
Isaiah 34-35	Diptych of judgment and salvation
Isaiah 36-39	Narratives

Prologue

Isaiah 1 demonstrates a thematic unity with Isaiah 66 and can be viewed as a prologue to the entire book. At the same time, this chapter introduces the most important themes dominating the first part of the book. Here, Israel is presented as a sinful nation that has forsaken the Holy One of Israel; the impending judgment is described; Zion is mentioned as a besieged city; the remnant surviving God's judgment is introduced; social injustice is pointed out; a future perspective of cleansing and purifying is proclaimed; and the redemption of Zion by justice and righteousness is announced. These representative themes will be worked out throughout the first part of the book. The second and third parts of the book of Isaiah will concentrate emphatically on the last mentioned theme of Zion's redemption.

Isaiah 2-12

A new heading introduces Isaiah 2-12 as a unified whole, marked at the beginning by a salvation prophecy concerning the coming of the nations to Mount Zion (2:1-4) and at the end by a song of thanksgiving in which Zion and the nations once again play a role (12:1-6). Central to these chapters are the stories about Isaiah's foundational vision and calling (ch. 6) and his preaching during the Syro-Ephraimite War (ch. 7-8), which perhaps once constituted "the Book of Immanuel" (6:1—8:18; often called Isaiah Memoir), probably co-edited by Isaiah's own disciples (8:16; cf. Dekker, 2009). This "Book of Immanuel" concludes in its present form with the messianic prophecy of 9:1-6 and is surrounded with woe-statements and judgment oracles that date from different times, interwoven with salvation oracles concerning the so-called remnant (4:2-6; 10:20-27; 11:11-16) and the shoot of Jesse (11:1-10). Isaiah 12 closes the first collection of prophecies in the book and at the same time functions as a transition to the next section.

Isaiah 13-23, 24-27

Isaiah 13-23 constitutes a collection of oracles against the foreign nations, dating from different periods, though a kernel of the collection probably originates from the Assyrian period as does the report of a symbolic act of Isaiah in the middle (Isa. 20). In its present form, however, this collection starts prominently with an explicitly authorized prophecy about the fall of Babylon, the empire that dominated the sixth century. These oracles against the nations are followed by the so-called Isaiah apocalypse of Isaiah 24–27 prophesying about God's judgment of the world, his universal reign on Mount Zion, and the ensuing hopeful perspectives for Israel. Some scholars prefer to take Isaiah 13–27 together as constituting one single collection, though Isaiah 24–27 focuses more on cities than on nations.

Isaiah 28–33

The next part of the book is held together by a framework of six woe-statements (28:1; 29:1; 29:15; 30:1; 31:1; 33:1). Though the first woe-statement is addressed to Samaria, it bears a paradigmatic character and ultimately concerns Jerusalem and its leaders, as do the following woe-statements. Only the last woe-statement exhibits a different character. Most of the judgment oracles enclosed in this collection can be understood in the context of the Assyrian crisis connected with the campaign of Sennacherib. Isaiah 28–31 is often considered to be the core of this collection. Together with Isaiah 1–12, these chapters contain most of Isaiah's original prophecies. In the present form it is striking that its judgment prophecies are interchanged once and again with prophecies of salvation. The concluding chapter of this collection of prophecies exhibits a more or less liturgical character and functions as a transition to the next sections (cf. the pivotal announcement of God's acting on behalf of Zion in 33:10).

Isaiah 34–35, 36–39

The remaining two redactional units, chapters 34–35 and 36–39, generally viewed as compositions of a relatively late date, can both be considered bridges to the second part of the book. Isaiah 34–35 form a diptych of a judgment oracle concerning Edom as a representative of all hostile nations and a salvation oracle about the return of the redeemed to Zion, thus anticipating a theme elaborated at length in the second part of the book. Isaiah 36–39 consists of narratives about the threat to and deliverance of Jerusalem during the Assyrian crisis (cf. 2 Kgs 18–19), concluding with an announcement of the Babylonian exile, that gives an indication of the historical context for the prophecies recorded from Isaiah 40 onwards.

Theology of the Book

It is not the biography of the prophet but the theology of the book that deserves our greatest attention. Characteristic for the book of Isaiah is that God is presented time and again as the Holy One of Israel. This indicates that God's holiness, referring to the absolute supremacy and purity of the Lord, constitutes a basic and unifying theme in the book. After describing the use of this divine name and the most important motives associated with it, four relationships the Holy One entered in will be highlighted: his relationship to Israel, Zion, Davidic kingship, and the nations. These four relationships are crucial for understanding the theological message of Isaiah 1–39.

1. God is the Holy One of Israel

Most names of God used in Isaiah are also found numerous times in the rest of the Old Testament. It is sometimes claimed that prophetic renderings of the deity are too polyvalent to be subsumed under any single heading. Nevertheless, for the entire book of Isaiah it is characteristic that God is specifically testified to as the Holy One of Israel (1:4; 5:19, 24, etc.). This divine name is only missing in the more or less apocalyptic sections Isaiah 24–27 and 34–35. Outside the book of Isaiah it occurs only once in the book of Kings (2 Kgs 19:22 // Isa 37:23), twice in the book of Jeremiah (Jer. 50:29; 51:5), and thrice in the Psalter (Pss. 71:22; 78:41; 89:19). This indicates that the divine name "the Holy One of Israel," if not already at home in the temple cult of Jerusalem, may have originated with Isaiah himself. In any case it represents a specific Isaianic way of talking about God.

Vision and calling

Probably it was the way in which Isaiah himself has been confronted with God during his foundational vision and subsequent calling, that has given the prophet a lasting impression of God's holiness. Williamson contests this hypothesis, for the divine name "Holy One of Israel" is not used in Isaiah 6 itself. He argues that Isaiah did not use the name during the first period of his preaching (Williamson, 2001). This depends, however, on redaction-critical arguments that are disputed. The prophet gives us a first person report of a visionary experience, in which he had seen the Lord himself, sitting on a high and lofty throne. Seraphs, winged snake-figures who were well known in the ancient Near East and often were venerated in popular religion, surround him and call to each other: "Holy, holy, holy is the Lord of hosts . . ." Suddenly Isaiah realizes that he is about to perish because he had seen "the King, the Lord of hosts," while he himself is a man of unclean lips, living among a people of unclean lips. Fortunately Isaiah's lips were cleansed through intervention by one of the seraphs, but the overwhelming impression of God's holiness, which must have been the impact of this threatening experience (cf. 1 Sam 6:20), apparently found its expression not only in the theme of Yhwh's exaltation as a central element in Isaiah's preaching, but also in the frequent use of the divine name "the Holy One of Israel," in first instance by the prophet himself and then also by the editors of the book that bears his name.

Sanctifying the Holy One

The linkage of the Holy One with the name of Israel corresponds with the preaching of Hosea (Hos 11:9) and underscores that God's holiness in and of itself does not prevent him from interacting with human beings. More specifically, God himself has chosen to interact with Israel. The ultimate goal of this interaction is described as the sanctification of his name, the Holy One of Jacob, and standing in awe before the God of Israel (29:23), just as the prophet Isaiah himself once had been called upon to do (8:13). This purpose, however, cannot be realized without the recognition that God's holiness constitutes a divine norm for ethical behavior (cf. Lev 19). In line with this, the uncleanness that Isaiah realizes he himself and Israel are infected with, does not refer to cultic but to ethical impurity. In the book of Isaiah it is not only the covenantal relationship between God and his people that forms the argument for expecting justice and righteousness (1:2-4; 5:1-7), but also the attributes of the Holy God himself, who is exalted by justice and shows himself holy by righteousness (5:16).

Justice and righteousness

In his ethical emphasis on doing justice and promoting righteousness in Israelite society, Isaiah shows himself to be in line with his predecessor Amos and with his contemporaries Hosea and Micah. The knowledge of Yhwh requires a way of living that corresponds to the attributes of Yhwh. Isaiah's denouncing of all forms of social injustice perpetrated by Israel's kings and leadership (cf. 1:10–17, 21–23; 3:1—4:1; 5:8–24) shows some basic resemblance with the ideal standards of Near Eastern kingship described in Mesopotamian literature. His constant emphasis on the holiness of God, however, adds an important theological perspective. When the Holy One is exalted by justice and shows himself holy by righteousness, then justice and righteousness are not optional for Gods people. On the contrary, Israel's rejection of these virtues can be summarized as pride (cf. 2:6–22) and in essence this is nothing short of rejection of the Holy One himself (1:4; 5:19, 24; 30:11). That is why Yhwh uses justice like a line and righteousness like a plummet when measuring and judging his people (28:17). And when judgment has been executed, it is only by righteousness and justice that there will be redemption again (1:27). In the context of the book of Isaiah as a whole this refers to righteousness and justice as brought about by God himself, indicating salvation (1:26; 33:5), mediated by his agent, the messianic king (9:6; 11:4–5; 32:1), or established by his spirit, poured out from on high (32:15–17).

2. The Holy One and his relationship to Israel

The connection between the Holy One and Israel is most striking, especially when one realizes that in the book of Isaiah Israel is presented from the outset as a sinful nation (1:4). The divine name "the Holy One of Israel," therefore, in itself already implies a confession of Israel's relationship with God as a relationship of grace. In essence this relationship is founded on election, starting with the redemption of Abraham, concretized in the offspring given to him (29:22; cf. 41:8). In the book of Isaiah "Israel" is a religious designation that in fact has both kingdoms in view (the Northern Kingdom is usually referred to as "Ephraim"), though its prophecies often focus on Judah and Jerusalem.

Vineyard of Yhwh

In the book of Isaiah the special relationship of Yhwh to Israel is expressed in a most remarkable way in the Song of the Vineyard (5:1–7). The designation of Israel as vineyard of the Lord reveals the love and care of Yhwh that constituted their relationship. In the first part of Isaiah, this relationship is not referred to as a "covenant"; yet mention is made of the covenant the inhabitants of the earth have broken (24:5) and of covenants within the realm of politics (28:15; 30:1; 33:8). Nevertheless, the metaphor of the vineyard comes close to the idea of the covenant mentioned elsewhere in the Old Testament. On God's initiative Israel was called into existence to share in a special relationship with Yhwh. Essential to this relationship, characterized by God's comprehensive care for his people, was his expectation that Israel would practice justice and righteousness. However, in the book of Isaiah it is clear from the outset that the relationship of the Holy One with Israel is in a state of crisis. God's expectations for his vineyard have not materialized (cf. 3:14), though the book of Isaiah expresses the hope that one day circumstances will change and the Song of the Vineyard can be sung anew (27:2–6). That may take a while, however.

This people

The first prophecy of the book already introduces children reared and brought up by Yhwh, who choose for rebellion and miss knowledge and understanding (1:2–3). Israel is still called "my people" here, but in the next indictment this already changes to "a sinful nation, people laden with iniquity." Though this does not exclude the continued use of the expression "my people" in the book, the crisis in the relationship between Yhwh and Israel is clearly illustrated in the use of the expression "this people." This expression is persistently used in the foundational vision and calling of Isaiah and during the two most crucial periods of Isaiah's preaching (6:9, 10; 8:6, 11, 12; 9:15; 28:11, 14; 29:13, 14), consciously indicating a certain distance between God and his people.

Unwillingness

Because Isaiah's call takes place in a period during which the relationship of the Holy One with Israel is in a state of crisis, much of his preaching falls under the heading of judgment. He is even called to harden the people in their unwillingness to convert. This commission has often been interpreted as Isaiah's own retrospective reconstruction in which he tried to deal with the disappointing results of his preaching. This hypothesis, however, has no ground in exegesis and originates from modern psychological and theological considerations. The idea that Yhwh hardens the hearts of human beings as a form of judgment is not foreign to the Old Testament (cf. Exod 4:21; Deut 2:30; etc.). It is better, therefore, to deal with the text as it presents itself. The judgment is described as hearing without comprehension and seeing without understanding (6:9–10). Throughout the first part of Isaiah the themes of hearing and seeing, blindness and lack of understanding, in all their variations, remain an important reference to Israel's sin and to the judgment Israel will face (cf. 29:9–12), until they are reversed definitively in the salvation promises that dominate the second part of the book (42:18–25; etc.; cf. 29:18; 32:3–4). This does not mean, however, that all salvation prophecies in Isaiah 1–39 must have been written by a later editor. When God calls Isaiah, he prepares him for the negative effect of his preaching, but Isaiah is not ordered to prophesy only judgment. Rather, Isaiah's theology was strongly rooted in the hopeful traditions of Zion and David. Even his salvation preaching, however, will have the effect of hardening the people in their unwillingness to listen. This unwillingness is signaled time and again. The people even openly ask seers and prophets to keep the Holy One of Israel away from them (30:10–11).

Hidden face

The theological consequence of this prevalent lack of trust in the promises of the Holy One is that God is revealed to Isaiah as "a stone one strikes against," "a rock one stumbles over," and even as "a trap and a snare" for his own people (8:14). This comes as a complete reversal of the credo of Israel, in which Yhwh is acknowledged as a rock to build on or to take shelter at (1 Sam 2:2; Deut 32; cf. Isa 17:10) and as a God who delivers his people from trap and snare (Ps 91:3). So how does one deal with this shocking self-revelation of Yhwh in the book of Isaiah?

Isaiah, Prophet in the Service of the Holy One of Israel

The prophet himself shows how he handled it. Confronted with God's pronouncements he himself professes to "wait for the Lord, who is hiding his face for the house of Jacob" (8:17). Calling Israel "the house of Jacob" instead of "this people," as Yhwh himself had done, and talking about Yhwh as "hiding his face" both give expression to Isaiah's belief in the ultimate abiding relationship of the Holy One with Israel. For this same reason the judgment Yhwh will execute among his own people is called his strange work (28:21; cf. 63:10). Thus Isaiah himself already testifies implicitly to the fact that the real face of Yhwh cannot be known from the experience of judgment (cf. 54:8).

Remnant

The belief in the abiding relationship between Yhwh and Israel is also the presupposition of the idea of the remnant that is elaborated upon in the book of Isaiah. At first glance the remnant idea underscores the seriousness of the judgment Israel has to undergo. The answer God gives to Isaiah when he asks how long the hardening would endure, reveals that there will not be much left after the execution of Yhwh's judgment, just as only a stump remains when a tree is felled (6:13a; cf. 17:4–6; 24:12–13; 30:17). Even a tenth part that has remained, will be burned again. It is concluded, however, that a stump can bear a holy seed (6:13b). Though this notion may not be original, for it is missing in the Septuagint, it is fully in line with the overall image of Isaiah's preaching in which an element of hope can clearly be associated with the idea of the remnant. The most existential illustration of this is incorporated in the name of one of Isaiah's sons: Shear-Jashub, which means "a remnant shall return" (7:3). When it is *only* a remnant that returns, the connotation is one of judgment. However, when it is *still* a remnant that returns, the connotation is one of hope. Both connotations are present in Isaiah's preaching to king Ahaz in the context of the Syro-Ephraimite War. The same ambiguity is present in the prophecy of 10:20–23, often ascribed to later editors of the book. The name Shear-Jashub recurs, but this time incorporated within a prophecy. This prophecy opens a future perspective on the remnant one day leaning in truth on Yhwh, the Holy One of Israel. Designating the survivors of judgment as a "returning remnant" is thus not a neutral saying. They are destined to be the beginning of a renewed Israel. The return of the remnant has to be a return to God. The importance of this double function of the remnant idea in the book of Isaiah can also be illustrated already from the opening chapter. The prophecy of 1:8 uses the striking metaphor of the daughter of Zion left as a booth in a vineyard. Here the remnant idea functions primarily as a sign of the severity of the judgment. But the remnant immediately becomes a sign of hope when reference is made to the fact that *there still is a remnant* of a few survivors (1:9). This outcome, essentially distinguishing Zion from Sodom, is afterwards elaborated in the prophecy of 4:2–6 (cf. 11:16). Surprisingly, the metaphor of the booth is then used again, but now referring to Yhwh who provides shade, refuge and shelter (4:6).

Salvation

In the end there will be salvation. In all its varied expressions that is undoubtedly a core-message of the present book of Isaiah. However, this salvation shall only be realized through judgment. That is what the remnant idea as well as the present composition of the book with its juxtaposition of judgment and salvation oracles are meant to teach. Moreover, when already in the first chapter the metaphor of a purging smelting process is used (1:25), this functions as a helpful guide for the readers of the book on how to interpret its often harsh prophecies of judgment in a theologically correct way. For in the end, the book of Isaiah preaches Yhwh as a God whom not only Isaiah himself, in the midst of judgment, could decide to wait for faithfully (8:17), but a God that the readers of the book of Isaiah, after being confronted with severe oracles of judgment, can also be called to wait for. The fact that Yhwh himself waits to be gracious (30:18) can even be an incentive for doing this. There is no room here to mention all the various ways in which the ultimate salvation of Israel is described. Theologically important are the expressions referring to the relationship between the Holy One and Israel. It is said of the survivors of the judgment, that they will lean on Yhwh, the Holy One of Israel, in truth (10:20), that they will regard their Maker and will look to the Holy One of Israel (17:7) and that even the neediest people shall exult in the Holy One of Israel (29:19). The scope of the work that Yhwh is doing among his children, bringing salvation through judgment, will ultimately lead to the sanctification of the Holy One of Jacob (29:23). Israel will sanctify his name, not despise it as it had done previously (1:4;

5:24; 31:1). Salvation thus brings a complete reversal in Israel's attitude towards God.

Faith

Already in his judgment preaching Isaiah points consistently and clearly to the attitude that should fit Israel's position as the people of God, but which regrettably was missing among them. Addressing the house of David, represented by king Ahaz, Isaiah says: "If you do not stand firm in faith, you shall not stand at all" (7:9), and during the Assyrian crisis Isaiah coined the important expression: "One who trusts shall not hurry off" (28:16). Both of these key texts indicate an attitude of faith and trust as the appropriate reaction to the promises that are included in Yhwh's choice for respectively the house of David and Zion. The saying in 30:15 comes close to this. Introduced explicitly as a saying of the Holy One of Israel the prophet says: "In returning and rest you shall be saved; in quietness and in trust shall be your strength." The present attitude of Israel, however, is characterized by unwillingness (28:12; 30:9, 15), even more manifest than was the case in the past, during the Syro-Ephraimite War. The reversal of Israel's attitude towards God is therefore promised with respect to the future (cf. 26:3–4; 32:17). In this context it is telling that the concept of faith expressed in these sayings—as trust in the midst of a highly existential and fear-engendering crisis—is constitutive for the way the New Testament concept of faith was developed.

3. The Holy One and his relationship to Zion

In the book of Isaiah, the continuing relationship of the Holy One with Israel is concentrated in his divine love for Zion. Zion is one of the most important theological themes in the entire book of Isaiah. Though it is not until 60:14 that we read the formulaic name "Zion of the Holy One of Israel," it is a theme that is central to the book of Isaiah as a whole. The first collection of the book already closes with an appeal to the inhabitants of Zion to sing for joy "for great in your midst is the Holy One of Israel" (12:6). Both of these texts are probably younger than Isaiah, but the centrality of this theological concept in the book undoubtedly goes back to the preaching of Isaiah himself. As a Jerusalemite prophet he was well acquainted with the so-called Zion tradition.

Zion tradition

Central to the Zion tradition is the conviction that Yhwh has chosen Zion as the place of his earthly dwelling. During the Syro-Ephraimite War, when king Ahaz refuses to trust in the Lord and his promises of deliverance, Isaiah himself puts his hope in "the Lord of hosts, who dwells on Mount Zion" (8:18), thus defining the essence of the Zion tradition in a nutshell. Several years later, when the Philistines send emissaries to Jerusalem to probe its readiness to rebel against the Assyrians, Isaiah again refers to the essence of the Zion tradition. The Philistine messengers should be answered that "the Lord has founded Zion and the needy of his people will find refuge in her" (14:32). In other words, the Jerusalemites should not make their future dependent on political maneuvers and expect their welfare from foreign nations, but would be better off to trust in the Lord who has founded Zion. The same appeal is implied when Isaiah reiterates these words, with a slight variation, during the campaign of Sennacherib. Then he refers to Yhwh's founding of Zion as a salvific act in the past in which the rulers of Jerusalem should have trusted (28:16). This time, however, the reference to the Zion tradition is incorporated in an oracle of judgment. In this text the reference to the Zion tradition functions as a kind of theological motivation for the judgment Isaiah has to proclaim (Dekker, 2007).

Judgment

His adherence to the Zion tradition thus did not prevent Isaiah from preaching judgment. On the contrary, the refusal of Israel's leaders to trust in the promises included in this tradition and their failure to practice righteousness, as this is inextricably connected with these promises, makes his judgment preaching even more harsh. Isaiah even compares the once faithful city with a whore (1:21). Elsewhere in the Old Testament such a comparison always refers to the sin of idolatry, but here it indicates that also in case of lacking justice and righteousness, the Holy One is offended personally.

Hope

In the context of the book of Isaiah, however, there is always also an element of hope connected to the name of Zion. Zion often fulfils a double role, being an object of judgment because of Israel's lack of faith, while at the same time being a symbol of hope. This double role of Zion can even be recognized as characteristic for the very composition of the book in which the oracles of Isaiah have been collected and elaborated upon. The first introductory chapter refers already to both roles that Zion will fulfill in the book of Isaiah (cf. 1:8, 27). These roles are confirmed immediately by the prophecies collected in the next chapters (cf. 3:16ff; 4:2–6). This first collection of oracles, however, is composed in such a way that in the end all emphasis is laid on the hopeful future for Zion. The remarkable positioning of the prophecy of all nations' pilgrimage to Mount Zion at the beginning of Isaiah 2, as well as the concluding song of thanksgiving in Isaiah 12, meant to be sung by the inhabitants of Zion, function as clear indications for the present readers of the book of Isaiah that in the end Zion will remain only as a symbol of hope. Admittedly, this hope then is "deeply postsuffering hope" (Brueggemann, 1998: 22), and only the believing remnant shall participate in. This element of hope in the concept of Zion, however, is not an invention of the editors of the book, though they elaborated on this element extensively. The element of hope is inherent to the Zion tradition and Isaiah himself makes critical use of it in his preaching. This can be seen most clearly in Isaiah 29–31 where we find an intriguing intertwining of judgment and salvation oracles concerning Zion, for the most part widely considered authentic and dating from the time of the campaign of Sennacherib. In the collection of Isaiah 28–33, however, the emphasis in the end is completely on Zion as a symbol of hope. Just as in the collection of Isaiah 2–12, here too all ambiguity is abandoned when we arrive at the concluding chapter (Isa 33). This chapter designates Zion as a city that in the future shall be filled with justice and righteousness (33:5; cf. 1:26). This already anticipates the rest of the book of Isaiah with its expanding attention to the hopeful future of Zion.

King on Mount Zion

At the centre of the Zion tradition is the depiction of YHWH as King dwelling on Mount Zion (cf. Ps 48:3). Hence, it is not surprising that also in the book of Isaiah the Holy One is revealed as King. Already in his foundational vision and calling Isaiah in awestruck fear says that he has seen the King, the Lord of hosts (6:5). When the book of Isaiah describes the future of Zion, the description of Y{HWH} as depicted in his glorious kingship is central. Thus the prophecy of Isaiah 24 ends with the eschatological announcement that the Lord of hosts will be King on Mount Zion and will manifest his glory (24:23). The same notion is inextricably connected with the Zion prophecy in the closing section of Isaiah 28–33. In the Zion of the future, Y{HWH} will be acknowledged by the righteous as Judge, Ruler, and King (33:22; cf. 52:7). It is even announced that the righteous will see a king in all his beauty (33:17). Though at first glance this would appear to refer to a messianic king from the house of David (cf. 32:1–8), when read together with the subsequent confession of Y{HWH} as "our King" this prophecy suggests that the righteous probably will see God himself as the King, just as Isaiah saw the Lord sitting on his high and lofty throne. In redeemed Zion this experience is apparently also granted to the righteous who will live there, without any need to fear for their lives, because "the people who live there will be forgiven their iniquity" (33:24).

4. The Holy One and his relationship to Davidic kingship

The prophecies of Isaiah often address the ruling classes of Israel. In the opening chapter of the book the leaders of Israel are typified as "rulers of Sodom" (1:10). In 1:23 and 3:14 the princes and elders are explicitly referred to as those who are responsible for the deplorable situation of God's vineyard and for the injustice the vulnerable have to suffer. That is why Israel's leaders, also the religious ones, will be removed (3:1–3; 9:13–15; cf. 28:7, 14). Even the failing royal house of David itself is explicitly addressed in its contemporary representative, king Ahaz (7:13). Nevertheless, in the book of Isaiah there is not any indication that God has decided to do away with the house of David.

David tradition

Next to the Zion tradition, Isaiah's preaching also draws from the so-called David tradition. The origin of this tradition, a tradition that gave rise to several messianic prophecies, is found in the prophecy of Nathan

(2 Sam. 7). After having rejected David's plan to build a house for the Lord, YHWH promised that he himself would build David a house, which means that David would always have an heir on the throne. It does not come as much of a surprise that Isaiah as a Jerusalemite prophet is also well acquainted with the concept of faith included in this David tradition. He was familiar with the idea that the Holy One had a special relationship with Davidic kingship.

House of David

The first time Isaiah clearly makes reference to the David tradition is during the Syro-Ephraimite War, which in fact had been an attack not just on Jerusalem, but on the house of David itself. Enemies had planned to conquer Judah, but it was their goal to make the son of Tabeel its king (7:6). It is for this reason that the house of David is mentioned as the addressee of the report of Aram's alliance with Ephraim (7:2). When the prophet subsequently announces that the plans of the enemies shall not come to pass, he adds the admonition to stand firm in faith (7:9). The presumed object of this faith cannot be anything else but God's promise to the house of David, the latter represented now by the unfaithful king Ahaz. This house of David is explicitly mentioned again when the prophet gives him the sign of Immanuel (7:13-14). Though some scholars think Immanuel could have been a son of the prophet himself, the sign is better understood as referring to a son born in the house of David, thus underscoring the faithfulness of God's promises to this house. Despite the latter's disappointing sinfulness, YHWH still upholds his promises. This does not exclude the possibility that in not standing firm in faith the kingdom of Judah and the house of David could lose their independence, which in fact happened with the arrival of the king of Assyria (7:17). However, the promise of Immanuel—God with us—guaranteed that the treacherous plans of Aram and Ephraim would not come to pass (8:10).

For the sake of David

The royal son whose birth is prophesied in the Immanuel prophecy has often been identified with Hezekiah. Historically this interpretation is a plausible one. In any case, in the narratives of the book of Isaiah, Ahaz and Hezekiah are intentionally depicted as opposing each other. Ahaz is presented as the unfaithful representative of the house of David (Isa 7) and Hezekiah as the faithful one (Isa 36–37). Reference to David becomes explicit when Jerusalem is promised to be spared for Yhwh's own sake and for the sake of his servant David (37:35). The appearance of these two motives together shows how Yhwh has committed himself to the house of David (cf. 38:5).

Throne of David

But even Hezekiah did not appear to be the one who could fulfill the expectations connected with the David tradition. At the end of the first part of the book of Isaiah Hezekiah is clearly pictured as a failing king, who ultimately is only concerned with his own peace and security (39:8). This stands in sharp contrast with the plan Yhwh himself has for the house of David. This comes to the fore once again after the prophecy of Immanuel and most expressively in the messianic prophecy of 9:1–6 in which the birth of a royal son is celebrated. As a sign of hope his just and peaceful reign is announced as everlasting. Though the birth of this royal child probably supposes the fulfillment of the Immanuel promise, perhaps looking forward to Hezekiah, this prophecy seems to have undergone a messianic elaboration with eschatological overtones. By not mentioning the newborn royal by name, expectations appear to focus on a future Davidic figure. The royal names given to the newborn son exceed a mere birth announcement and evoke thoughts of the enthronement of a new king (cf. Ps 2:7). There is no consensus about the Isaianic authenticity of 9:1–6. It is often thought that the reign of Josiah had given rise to this prophecy. Even this pious king, however, despite the expectations that surrounded him, could not bring everlasting peace to the throne of David and his kingdom. In any case, an important and recognizable Isaianic element of this prophecy is the announcement that the throne and kingdom of David are said to be established with justice and righteousness (9:6). This corresponds with the potentially messianic prophecy of 16:5.

Root of Jesse

Another messianic prophecy relates the expected reign of a new Davidic king to the root of Jesse, underlining the radical way in which the new start has to be made with Davidic kingship (11:1–10). Strong emphasis is put on the expectation of social justice regarding the vulnerable, resulting eventually in a transformed creation from which even the animals will benefit. At this point a new element expressed is the reference made to the spirit of Yhwh who will rest on the new Davidic king. The effect of his reign is directly related to the holy mountain of Yhwh, which means that the reign of this new Davidic king is directly related to the kingship of the Holy One himself, centered on Mount Zion.

Davidic references

Less messianic, but full of expectations connected with the David tradition, is the prophecy concerning Eliakim (22:20-25). In the end, however, even Eliakim cannot bring salvation, for the present text of the prophecy concludes with an announcement of downfall and ruin. Salvation apparently has to be brought from elsewhere. Without mentioning the name of David, the prophecy about a king who will reign in righteousness and princes who will rule with justice (32:1-8) is loaded with messianic perspectives. Though this prophecy can also be interpreted in the more general sense of a wisdom proverb, in the context of the book of Isaiah the Davidic connotations may not be overlooked. The mention of righteousness and justice corresponds with the announcement about the foundations of the throne of David (9:6). A new age of peace will be inaugurated which will bring even the judgment of hardening to an end (32:3).

5. The Holy One and his relationship to the nations

Though the book of Isaiah often characterizes Yhwh as the Holy One of Israel, this does not mean that there is no room for the interaction of God with the nations. On the contrary, from the outset the nations play an important role in God's dealings with Israel. Primarily the nations function as the objects of his judgment, because of their pride and arrogance. For a while they are used as the instruments of his judgment. In the end, however, the nations can also be pictured as participants in his plan of salvation. Outside the collection of oracles against the foreign nations (Isa 13-23), the nations most frequently referred to in Isaiah 1-39 are Assyria and Egypt. They need individual attention in this paragraph, but first we take a closer look at the divine name Yhwh Tsebaot and the notion of the plan of God, both related to the Holy One and his dealing with the nations.

Yhwh Tsebaot

When the book of Isaiah talks about the Holy One of Israel, it often uses the name Yhwh Tsebaot, "Lord of hosts." Already in his foundational vision and calling Isaiah heard the seraphs calling to each other, exalting the holiness of Yhwh Tsebaot (6:3). Isaiah at this point also characterized the King he had seen as Yhwh Tsebaot (6:5). Sometimes this name can even be used in parallel with the Holy One (5:16, 24; cf. 8:13). Whatever its origin, in the book of Isaiah the name Yhwh Tsebaot evokes the sovereign power of Yhwh to fulfill his plans in history, with respect to his own people and other people as well. The seraphs can represent his armies and can be used to express his sovereignty, but Yhwh Tsebaot can even make use of the nations for whatever purpose he wants (cf. 10:5–6; 13:17). With regard to the nations the picture of 13:2–5 is striking. Yhwh Tsebaot is presented here as a military commander mustering his army for battle. The nations are even explicitly mentioned as his consecrated warriors. "The Holy One of Israel is, in Yahweh's own person, a dangerous military power" (Brueggemann, 1998: 17).

Plan of God

In the book of Isaiah, the work of Yhwh Tsebaot in history is not something he does at random, but something that is part of his plan. This concerns his work of judgment as well as his work of salvation, for Israel as well as for the nations (5:19; 14:26). Characteristic of Yhwh's plan is that he has the capacity to execute it and that no one is able to annul it (14:27; 28:29). The problem with Israel, however, is that they do not see and understand the plan of God (22:11). On the contrary, they audaciously challenge the Holy One of Israel to speed up his work and to hasten the fulfillment of his plan so that they can see and know it (5:19). Apparently they are unaware of the fact that the first element of God's plan will be the execution of judgment by a foreign nation. In contrast to the plan of Yhwh Isaiah also mentions the plans the nations and the people of Israel are making on their own, and criticizes them, because these plans are made without consulting Yhwh (19:3; 29:15; 30:1). Such

Isaiah, Prophet in the Service of the Holy One of Israel

plans will not stand. The same, however, concerns the plans the hostile nations have been making to threaten Israel (8:10).

Assyria

Making use of the nations, and Assyria in particular, to judge his own people is part of the plan of God. In the book of Isaiah the king of Assyria is first mentioned explicitly in 7:17 as the agent of God in the execution of his judgment. Yhwh is pictured as one who whistles for the flies from the Nile delta in Egypt and for the bees from the land of Assyria, and who hires a razor beyond the river Euphrates (7:18, 20; cf. 5:26). The focus of Isaiah's preaching is on Assyria, but the flies of Egypt are probably mentioned to underline the threat by alluding to the story of the plagues in Egypt (cf. 10:24). Damascus and Samaria shall be the first to suffer under the king of Assyria (8:4), but Judah and his helpers will have to face him too (8:7; 20:4, 6; cf. 36–37). Elsewhere Assyria is compared to a storm of hail and a destroying tempest that Yhwh shall pour out on Israel (28:2, 17). Assyria is even referred to as "the rod of his anger" (10:5). This does not mean, however, that the Holy One has given Assyria *carte blanche* to destroy and annihilate. Because of his arrogance and pride (the essence of sin in the book of Isaiah), and because of his lack of respect for the divine majesty of Yhwh, the king of Assyria himself will also be punished, as soon as Yhwh has finished all his work on Mount Zion and in Jerusalem (10:1–19). The expectation of Yhwh's judgment on Assyria is elaborated upon extensively in the book of Isaiah (14:25; 30:31–32; 31:8-9; etc.). Also for Assyria the Holy One of Israel will become a burning fire and a devouring flame (10:17).

Egypt

The first time Egypt is alluded to in the book is in the above mentioned comparison with the past experience of plagues and slavery in the context of judgment for Israel. During the days of Isaiah Egypt primarily came into view as the world power Judah leaned on for help against the Assyrians. The prophet time and again warned against relying on Egypt as a helping force (30:1–7; 31:1–3; cf. 28:15, 18). Even the Assyrian Rabshakeh prophesied that Egypt is no more than a broken reed of a staff (36:6). The fact that Israel continuously looks to Egypt for help is also the background of the prophecies in which the downfall of Egypt is prophesied (Isa. 18–20).

Oracles against the nations

Though Assyria is the only real superpower in the days of Isaiah, little space is given to it (14:24–32) in the collection of oracles against the nations (Isa 13–23). This is possibly due to the fact that an original anti-Assyrian oracle has been reworked (14:4b–23). Instead of focusing on Assyria, the collection now opens with lengthy oracles concerning the day of YHWH and the downfall of Babylon (13:1—14:23), reiterated in 21:1–10, and presupposing a time in which Babylon will have long since replaced Assyria as a world power. Babylon is already pictured paradigmatically as the anti-God power *par excellence*. This means that this part of the book of Isaiah has undergone a considerable amount of updating and editing, becoming a monument of eschatological hope for Israel suffering from her enemies, of which several are mentioned by name in this collection. The theological significance of these oracles against the nations is their proclamation of the sovereign authority of YHWH over all the nations. In essence that is also the theological message of the Isaiah Apocalypse (Isa 24–27) where no nations are mentioned by name anymore and the focus is more on the certain inauguration of the kingdom of God on earth.

Hope for the nations

Though most of the oracles concerning the nations are judgment oracles, it is characteristic of the book of Isaiah that the Holy One can also have a positive relationship with the nations. It is a subject for discussion whether Isaiah himself had prophesied in a positive way concerning the destiny of the nations, but in the present context of the book the prophecy of 2:2–4 is explicitly ascribed to him and deliberately placed in the beginning. In this prophecy the nations come to Mount Zion to be instructed by YHWH. In the prophecy of 11:10 the root of Jesse himself becomes a banner for the peoples. The nations are said to inquire after him. This clearly opens up a hopeful perspective, though in the following prophecy it is elaborated in such a way that the nations are destined only to bring home the survivors of the people of Israel (11:11–16). When the editors of the book close the first collection of prophecies (1–12) with a song of thanksgiving, elaborating on the name of Isaiah ("Yhwh is my salvation"), there is a positive perspective on the nations again (12:4). Though probably dating to a much later period, the most impressive witness to Yhwh's positive relationship to the nations are the oracles concerning Egypt. A clearly Isaianic judgment oracle (19:1–15) is followed by five announcements about a future day (19:16–25). It is prophesied that Yhwh will send a savior to Egypt and make himself known to the Egyptians. If translated correctly, it is even said that the Egyptians and Assyrians will worship together (cf. 18:7). Yhwh will bless Egypt and Assyria, calling them "my people" and the "work of my hands" respectively, aligning them with Israel (cf. 23:17–18).

Future feast

Remarkably, the future destiny of the nations is not always pictured with hope. Sometimes the nations are said to become possession of Israel (14:2). That the present book of Isaiah, however, is definitely shaped to reinforce the Isaianic message that the nations ultimately will be included in the salvation of Yhwh, is underscored by the prophecy of the future feast on the mountain of Yhwh (25:6–8). This feast will be organized for all the nations which at the same time will be freed from the shroud and sheet that is still spread over them. Even death will be swallowed up forever. Only Moab (25:10–12; cf. 16:13–14) and the overtly godless nations, of which Babylon and Edom are the most recognizable representatives, seem to be excluded from this hopeful perspective (cf. 14:21–23; 34). The message that ultimately there is also hope for the nations, is developed further in the second part of the book of Isaiah. In the end the Holy One of Israel shall be known as the God of the whole earth (54:5). Though this may appear to be a theological paradox, it is in fact the realization of the call of the Seraphs in the realm of history: "Holy, holy, holy is Yhwh Tsebaot; the whole earth is full of his glory" (6:3).

Bibliography

Barton, John. *Isaiah 1–39*. 1995. Reprint. Sheffield, UK: T. & T. Clark, 2003.
Beuken, Willem A. M. *Jesaja 1–12. Jesaja 13–27. Jesaja 28–39*. Herders Theologischer Kommentar zum Alten Testament. Freiburg: Herder, 2003, 2007, 2010.
Blenkinsopp, Joseph. *Isaiah 1–39*. The Anchor Bible 19. New York: Doubleday, 2000.

———. *Opening the Sealed Book: Interpretations of the Book of Isaiah in Late Antiquity.* Grand Rapids: Eerdmans, 2006.

Brueggemann, Walter. *Isaiah 1–39.* Westminster Bible Companion. Louisville, KY: Westminster John Knox, 1998.

Childs, Brevard S. *Isaiah.* The Old Testament Library. Louisville, KY: Westminster John Knox, 2001.

———. *The Struggle to Understand Isaiah as Christian Scripture.* Grand Rapids: Eerdmans, 2004.

Dekker, Jaap. "Bind Up the Testimony: Isaiah 8:16 and the Making of the Hebrew Bible." In *The Impact of Unit Delimitation on Exegesis.* Pericope 7: Scripture as Written and Read in Antiquity, edited by Raymond de Hoop et al., 63–85. Leiden: Brill, 2009.

———. *Zion's Rock-Solid Foundations: An Exegetical Study of the Zion Text in Isaiah 28:16.* Oudtestamentische Studiën 54. Leiden: Brill, 2007.

Firth, David G., and H. G. M. Williamson. *Interpreting Isaiah: Issues and Approaches.* Downers Grove, IL: InterVarsity, 2009.

McGinnis, Claire M., and Patricia K. Tull. *"As Those Who Are Taught": The Interpretation of Isaiah from the LXX to the SBL.* Symposium Series 27. Atlanta: Society of Biblical Literature, 2006.

Roberts, J. J. M. "Isaiah in Old Testament Theology." *Interpretation* 36 (1982) 130–43.

Sawyer, John, F. A. *The Fifth Gospel: Isaiah in the History of Christianity.* Cambridge: Cambridge University Press, 1996.

Williamson, H. G. M. "Isaiah and the Holy One of Israel." In *Biblical Hebrew, Biblical Texts: Essays in Memory of Michael P. Weitzman,* JSOT Suppl. 133, edited by Ada Rapoport-Albert and Gillian Greenberg, 22–38. Sheffield: JSOT, 2001.

Chapter 5

Micah, Prophet of Hope through Judgment

Historical Setting of the Book

The prophet

WE DO NOT KNOW very much about Micah as a person. He comes from Moresheth (1:1), a small town halfway between Jerusalem and the Mediterranean Sea. We may speculate about his family background or his prophetic ministry, but the only thing we have is his message. Actually, the name "Micah" is a sentence. It means "Who (*mi-*) is like (*-ca-*) Yhwh (*yah*)?" Obviously, this name conveys the message of the prophet. There is no other god like Yhwh. Beside Yhwh, there is no other king in heaven and on earth. After the announced judgment, this sovereignty of Yhwh will eventually be Israel's hope, because the uniqueness of Yhwh leads the way to the forgiveness of her sins (7:18–20).

The time of Micah

Micah delivered his message of judgment and hope to Samaria and Jerusalem during the reigns of Jotham (750–731 BCE), Ahaz (735–715 BCE), and Hezekiah (729–686 BCE) (1:1). Amos and Hosea had started their prophetic ministries in Israel one generation before the appearance of Micah on the prophetic stage (ca. 740–690 BCE). The ministry of Isaiah (745–700 BCE) falls within Micah's time (cf. the remarkable parallel of Mic 4:1–5 in Isa 2:2–5).

The Lion Has Roared

Time bar (BCE)	800	750	700	650
Prophets		Micah		
	Hosea			
	Amos	Isaiah		
Kings in Judah		Jotham – Ahaz – Hezekiah		
Kings in Israel	Jerobeam II	Menahem Pekah – Hoshea		

The Assyrian threat

During Micah's time it became very clear that the Assyrian Empire was on the rise. Tiglath-Pileser III had aggressively pushed ahead the re-expansion of Assyria in the ancient Near East (745–727 BCE). Under Rezin (732 BCE), Israel and Judah had witnessed the fall of their northern neighbor Aram. Then Shalmaneser V (727–722 BCE) and Sargon II (722–705 BCE) ultimately defeated Israel when Samaria fell in 722 BCE. Subsequently, even the Southern Kingdom of Judah was threatened by the Assyrian army. This time it was Sennacherib (705–681 BCE) who carried forward the establishment of Assyrian power as the dominating number one in the Middle East. But Hezekiah escaped the horrors of the Assyrian danger once again by the skin of his teeth (see Isa 36–37).

The social and moral situation

Micah had learned from the fate of Samaria that the messages of Amos and Hosea had come true. He had seen the social and ethical decline of Samaria, and now he witnessed the same things taking place in her "prostitute" sister, Jerusalem. The upper-class leadership did not assume responsibility for guiding and caring for the people and the land. Farmers were driven off their land (2:1–2), people lost their property, and even basic needs like housing and clothing were threatened (2:8–9). The leading judges did not exercise justice, but were corrupt and easy targets for taking bribes (3:11). Neither the priests nor the prophets intervened because they, too, administered their offices for financial gain (3:11). The social and moral decline of Judah continued without restraint, while the leaders did not realize that a disaster was about to hit Jerusalem.

Micah, Prophet of Hope through Judgment

Content and Structure of the Book

A popular approach for structuring the book of Micah is that of Willis and Waltke (see also the recent overview of Decorzant, 2010: 37–44) who recognize an alternating pattern of doom and hope dividing the book of Micah into three units (Mic 1–2, 3–5, 6–7). Accordingly, each of these units is, again, made up of two subunits dealing with the topics of judgment and hope respectively. However, these two topics make only for a very general outline. A closer look into the book of Micah makes it clear that there is a logical and more detailed line of argumentation that is not so easy to grasp. It is difficult to decide how the several units function as parts of an assumed larger unit. There seem to be several structural markers, but it is a matter of discussion whether and to what extent they determine the parting lines between (sub)units. Thus, the scholarly proposals for structuring the book of Micah range from only two to up to six units (cf. the overview by Jacobs, 2001: 60).

The following list shows those expressions at the beginning or at the end of a section that may function as structural devices:

1. The whole book of Micah is framed by Yhwh dealing with the *sins* of his people. Yhwh who rules the world will forgive the *sins* of the people according to the covenant with Abraham for the whole world – from the top of the earth to the depths of the sea (1:2–5; 7:18–20).
2. The word *"ruin"* brackets chapters 1–3. Zion becomes a *ruin* like Samaria (1:2, 3:12).
3. Yhwh's anger addresses even the *nations*. These nations have to *hear* what Yhwh says (1:2), but they do not *hear* (5:14 [15]). Furthermore the word *"hear"* appears at the beginning of several units (1:2; 3:1; 6:1; 7:7). But it is not clear to what extent it functions as a structural device.
4. The *nations* go up to the mountain of Yhwh (4:1–2) and turn in fear to Yhwh and the end of the book (7:16–17).
5. Yhwh takes vengeance in *anger* (5:14 [15]). But Yhwh does not stay *angry* (7:16–17).

Obviously, the first subdivision on the macro level comprises at least two units. These are chapters 1–5 and chapters 6–7. Up to this point, most scholars agree (cf. Hagstrom, Mays). Chapter 1 commences with the announcement of YHWH's judgment over Samaria and Jerusalem. The nations shall listen to the Lord of the earth (1:2). But YHWH is angry with the nations that have failed to listen to his words (5:14 [15]).

One may also suppose divisions between chapters 1–2, 3–5, and 6–7 (cf. Allen, Jacobs, Waltke, Willis). Many commentators, however, prefer a different subdivision into three parts: chapters 1–3, 4–5, 6–7 (cf. Dreytza, Kessler, Mason, Smith). Zenger (2008: 554) splits even chapters 6–7 into two units: 6:1—7:7 and 7:8–20. In this division he identifies a thematic alternation between judgment (chs. 1–3; 6:1—7:7) and hope (chs. 4–5; 7:8–20). Finally, the outline of the book of Micah might be understood as consisting of four major parts (cf. also Wolff):

- A. YHWH comes to judge Samaria/Jerusalem; this also includes a charge against the present leaders of the people (1–3)
- B. YHWH, as the King, brings salvation and victory for Zion and purifies Zion in the midst of the nations (4–5)
- C. In a lawsuit YHWH appears as the accuser of his people (6:1—7:7)
- D. Final victory of YHWH and his mercy towards his people (7:8–20)

Chapter 1 starts with "Hear" (שִׁמְעוּ; v. 2). This unit begins with the announcement of the coming destruction of Samaria and, likewise, Jerusalem. However, the reader has to wait for the fulfillment of this message until the end of chapter 3. Finally Jerusalem, like Samaria, becomes a "ruin" (עִי), a word that appears in 1:6 and in 3:12. This connection is underscored by the word "field" (שָׂדֶה) that also occurs in 1:6 and 3:12. Thus, these expressions frame the unit stretching from chapters 1–3.

This judgment affects Zion. But as we move on to the next unit comprising chapters 4–5 the judgment against Zion is placed in a wider context: YHWH will judge "the nations that have not heard" in 5:14 [15] (אֶת־הַגּוֹיִם אֲשֶׁר לֹא שָׁמֵעוּ) in order to bring salvation to Zion (5:1ff [2ff]). These chapters focus on the current political situation of Judah and Jerusalem in order to show a new dimension of the coming kingship of YHWH. The first part declares the unification of the nation in Zion (4:1–8). At the end we see YHWH as king (4:7–8). At the centre of chapters 4–5 we look at the weak 'no-king' in Jerusalem (4:9–14). Chapter 5 shows the new Davidic king and the remnant reigning in the name of YHWH. This also includes the judgment of the nations (5:1–14 [2–15]).

In sum, chapters 4–5 can be seen as a bridging unit (for further study cf. Renaud). In chapter 1 YHWH descends in order to judge Judah for their sins and transgressions. The end of the book shows how Yhwh will forgive the sins of the remnant (7:18). But the final vision is about a transformation of the remnant into a strong nation together with all the nations before Yhwh in Zion (chs. 4–5). Thus, according to Dorsey (1999: 299) and Allen (1974: 260), the book as a whole displays a chiastic pattern with chapters 4–5 as the central unit (cf. also Richelle). This structure highlights the above outline theologically:

A   Coming judgment and destruction (1)
    B   Accusation against the leaders of Yhwh's people (2–3)
        C   The future restoration under the strong and righteous reign of Yhwh (4–5)
    B'   Accusation against the people of Yhwh (6:1—7:7)
A'   Future hope and renewal (7:8–20)

Theology of the Book

1. Overview

Based on these structural devices one can highlight the theological themes and, thus, come to grips with the theology of Micah.

1. Yhwh as the ruler of the entire earth and all the nations
2. The judgment of the present leaders in Israel and Judah
3. Yhwh dealing with Samaria and Jerusalem in view of their sins
4. The overcoming grace of God and the appointment of the new David

These four thematic threads are mutually dependent, as they develop within a theological cycle. The following outline gives an illustration of the thematic progression:

The Lion Has Roared

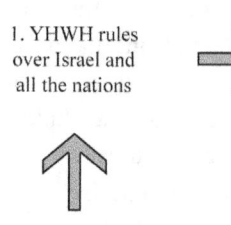

1. YHWH rules over Israel and all the nations

2. YHWH judges the rulers of Israel who are responsible for his firstborn people

3. YHWH has to punish his people because of the persistency of their sins

4. By overcoming their sins YHWH will renew his kingship in Zion for Israel and all the nations

Clearly, the initial point of departure is Yhwh, the king who established a relationship with his people. As God of all creation he is also king over all the nations (1). Because Yhwh has chosen Israel as his firstborn people among all other peoples, he has to judge the leaders of his flock because they have led them astray (2). The sin of his people stands in stark contrast with the love of Yhwh. Despite the covenantal gifts of grace and salvation Israel is unwilling to listen to God. However, Yhwh has shown his love again and again throughout the entire history of Israel. Therefore, Israel has to suffer the punishment as a consequence of their sins (3). But this judgment is not the end of the road. Yhwh overcomes the sin of his people by his grace according to his covenant. Yhwh has the purpose to build up his kingdom in Zion for all the nations through a new king who will reign in peace eternally (4).

2. Yhwh as the ruler of the entire earth and all the nations

As mentioned above, the starting point for a theology of Micah is the evaluation of the kingship of Yhwh. This gives the book its thematic frame, as can be seen in the first and the last verses (1:2–4; 7:16–20). The theological meaning of Yhwh being the King over Jerusalem and the nations is then portrayed and characterized in detail in chapters 4–5. The core statement about Yhwh is located at the centre of this thematic unit: He is the Lord of all the earth (4:13). In the face of the Assyrian invasion this theological idea of Yhwh challenges the faith of Judah. Within the dominant theological concept of the Assyrian king as a servant of the god Assur, under the mandate of whom he is about to subdue the

Micah, Prophet of Hope through Judgment

ancient Near East, the belief in a faithful and mighty Yhwh is on the brink of collapse. Micah, however, unequivocally sets the supremacy of Yhwh on top of the agenda. Thus, 1:2–4 pictures Yhwh as descending from his heavenly realm in order to destroy Samaria. Yhwh is not only a national God of Jerusalem or Samaria. Though the judgment takes place locally, Yhwh's intervention has a universal perspective for all the nations. Finally, all the nations are gathered for judgment (5:14 [15]). Even though the judgment starts with the people of God in Jerusalem, Yhwh exercises his judgment by his claim that he is indeed the universal King. The victory of the Assyrians is neither due to their military power nor the result of their god Assur. It is Yhwh who grants power to nations. The nations, for their part, have to obey. If they do not they will have to bear the consequences (5:4 [5], 14 [15]).

At the very heart of the book the universal lordship of Yhwh is pictured in terms of its restoring and renewing dimension, not only for Israel and Judah, but for all the nations. The people of Israel who walk in pilgrimage to the temple in Jerusalem present a model for the nations to join this track on the road to mount Zion (4:1–5). Finally, Yhwh is pictured as a righteous judge over all the nations who will unite them in peace (4:3).

Yhwh as the creator is the only God who can guarantee the reliability of his plans. In chapters 4–5 we see how the salvation of his chosen people on the national level is paralleled to the salvation of all the peoples on an international level. These two aspects cannot be separated. The kingship of Yhwh is the starting as well as the finishing point (4:7). This heavenly King will reestablish an earthly king in Jerusalem (4:8) who will reign in peace after the victory over Assyria (5:1–5 [2–6]). But the current situation in Judah stands in sharp contrast to the claim of Yhwh and his view of the future: There is no king in Jerusalem who is able to protect Judah from the danger. The nations have gathered in order to bring Zion down. Judah will go into captivity (4:9–11). Despite this desperate situation, Yhwh states that he is in control, even during the time of the exile (4:10), because Yhwh himself has gathered the nations "like a sheaf to the threshing-floor" (4:12). Yhwh will leave a remnant among the nations. Through this remnant, that will become a strong nation, Yhwh will execute his judgment over the nations (5:6–14 [7–15]). Both Israel and the nations have to suffer through the judgment of Yhwh in order to be united under Yhwh as their king ruling in Zion. Then Yhwh will have destroyed all military equipment (4:3, 5:9 [10]) and all aspects of idol worship (5:11–13 [12–14]). Eventually, Israel and the nations will gather in Zion as peaceful nations under God, obedient to the instructions (תּוֹרָה) of the king Yhwh (4:2).

3. The judgment of the leaders of Israel and Judah

In the ancient Near East the king is often portrayed in the role of a shepherd. Accordingly, Yhwh, being the King, is portrayed as gathering his sheep (2:12). As shepherd and king he is also the judge of Israel. Therefore, he challenges the leaders of his flock. Noticeably in 2:13 Yhwh passes through "at their head" (בְּרֹאשָׁם) and accuses "the heads of Jacob" (רָאשֵׁי יַעֲקֹב) directly in the following verse (3:1). As the great King and Judge he is responsible for the keeping and the enforcement of his laws through the appointed leaders. But all the leaders of Israel are acting contrary to his decree. This is the reason why not only the king is confronted with his false attitudes towards and deeds against Yhwh's flock, but also the judges, counselors, leaders, rulers, prophets, seers, diviners, and priests (2:11; 3:1, 5–11; 4:9, 14; 7:3). Finally, the transformation of the people also contains the judgment of the leaders that are responsible for the social, ethical and spiritual condition of the people in Judah and Jerusalem. After the judgment there will be room for a new ruler (5:1[2]) who will represent the kingship of Yhwh (4:7) in the strength of Yhwh in order to shepherd his flock (5:3[4]).

4. Yhwh dealing with Samaria and Jerusalem in view of their sins

The above-mentioned future is only possible if Yhwh creates a new people. This hope is rooted in the belief that Yhwh is the creator and ruler of the entire earth. He addresses the earth and its inhabitants. The nations have to listen to the only king in heaven and on earth (1:2–4). As king of Israel he is also the God of the covenant, but his holy nation has forgotten its status before Yhwh. Therefore, Yhwh has to remind them of his mighty acts of salvation in the course of history (6:3–5). Obviously, the mercy of Yhwh has not led Israel to merciful deeds. They do not show justice to the members of their own community (6:8–12), but they still feel secure in Jerusalem due to the Davidic promise for Zion. Their sinful behavior forces the curses of the covenant upon them instead of blessings (1:6–7; 6:13–16).

Throughout the book Micah uses different expressions explaining the destructive behavior of Israel: "sin" (חַטָּאת), "transgression" (פֶּשַׁע), "iniquity" (עָוֹן), "wickedness" (אָוֶן) and "evil" (רָע / רָעָה). By its sin Israel has broken the relationship with Yhwh and has provoked his wrath. Therefore Micah has to pronounce the final judgment on them (6:1–2). Yhwh as a God of both anger and mercy is able to maintain his covenant not only with his people Israel but he also keeps his promise for them to be a blessing for all the peoples. The harmful behavior of Israel that is displayed throughout the book of Micah is overcome by Yhwh himself as can be seen in the closing section (7:18–20).

The following chart shows the use and distribution of the expressions concerning the sinful attitudes and deeds of God's people:

	Ch. 1	Ch. 2	Ch. 3	Ch. 4	Ch. 5	Ch. 6	Ch. 7
Sin	1:5, 13		3:8			6:7	7:19
Transgression	1:5, 13		3:8			6:7	7:18
Wickedness		2:1					
Evil		2:1, 3	3:2, 4				
Iniquity							7:18, 19

At the end of the book we see Yhwh's triumph over his own anger (7:18, cf. 5:14 [15]) and the victory of his own "truth" (אֱמֶת) and "mercy" (חֶסֶד). He finally "shows compassion" (יְרַחֲמֵנוּ) and "pardons sin and forgives the transgression" (נֹשֵׂא עָוֹן וְעֹבֵר עַל־פֶּשַׁע).

5. The overcoming grace of God and the appointment of the new David

We have seen Yhwh approaching all the peoples of the earth. He is not only the God of Jerusalem or Samaria but the Lord who reigns in his holy temple universally. From this position he descends in order to accuse and judge Jacob (1:2–5). Since Yhwh rules over the entire earth he is the only God who is able to destroy and restore, punish and pardon. As the only ruler Yhwh is able to guarantee his grace, which is pictured as one of his characteristics. There are two aspects to his grace. On the one hand, it stands for his steadfast faithfulness. He is consistent. Nobody can change his ways. On the other hand, we see his passion for mercy in order to forgive. Thus, Yhwh himself does change his plans in order to renew his relationship with Israel and the nations.

Yhwh approaches Samaria/Jerusalem and even the nations on the basis of this claim. They all have to hear and listen to the words of the judge. Micah's message does not end in doom. Rather, the predicted doom is the foundation for transformation, hope and peace. Certainly, the oracles of judgment are many and severe in their dimension. But there is hope because of the new covenantal initiative of Yhwh. Because the king and the people of God have constantly failed, God is going to renew the relationship. Zion will become the centre for all the nations of the world. They will meet in Jerusalem to experience the new *shalom* under the new king David. Jerusalem will experience a transformation out of judgment to restoration and enduring freedom. Jerusalem will be turned from the heap of stones in a field (3:12) into the highest mountain to which the nations will flock and experience blessing (4:1–5). "These prophecies become powerful messages of hope in exile, when Babylon is the highest 'mountain' and Jerusalem lies shattered and depopulated. The tables will be turned" (Dempster, 2003: 188). God judges Israel because of its sin. But this judgment is described as a precondition for creating new hope. In this case judgment is the indispensable condition for hope. This can be illustrated by the two aspects of the word "through." Firstly, hope carries *through* in the face of judgment. Secondly, the renewal of hope only becomes true *through* the experience of judgment. The kingship of David in Zion will be renewed because the kingship of Yhwh lasts forever. The new Davidic king is appointed to reign in the name of Yhwh. His majesty will reach as far as the ends of the earth (5:3 [4]).

Bibliography

Allen, Leslie C. *The Books of Joel, Obadiah, Jonah and Micah*. NICOT. Grand Rapids: Eerdmans, 1974.

Decorzant, Alain. *Vom Gericht zum Erbarmen: Text und Theologie von Micha 6–7*. Forschung zur Bibel. Würzburg: Echter, 2010.

Dempster, Stephen G. *Dominion and Dynasty: A Theology of the Hebrew Bible*. NSBT 15. Downers Grove, IL: InterVarsity, 2003.

Dorsey, David A. *The Literary Structure of the Old Testament: A Commentary on Genesis-Malachi*. Grand Rapids: Baker, 1999.

Dreytza, Manfred. *Das Buch Micha*. Edition C Altes Testament. Witten: R. Brockhaus, 2009.

Hagstrom, David G. *The Coherence of the Book of Micah: A Literary Analysis*. SBLDS 89. Atlanta: Scholars, 1988.

Jacobs, Mignon R. *The Conceptual Coherence of the Book of Micah*. Sheffield, UK: Sheffield Academic Press, 2001.
Kessler, Rainer. *Micha*. HThAT. Freiburg: Herder, 1999.
Mason, Rex. *Micah, Nahum and Obadjah*. T. & T. Clark Study Guides. London: T. & T. Clark, 2004.
Mays, James L. *Micah: A Commentary*. OTL. Philadelphia: Westminster, 1976.
Renaud, Bernard. *La Formation du Livre de Michée: Tradition et Actualisation*. Étude Biblique. Paris: Gabalda, 1987.
Richelle, Matthieu. "Un triptyque au coeur du livre de Michée (Mi 4-5)." *Vetus Testamentum* 62 (2012) 232–47.
Smith, Ralph. *Micah-Malachi*. WBC 32. Waco, TX: Word, 1984.
Waltke, Bruce K. *A Commentary on Micah*. Grand Rapids: Eerdmans, 2007.
Willis, John T. "The Structure of the Book of Micah." *SEÅ* 34 (1969) 5–42.
Wolff, Hans W. *Micha*. BKAT Dodekapropheton 4. Neukirchen-Vluyn: Neukirchener, 1982.
Zenger, Erich. *Einleitung in das Alte Testament*. 7th rev. ed. Stuttgart: Kohlhammer, 2008.

Seventh-Century Prophets

Chapter 6

Nahum, Prophet of the God Who Avenges Injustice

Historical Setting of the Book

Judah

THE ORIGINS OF THE book of Nahum fall between 664/3 (the date of the fall of Thebes to which Nahum refers as past, 3:8) and 612 (the date of the fall of Nineveh that Nahum anticipates, 3:5–7). Because Assyria overextended itself in suppressing the rebellion of Babylon (652–648) and never recovered, the book probably dates more precisely to about 664–650 (cf. 1:12, which represents Assyria as being at full strength). These were turbulent years for the kingdom of Judah, particularly since the Assyrian empire had conquered the Northern Kingdom of Israel less than hundred years earlier, in 722. That kingdom's entire territory had become the Assyrian-administered province of Samerina, largely devoid of its original Israelite inhabitants and peopled instead by deportees from elsewhere in the Assyrian empire (2 Kgs. 17:24, 30–31). The abortive siege of Jerusalem led by the Assyrian king Sennacherib in 701 was surely no less traumatic as Sennacherib shut up Hezekiah (715–686) and those in the city "like a bird in a cage," "besieged forty-six of his fortified towns and surrounding smaller towns, which were without number" (as Sennacherib's official description of his campaign puts it, Cogan: 302–3), and annexed significant tracts of Judah's territory.

Manasseh's reign (686–642) saw Assyria's domination continue, and he was obliged to contribute both forced labor and military conscripts (cf. *ANET* 291, 294). The biblical record makes clear that this was an extremely low point in Judah's religious and moral life, with Manasseh being the primary instigator (2 Kgs 21:1–18; cf. 2 Chr 33:10–17). Amon (642–640) and Josiah (640–609) followed Manasseh, and by the time of Josiah's death Assyria had herself fallen to Babylon and its allies, partially fulfilling Nahum's prophecy.

Assyria

The Assyria of which Nahum spoke was in full possession of all its powers (1:12), and so was a terrifying presence in the ancient Near East. Since its resurgence near the end of the tenth century BCE, Assyria had managed to greatly expand its empire, aided by its highly effective intimidation of its opponents by torture and barbarism and by its sophisticated military apparatus (De Backer, 2007). This violent imperialism is attested in numerous written records produced by the Assyrian kings and in Assyrian reliefs that presented "the problems, contortions and maltreatment of dead or doomed enemies" on the walls of royal palaces (Reade, 2005: 20). In his official description of his campaign against the rebellious Yau-bi-di of Hamath, Sargon II (721–705) recounts that "I mustered the masses of Assur's troops and at Qarqar, together with his warriors, I burned Qarqar. Him I flayed. I killed the rebels in the midst of those cities" (Younger: 296). Sennacherib's account of his 701 campaign against a number of nations and city-states in the Levant for their rebellion shares the same tenor: "I advanced to Ekron and slew its officials and nobles who had stirred up rebellion and hung their bodies on watchtowers all about the city" (Cogan: 303). During this same campaign the Judean city of Lachish fell to Assyria, an event depicted in gruesome detail on extensive reliefs now housed in the British Museum. As a final example, Assurbanipal (668–627), who was in power during Nahum's ministry, recounts how he punished by killing, impaling, and flaying not only unfaithful rulers but their subjects as well, "small and great" (Melville, 2006a: 364). At the time of Nahum's ministry, therefore, Judeans might well have feared that Assyria's domination of them would prove fatal, and Nahum addresses this concern directly.

Content and Structure of the Book

The possibility that Nahum 1:2–8 is a broken acrostic has not met with widespread acceptance, but despite uncertainty on that point the structure of the book remains fairly clear. As these literary units show, the book focuses on Nineveh as God's enemy and God's opposition to her.

1:1	Superscription
1:2–8	Hymn on God the Divine Warrior
1:9–2:2[3]	Oracles of judgment against Assyria, salvation for Judah
2:3[4]-10[11]	Vision of Nineveh's demise
2:11[12]-13[14]	Lion taunt
3:1–3	Woe oracle against Nineveh
3:4–7	Sorceress-harlot taunt
3:8–11	Historical taunt
3:12–15c	Insults against Nineveh
3:15d–17	Locust taunt
3:18–19	Final dirge

Theology of the Book

Nahum announces that God as the Divine Warrior will exercise his righteous vengeance against the powers of evil that oppose him and his people while delivering those that trust in him. The following themes explore various facets of this summary, following the literary order of the book when possible. The allusion to Exodus 34 in 1:2–8 merits special attention due to that passage's prominence in the Old Testament.

1. God as a warrior and Assyria as his enemy

The book presents itself as an oracle of judgment against Nineveh (1:1). While such oracles typically have the prophet speak on God's behalf, God himself inveighs against Nineveh more than once (2:13; 3:4–7) and explains that he is her opponent (2:13; 3:5). Nahum's thinking is strongly marked by this divine commitment to retribution, leading him to portray God as the Creator, King, and Judge of all: note the threefold repetition of נקם in 1:2 (see further Peels, 1995: 199–207).

The Lion Has Roared

While at first glance Nahum's message that God is the foe of Judah's most dangerous enemy might appear to be mere nationalism, Nahum's description of God's vengeance against Assyria is quite sophisticated and should not be dismissed so lightly. It consists of at least three elements. First, the prophet sees Assyria's aggression against other nations, Israel and Judah included, as religiously motivated (cf. Holloway, 2002: 73–74). This would hardly surprise an Assyrian: Adad-Nirari II (911–891) states that after the gods made him "illustrious" and gave him kingship, "they called me to plunder the property of all the lands" and that he "tramples evildoers" in obedience to that commission. This is consistent with sentiments found throughout Neo-Assyrian royal inscriptions (Melville, 2006b: 282) and prophetic texts (e.g., Nissinen, 2003: 104–5).

Second, religiously motivated Assyrian aggression is not simply directed against other nation-states: in the case of Judah (if not more broadly) it is direct opposition to God himself. This is how Nahum describes Assyria's wrongdoing in detail, in particular its anti-Yhwh nature:

1. conspiracy against Yhwh (1:9–11);
2. idolatry (1:14);
3. violence (2:11–13; 3:1);
4. materialism (2:11–13; 3:16; cf. the same term (רעה) summarizing Nineveh's behavior in Jon. 3:8);
5. harlotry (3:4–7) because of the integration of her religion, warfare, and economic activity (cf. 3:16–17, and Gwaltney, 1998);
6. "emptying" Judah (2:2).

Third, and most importantly, while the historical setting of the book makes clear that Assyria was indisputably Judah's oppressor, Nahum sets Assyria's actions in the context of Yhwh's redemptive-historical acts against evil and so presents that empire as a stereotyped manifestation of ungodly evil (1:11). Although it is unlikely that בליעל ("evil/wicked") is personified here as "Belial" (Floyd, 2000: 46–48), the anti-God element is clearly present in the context. In the same vein, it is crucially important that Nahum characterizes the non-Israelite nations other than Assyria (many of whom other biblical prophets condemn for violations of God's universal moral rules [e.g., Amos 1:3—2:3, where God enforces his will as universal King against many nations around Israel and Judah] and often for aggression against Israel and Judah [e.g., the "oracles against the nations" that appear in almost every writing prophet]) simply as victims of Assyrian violence (3:4). In other words, they too are stereotyped, for Nahum atypically overlooks their sins (contrast Amos 1:3—2:3). Yhwh will judge Assyria not because it is nationally or culturally different from Judah, but because it is the primary expression of obdurate opposition to the God of Israel in the seventh century.

This point is important enough to explore in some detail. Early in the history recounted by the OT God is opposed to individuals or lines within a family (e.g., the serpent's seed, Gen 3:15; the line of Cain, Gen 4:16–22, which ends in the flood; Canaan, Gen 9:25), while graciously delivering the line of promise, including Seth, Noah, and Shem, whose line forms an inclusion around the Table of Nations (Gen 10:1, 21) and is immediately followed by the genealogy of Abram (Gen 11:10-26). Once Israel becomes a clan, and later a nation, various groups begin to oppose her, and in that capacity they are treated as God's enemies even as the divine plan envisions their long-term benefit (cf. Gen 12:3). These enemies include the Egyptians and Amalekites in Exodus, the Canaanites in Joshua, and so on.

This Israel—enemies antithesis, expressed differently in the Sinai covenant's call for holiness in all spheres of life, required that Israel remain distinct from the nations around her. This proved difficult from the earliest stages of Israel's national existence (e.g., the severe religious decline described in Judges), and with time her uniqueness disappeared, especially in religious terms. Many of the writing prophets therefore develop the concept of a "remnant" within Israel. Not only do their oracles of judgment against Israel foresee that she (or parts of her) will suffer the same fate as the nations, but many prophetic oracles of salvation also announce that at least some from among the nations will share in the same deliverance as (the remnant of) Israel. Nahum's approach to these issues is closer to a sharp distinction between Judah and her enemies than it is to a distinction within Judah between a remnant and the rest of the Judeans. Judah is presented in Nahum in a stereotyped way that overlooks its religious flaws (there is thus no need for a remnant concept in Nahum) in order to sharpen the contrast between Judah and Assyria, while allowing for substantial similarity between Judah and nations other than Assyria.

2. God as a refuge and those whom he delivers

Nahum's immediate concern is to assure his audience that God will deal definitively with Assyria, whose arrogance and violence have reached a critical point and call for the exercise of his justice. Yet, although this is a message of salvation for Judah, also with regard to this salvation Nahum is not nationalistic or xenophobic. There are even hints that God's deliverance of Judah is selective. The book's first mention of Yhwh's deliverance is not promised to "Judah," but to those who "take refuge in him"(1:7; the idiom "trust in" [חסה + ב] with God as its object consistently denotes those in Israel or outside it, who seek refuge in him from the threat of the wicked; cf. 2 Sam 22 // Ps 18; Ps 2:12; 5:11; 31:19; 37:40; 64:10). It is also striking that Carmel and Bashan are among the areas affected by Yhwh's cosmic judgment, since both are in (northern) Israelite territory (although now an Assyrian province; cf. Isa 2:13; 33:9; Amos 1:2; Zech 11:2). There may also be an oblique reference to Jacob's new name in 2:2 such that God will restore to "Jacob" (Judah in a lackluster spiritual condition) the excellence and blessing that were associated with Israel/Jacob after his struggle with God (cf. Gen 32:27–28; Hamilton, 2000: 588).

This type of distinction, however inchoate it is in Nahum, would have been almost unavoidable in the ministry of a prophet of Yhwh in seventh-century Judah. The OT itself (e.g., Zech 1) and archaeological evidence both clearly show that not all Judahites were faithful to the God who had called his name over them (cf. Stavrakopoulou and Barton, 2010). Since the referent of "Judah" has some flexibility by virtue of the opening section's emphasis on those "trust in Yhwh," God's promised deliverance to "Judah" in 1:15 should not be conceived of as a *carte blanche* guarantee of deliverance for all Judahites regardless of their religious commitments.

3. Judgment and deliverance in the day of Yhwh

In Nahum, this deliverance spares those who trust in Yhwh from the "day of distress" (1:7). This "day" appears as part of a larger context (1:2–8) that describes God's vengeance against his enemies on a scale that affects the seas, Israel, Lebanon, and the earth and all its inhabitants (1:4–5). This complex of events forms the final horizon against which to understand the book's message.

Most of the other writing prophets refer frequently, most often with the term "Day of the LORD," to a complex of events in which God definitively reveals his righteousness, destroys the wicked, and delivers his people (Beasley-Murray, 1986: 11–16). While Nahum uses the term "day of distress," his vision of the future overlaps significantly with what other writing prophets mean by the "Day of Yhwh," and other prophets occasionally use "day of distress" in describing the same climactic divine intervention (Obad 12, 14; Hab 3:16; Zeph 1:15). Accordingly, although Assyria's punishment is important and inevitable in Nahum (repentance is neither offered nor contemplated), the "day of distress" extends beyond her to *all* of Yhwh's "enemies" (1:2).

For this reason it is preferable to refer to the fall of Nineveh as a *partial* fulfillment of Nahum's message. The Day of Yhwh cannot be reduced to one event (Nogalski, 2003: 196). Beyond the fall of Nineveh (3:18–19) lies a cosmic denouement by which God's kingdom will be fully established, his enemies vanquished, and his people delivered.

Conclusions and New Testament Trajectories

Nahum encourages his Judahite audience by affirming that God will deliver those who trust in him from Nineveh's clutches. His representation of Assyria as a chiffre for all evil also provides hope that God will ultimately deliver from evil itself. Accordingly, Paul focuses on God's superlative revelation of his righteousness in Christ's death and resurrection while arguing that Gentiles can receive this righteousness in the same way as Jews (Rom 3; 9). Other New Testament documents show that the destruction that Nahum announced against the Neo-Assyrian empire is indeed part of an epoch-long battle which God will decisively conclude by defeating and destroying "Babylon" and the "nations," titles that Revelation defines in religious/spiritual rather than ethnic/national terms. Since this battle is still being waged, the message of Nahum remains as pertinent today as when first delivered, and its promise of deliverance helps sustain the faith and fidelity of all those who face opposition for the sake of Jesus and the gospel (Mark 8:35).

Bibliography

Beasley-Murray, G. R. *Jesus and the Kingdom of God*. Exeter, UK: Paternoster, 1986.

Christensen, D. L. *Nahum*: A New Translation with Introduction and Commentary. Anchor Yale Bible 24F. New Haven: Yale University, 2009.

Cogan, M. "Sennacherib's Siege of Jerusalem." *Context of Scripture* 2.119B (2: 302–3).

De Backer, F. "Some Basic Tactics of Neo-Assyrian Warfare." *UF* 39 (2007) 69–115.

Floyd, M. H. *Minor Prophets, Part 2*. FOTL 22. Grand Rapids: Eerdmans, 2000.

Gwaltney, W. C. "Assyrians." In *Peoples of the Old Testament World*, edited by Alfred J. Hoerth, Gerald L. Mattingly, and Edwin M. Yamauchi, with a foreword by Alan Millard, 77–106. Grand Rapids: Baker, 1998.

Hamilton, V. P. "Jacob." In *New Dictionary of Biblical Theology*, edited by T. D. Alexander and B. R. Rosner, 587–89. Leicester, UK: InterVarsity, 2000.

Holloway, S. *Assur is King! Assur is King! Religion in the Exercise of Power in the Neo-Assyrian Empire*. CHANE 10. Leiden: Brill, 2002.

Longman, T. "Nahum." In *The Minor Prophets: An Exegetical and Expositional Commentary*. 3 vols., edited by T. McKomisky, 765–829. Grand Rapids: Baker, 1993.

Melville, S. "Apology and Egyptian Campaigns." In *The Ancient Near East: Historical Sources in Translation*, edited by M. Chavalas, 363–65. Blackwell Sourcebooks in Ancient History. Oxford: Blackwell, 2006a.

———. "Neo-Assyrian Texts 1." In *The Ancient Near East: Historical Sources in Translation*, edited by M. Chavalas, 280–85. Blackwell Sourcebooks in Ancient History. Oxford: Blackwell, 2006b.

Nissinen, M., with contributions by C. L. Seow and R. K. Ritner. *Prophets and Prophecy in the Ancient Near East*. Writings from the Ancient World. Atlanta: SBL, 2003.

Nogalski, J. D. "The Day(s) of Yhwh in the Book of the Twelve." In *Thematic Threads in the Book of the Twelve*, edited by P. L. Redditt and A. Schart, 192–213. BZAW 325. Berlin: de Gruyter, 2003.

Peels, H. G. L. *The Vengeance of God: The Meaning of the Root NQM and the Function of the NQM-Texts in the Context of Divine Revelation in the Old Testament*. OTS 31. Leiden: Brill, 1995.

Reade, J. "Religious Ritual in Assyrian Sculpture." In *Ritual and Politics in Ancient Mesopotamia*, edited by B. N. Porter, 7–61. AOS 88. New Haven: American Oriental Society, 2005.

Spronk, K. *Nahum*. Historical Commentary on the Old Testament. Kampen: Kok Pharos, 1997.

Stavrakopoulou, F., and J. Barton, editors. *Religious Diversity in Ancient Israel and Judah*. New York: T. & T. Clark, 2010.

Younger, K. L. Jr. "The Great 'Summary' Inscription." *Context of Scripture* 2.118E (2: 296–97).

Chapter 7

Zephaniah, Prophet of the Day of Yhwh

Historical Setting of the Book

Zephaniah is the only Old Testament prophet introduced by an extensive genealogy, with Hezekiah as the first forefather (1:1a). Quite likely this Hezekiah is the famous king of Judah and reference to him is a possible reason for the genealogy going back four generations. Zephaniah's membership of the royal family probably also gave him access to the royal court, a position from which he could observe Judah's leaders (1:8, 12–13; 3:3–4). His name is a cognomen borne by three other individuals in the Old Testament (1 Chr 6:36; Jer 21:1; Zech 6:10). Usually it is explained as "Yhwh hides."

The prophecies of Zephaniah are dated during the reign of king Josiah, son of Amon of Judah (1:1b) circa 640–609 BCE. The downfall of Nineveh, announced in 2:13–15, occurred in 612 BCE, a few years before the death of Josiah.

In the eighteenth year of the reign of king Josiah, in 622 BCE, a law book of Moses was found in the temple (2 Kgs 22:3–20; 2 Chr 34:8–28). Usually this find is identified as (the main part of) the book of Deuteronomy. The book of Zephaniah does not contain any clear allusion to the discovery of the law book or to the reform activities associated with it. The book of Kings describes the reform thematically, centered around the discovery of the book, while the book of Chronicles gives a chronological sequence. It seems very likely that the extensive reforms took place over the span of many years. The official reforming activities of the king could not speedily stop the abuses among the wealthy inhabitants of

Jerusalem. Maybe the expression "remnant of Baal" (1:4) is an indication of an earlier purging, but the phrase may simply mean that God would remove the worship of Baal. Hence, the description of the sins in the book cannot reliably be used to determine whether Zephaniah was active before or after Josiah's reform.

Yet, the book of Zephaniah contains a wealth of phraseology reminiscent of paralleling expressions in the book of Deuteronomy (see examples in "Theology of the book," 3). These parallels suggest that Zephaniah used the recently found law book and helped to advance the reform instituted by Josiah. If this was the case, we could then date the prophecies of Zephaniah after 622 BCE and before the downfall of Nineveh in 612 BCE.

It is notable that Zephaniah expects a foreign invasion that will bring about the destruction of Jerusalem (1:4, 10–13; 2:1; 3:1–4). Scholars disagree on the identity of the enemy anticipated. In the above mentioned period the Assyrians are no longer a likely option, as the prophet already announces the destruction of Assur and Nineveh (2:13–15). A second possibility is the Scythians, a group of tribes described by Herodotus (*Histories* 1: 105). However, their raids were apparently brief and may have been confined to sites along the international coastal highway (Via Maris) with little direct impact on Judah. The disaster as announced by Zephaniah would also have affected the surrounding nations (2:4–12) and even Assyria itself (2:13–15). He appears to expect the destruction of Jerusalem and the deportation of the population. The remaining candidate would be the upcoming Babylonian Empire. The author of Kings reports that the coming invasion by Babylon was already anticipated at the time of Hezekiah (2 Kgs 20:17) and of Josiah (2 Kgs 22:15–20). The Babylonian incursions into this region started after the battle of Carchemish (605 BCE). We do well to read the prophecies of Zephaniah in this historical context.

Content and Structure of the Book

The structure of the book of Zephaniah compares fittingly with structures found in the Books of Isaiah, Jeremiah (shorter LXX version), and Ezekiel. These oracles all begin with the immediate historical situation of Judah, then turn to foreign nations, and end with a future eschatological blessing.

Superscription (1:1)

I. Oracles against Judah (1:2—2:3)

    A. Universal judgment, 1:2–3

    B. Judgment of Jerusalem, 1:4–13

    C. The Day of Yhwh, 1:14–18

    D. Means of avoiding judgment, 2:1–3

II. Oracles against foreign nations and Judah (2:4—3:8)

    A. Philistia, 2:4–7

    B. Moab and Ammon, 2:8–11

    C. Cush (Nubia), 2:12

    D. Assyria, 2:13–15

    E. Jerusalem, 3:1–7

    F. Universal judgment, 3:8

III. Oracles of blessing (3:9–20)

    A. Universal worship, 3:9–10

    B. Remnant in Zion, 3:11–20

The book of Zephaniah is characterized by a logical, orderly flow of thought, and reveals a carefully constructed unity. Several exegetes qualify the hopeful outlook of the last part of the book as a later addition, or assume three stages in the growth of the book: original material, redacted texts, and later additions (Vlaardingerbroek, 1999). However, the theological criteria for such reconstructions are not convincing. The theme of final salvation of the remnant (3:8–13), purified from sin in the coming judgment, was already familiar to the eight-century prophets, notably Isaiah. Other prophecies of judgment commonly concluded with an expectation of restoration and final felicity, for instance in the closing parts of the books of Amos, Micah, Nahum, and Habakkuk. If we assume a covenantal background as formulated in Deuteronomy 28–30, then the coherence can be demonstrated between the prophecies of doom and the prophecies of salvation.

Theology of the Book

1. The word of Yhwh

The message of the prophet begins with "The word of Yhwh which came to Zephaniah." The prophet's opening phrase positions him within a stream of servants of God, who were receptive to his message and did not speak their own words (cf. Deut 18:15-20). The admission of this book into the Old Testament canon confirms that the Israelites have accepted this high claim. The booklet presents itself as the word of the God of Israel and not merely as the word of an individual with a message.

2. The Day of YHWH

The theme unifying the entire book of Zephaniah is the notion of יום יהוה (*yôm* YHWH, "Day of YHWH"). Especially in the first chapter, this Day marks the message of the prophet. Related to this Day are the features of the destruction of the cosmos, the judgment on God's own people, the sacrificial feast of YHWH, and the terrors of a finalizing theophany (Robertson, 1990: 257). Zephaniah described the nature of the divine judgment by adopting ideas from older prophetic sources and in particular by employing the concept of the Day of the Lord as is found in Amos (5:18f.) and Isaiah (2:7-22).

The first two verses of Zephaniah's message form confronting statements about the destruction of this world (1:2-3). The order pertaining to humans and animals is a reverse from the creation narrative (Gen 1:20-27). Rather than leading up to a pronouncement of judgment by listing sins first, Zephaniah begins with a striking statement of total and devastating punishment. The Day of YHWH involves a theophany in which God manifests his power. It can be compared to a gathering for a sacrificial feast with consecrated guests, at which, however, the officials, the royal household, and many inhabitants of Jerusalem will be punished (1:7-13; cf. Isa 34:5-8; Ezek 39:17-20). Other features of the message are frightful images of God's appearance with darkness and gloom, clouds and blackness, a day with a trumpet sounding, and a war cry. These aspects remind us of the phenomena accompanying the establishment of the Sinai covenant (Exod 19:16-19), but now associated with war and punishment (cf. Judg 5:4-5; Joel 2:1-2; Amos 5:18, 20). The rather immediate expectation of this Day is indicated by the references to its nearness (1:7, 14) and to specific peoples. Other aspects suggest a later time of fulfillment, namely by the description of the cosmic proportions of the theophany. Zephaniah blended—as did other prophets—events near at hand and events expected in the future. The Day not only entails negative aspects, but also such positive aspects as the salvation of those people from Israel and all the nations who will come to worship Yhwh.

3. God's covenant

The dark and light sides of the message of the prophet are based on the covenant of God with Israel. The many parallels with passages from Deuteronomy include the following: to build houses, but not dwell in them (Zeph 1:13; cf. Deut 28:30); to plant vineyards, but not drink their wine (1:13; cf. Deut 28:39); a day of constraint and distress (1:15; cf. Deut 28: 53-57); a day of thick darkness (1:15; cf. Deut 4:11); to walk as blind men (1:17; cf. Deut 28:29); in the fire of his jealousy all the earth shall be consumed (1:18; cf. Deut 32:21-22); Yhwh is righteous; . . . he will not commit iniquity (3:5; cf. Deut 32:4); rejoice over you with singing (3:17; cf. Deut 28:63); a praise and a name among all the peoples of the earth (3:19-20; cf. Deut 26:19). More expressions such as "the scattered ones," the concentration on the "love" of God for Israel, and the representation of God as the king, a mighty hero, can be added (Robertson 1990: 69, 254-55).

4. God as universal judge

The opening chapters of Zephaniah reveal God as a righteous judge, who is offended by moral and religious sins. The people of Judah had blurred the essential distinction between Yhwh and the gods of the nations (1:4-5). They regarded God as indifferent and assumed that he would do neither good nor evil. However, Zephaniah announces the activity and wrath of God (1:12). God is pictured as the creator, who may destroy his creation. He is the God of the whole earth who judges all the peoples according to their behavior. As a result of all the punishments and his further activities, a purified remnant will remain on earth. Amidst of God's wrath there is always his mercy and the possibility of redemption. This view of punishment fits the patterns already set in Genesis 1–11, Deuteronomy 27-28, Isaiah 40-66, Jeremiah 31-34, and other texts. God always retains a remnant.

5. Idolatry

Because of their sins, Judah and in Jerusalem, both the city and its temple, will experience a devastating future. The ultimate reason is their prevailing idolatry. Five objects of extermination are mentioned: the remnant of Baal, the name of the idolatrous priests, those who bow down on the roof to the host of heavens, those who swear by Milcom, and those who have not sought Yhwh (1:4–6). This enumeration has striking similarities with the listing of reforms by Josiah in 2 Kings 23:4–5, 10–13. Zephaniah denounces the idolatry that he had witnessed in Jerusalem, where there had been no spiritual revival since the time of his ancestor Hezekiah. The royal court (not only the literal sons of the king) and the officials are mentioned, but not the king himself. Because of the reforming activities of King Josiah, it seems that this is an intended exclusion. Several idolatrous habits of the inhabitants of Jerusalem are listed, such as dressing in foreign attire (maybe priestly garments, 2 Kgs 10:22), a leaping over the threshold (cf. 1 Sam 5:5), as well as violence and fraud (1:8–9). The searching of Jerusalem with lamps means that no one can escape the pending judgment (1:12; cf. Amos 9:2–4). After dealing with the surrounding nations, also the officials, the judges, the prophets, and the priests are declared guilty (3:1–8). Now Yhwh explicitly indicates his intention to devastate other nations as well as to chasten Judah. These measures would hopefully incite Israel to lead a God-fearing life. However, the inhabitants display eagerness in making all their deeds corrupt (3:7; cf. Deut 31:29). As a consequence, Jerusalem will be included in the destruction of the earth (3:8).

6. Repentance

The second chapter portrays a call to repentance. This call does not imply that the arrival of the Day can be averted. However, a possibility exists for the repentant to gain protection on that Day ("perhaps," cf. Lam 3:29b). The prophet holds out this hope as primary motivation for urging the people to turn from their sinful ways (2:1–3). Three times the word "to seek" is used (cf. Jer 29:13). The people have to seek Yhwh, righteousness and humility. The turning to God has consequences with regard to the daily behavior. Humility is a characteristic of listening to God and the opposite of the dismissive pride (2:10, 15; 3:12; cf. Matt 11:28–30). Another motivation for repentance to be displayed by Judah is found in

Zephaniah, Prophet of the Day of Yhwh

God's word of judgment on the nations (2:4–15). Judah has to realize that righteous retribution is coming about. The prophecy demonstrates Yhwh's righteous character, his sovereign power over the nations and his redemption of the faithful.

7. The nations

Also in the second chapter, five foreign peoples are mentioned: Philistia to the West, Moab and Ammon to the East, the Cushites to the far South, and the Assyrians to the North (2:4–15). All four main directions are thereby covered, which speaks of the Day's comprehensive judgment. In the announcement of the desolation of the Philistine's cities, a remarkable comment is made. The seacoast will become the possession of the remnant of the house of Judah, for Yhwh will restore their fortunes (2:7). The prophet does not identify this remnant that will survive the devastating judgment of God. Apparently, they are the "humble," as mentioned in verse 3.

The Moabites and Ammonites are treated next. These peoples, living in the vicinity of the Dead Sea, will experience the same fate as witnessed by their ancestor Lot (Gen 19:24–38). Now, Moab will become like Sodom and the Ammonites like Gomorrah (2:9). Again a positive message is added, the remnant of Judah will repossess their land. In these events, Yhwh will destroy all the gods of the earth. Very striking is the fact that the nations of the world will worship Yhwh. Not only in Judah, but also in defeated countries will the worship of the God of Israel be performed (cf. Isa 19:19–23; Mal 1:11). In the South the far-off Cush (Nubia) is mentioned. Its inhabitants are personally addressed in a very short message. Although only threatening words are used here, in 3:10 a hopeful perspective is offered to the same nation.

The last of the peoples mentioned concerns Assyria, the mighty empire that for centuries had terrorized the ancient Near East. Almost unconceivable is the description of desolation that is to characterize the cultural metropolis Nineveh. The city will be dry as a desert and herds of cattle will lie down in it. A similar message had been delivered by the prophet Nahum. In 612 BCE the Babylonians indeed destroyed that city. In about 401 BCE, the Greek writer Xenophon passed the city of Nineveh and found not any trace of it in the shifting desert sands (*Anabasis*

3.4.8–12). The pride of Assyria as expressed in the words "I am, and there is no one else" (2:15) had come to naught.

8. The remnant and the future

The prophet depicts the formation of a new community of holy people, purified by God (Robertson, 1990: 327). This restored remnant (cf. Isa 7:3) will not be limited to only a purged group from Israel (cf. 2:9; 3:11–13). The converted from the nations will join with his people in worship and service of Yhwh (3:9–10; cf. 2:11). Zephaniah does not resolve the tension that might be felt among various aspects of his teaching, destruction of the nation, and the hope for a remnant. God converts the heart of the nations and makes them serve in unison. Even from beyond the rivers of Cush, scattered people will bring offering (3:9–10). Usually "scattered ones" is an expression used for Israelites, but here they come from the nations. On that day, the Day of Yhwh, the remnant of Israel will be purged of sin and the wicked will be destroyed. Jerusalem will become free from shame, in contrast to the earlier situation (3:11; cf. 2:1; 3:5). Only a people humble and lowly will be left (cf. Ps 37:11; Matt 5:5). They will seek refuge in the name of Yhwh, they will pasture and lie down in peace (3:12–13, cf. 2:7).

The closing verses of the book provide us with a moving description of the love of God for his people (3:14–20). Daughter Zion can sing, shout, rejoice, and exult, because the King of Israel is in her midst (cf. Deut 33:2–5; Ps 93). The absence of any reference to the house of David is rather remarkable, although, however, the phrase "a mighty hero who saves" (3:17) may refer to a (royal?) helper of God (cf. Isa 9:5). In his love, he will renew the people and he will rejoice over her (cf. Deut 28:63). All the external and internal problems will be solved. Even the lame and outcast will be changed (cf. Mic 4:6–7). The "gathering" implies more than simply returning to their land. They will be assembled as a reconstituted community. Instead of being shamed, God will make them renowned and praised among all the peoples of the earth. This is not only a restoration of Israel after the exile, but a paradise restored. The book of Zephaniah starts with a cataclysmic overthrow but ends with a glorious new order. The goal of God's judgment is redemptive, not just punitive.

Relevance for Our Time

Zephaniah's Day of Yhwh, in which the wrath of God would be poured out on Judah, became true with the destruction of Jerusalem by the Babylonians. The five other peoples mentioned by Zephaniah received their punishment and disappeared as nations from the scene of history. However, the destruction was not as thorough as depicted, and the promised renewal of Judah has not yet totally been fulfilled. The earth is not up till now a paradise restored. The ultimate "day of wrath" is yet to come (Rev 6:16–17). Many will be consumed, but it remains possible to be saved. The both sides of God's revelation and covenant are still relevant today and urge us to believe and to obey. A remnant will be saved by the Messiah (cf. Matt 3:7; 1 Thess 1:10; Rev 11:18; 14:10; 19:1–16) and the coming of a new heaven and earth is announced.

Bibliography

Baker, D. W. *Nahum, Habakkuk, and Zephaniah*. TOTC. Leicester, UK: Inter-Varsity, 1988.
Barker, K. L. and W. Bailey. *Micah, Nahum, Habakkuk, Zephaniah*. NAC. Nashville: B&H, 1998.
Ben Zvi, E. *A Historical-Critical Study of the Book of Zephaniah*. BZAW 198. Berlin: de Gruyter, 1991.
Berlin, A. *Zephaniah: A New Translation with Introduction, Notes and Commentary*. Anchor Bible 25A. Garden City, NY: Doubleday, 1994.
Bruckner, J. *Jonah, Nahum, Habakkuk, Zephaniah*. NIVAC. Grand Rapids: Zondervan, 2004.
Floyd, M. H. *Minor Prophets*, Part 2. FOTL. Grand Rapids: Eerdmans, 1999.
House, P. R. *Zephaniah: A Prophetic Drama*. Sheffield, UK: Almond, 1988.
Patterson, R. D. *Nahum, Habakkuk, Zephaniah*. Wycliffe Exegetical Commentary. Chicago: Moody, 1991.
Roberts, J. J. M. *Nahum, Habakkuk and Zephaniah*. OTL. Louisville, KY: Westminster John Knox, 1991.
Robertson, O. P. *The Books of Nahum, Habakkuk, and Zephaniah*. NICOT. Grand Rapids: Eerdmans, 1990.
Sweeney, M. A. *Zephaniah*. Hermeneia. Minneapolis: Fortress, 2003.
Vlaardingerbroek, J. *Zephaniah*. HCOT, Leuven: Peeters, 1999.

Chapter 8

Jeremiah, Prophet of Ultimate Ruin and New Hope

Historical Setting of the Book

MORE BIOGRAPHICAL INFORMATION IS available for Jeremiah than for any other Old Testament prophet. According to the heading in 1:1, he was a member of a priestly family in Anathoth, a village just north of Jerusalem. His prophetic activity in Judah and Jerusalem is said in 1:2–3 to have stretched over a period of exactly forty years. He was called in 627 BCE, during the reign of king Josiah (640–609), and notwithstanding certain periods of silence he prophesied until the definitive fall of Jerusalem in the disastrous year 587, and shortly thereafter. The major part of his activity took place during the reigns of Jehoiakim (608–598) and Zedekiah (597–587). The "weeping prophet" remained unmarried, and had to fight opposition throughout his life. A controversial figure, Jeremiah was rejected in the midst of the theo-political tumult of his days by both the common people as well as the elite at the Judean court, in spite of support received from several highly placed people (e.g., Baruch, Seraiah, Ahikam). Not long after the fall of Jerusalem in 587, he was taken off to Egypt by a remnant of Judeans from Mizpah who were afraid of reprisals after the murder of Gedaliah (Jer 40). According to an old tradition, Jeremiah met a sad death in Egypt ca. 580 (?). While he lived to see his many prophecies of doom fulfilled, he did not see the few salvation prophecies he also made reach their fulfillment.

Scholarship of the past decades has been increasingly skeptical regarding the historical reliability of the biographical details in Jeremiah. Under the lead of scholars as W. McKane and especially R. P. Carroll it is argued that Jeremiah as a prophetic figure is largely or entirely a later literary creation, a constructed presentation in the interest and service of an imposed ideology of the Deuteronomists. Other, however, still argue for a close connection between historical reality and text, among whom are W. L. Holladay, D. J. Reimer, and J. R. Lundbom. Admittedly, it cannot be denied that Jeremiah as a book came into existence well after the prophet's death (see, e.g., the historical epilogue in 52:31–34), and that the struggles of (post-)exilic Israel are reflected in its composition and redaction. In the weeping prophet's "I" we constantly hear the pain and questions of the later Jewish community. Jeremiah is a book with many layers, as is also evident from the remarkable number of doublets and quotations from other books of the Bible. All the same, however, criticism is pressed too far if the historical Jeremiah is made to disappear behind the literary Jeremiah, or if the Bible's depiction of Jeremiah is treated as a later invention and as the embodiment of an ideology. The direct historical references contained in this biblical book are simply too concrete.

Jeremiah lived and worked at a crucial time period in Israel's history. It was an era of suspense when world powers were rising and falling. The neo-Assyrian empire that had terrorized the ancient Near East for centuries met a quick end in the second half of the seventh century. While officially still a vassal state of Assyria, Judah gradually manages to regain its independence and to expand its territory under king Josiah. In 622 the temple in Jerusalem is even restored, a restoration which brings great revival to the worship of Yhwh. Remarkably, the book of Jeremiah hardly mentions anything about this restoration (but cf. 3:6 and 22:15f.); the impression we get from his prophecies is that the reform lasted for only a short time and had little socio-religious effect. During this time, a new power was beginning to rise in Mesopotamia: the "enemy from the north" under the leadership of Nabopolassar (crowned as king of Babylon in 625) and later his son Nebuchadnezzar. With help from the Medes, the Babylonians defeat their old archenemy Assyria so that Assur falls in 614 while the capital of Nineveh follows two years later in 612. When the Assyrians retreat to Haran, Pharaoh Neco in 609 hastens to their aid with an army. On his way up, Neco near Megiddo defeats the Israelite army led by Josiah, who dies in the battle (2 Kgs 23:28–30). Subsequently, Neco deposes Jehoahaz whom the people of Judah named to succeed Josiah, and sets Jehoiakim up as king in his place. The Babylonians then defeat the Assyrian-Egyptian coalition in 609 at the battle of Haran, and this leads to a long standoff along the Euphrates River.

The Egyptian hegemony over the Syro-Palestinian territories ends in 605 with the battle of Carchemish, where Nebuchadnezzar hands the Egyptians a crushing defeat (cf. 46:1–12). In the years that follow he expands his power to extend over all of Israel. A Babylonian invasion is nevertheless checked in Egypt in 601, and Nebuchadnezzar must withdraw temporarily. Then Jehoiakim refuses to pay him tribute any longer in spite of Jeremiah's persistent warnings not to rebel against Nebuchadnezzar, God's "hammer" (51:20). The Babylonians return soon, and in 598 Jerusalem is put under siege. Jehoiakim dies and is succeeded by Jehoiachin, who surrenders to the Babylonians and is deported to Babylon in 597, along with a part of the elite class (2 Kgs 24:8–17). Zedekiah, Judah's last king, wavers between loyalty to Babylon and rebellion with help from Egypt. Jeremiah's voice is drowned out by his opponents (37:11–16; 38:1–6), and in 588 Zedekiah opts for the latter policy. The so-called Lachish ostraca are probably to be dated to this period. Then, in 587, the Babylonians capture Jerusalem again; they destroy city and temple, and deport a part of the population. Jeremiah is released by the Babylonians (!) and goes to Mizpah, where the Babylonians have appointed Gedaliah to lead the people in their attempt to overcome the disastrous circumstances. However, the restoration is only temporary. Gedaliah is murdered and some of the Judeans move to Egypt, taking Jeremiah and Baruch along with them (43:6). Later the Babylonians also attack Egypt (43:8–13; 46:13–26).

The events in and around the years 609, 605, 597, and 587 had an enormous impact on Jeremiah's prophetic preaching on the life of God's people. Judah is tossed to and fro on the waves of the history of the surrounding nations (i.e., the fall of Assyria, the rise and fall of Egypt, the dominion of Babylon) and is finally inundated. That which had for centuries offered certainty to them (cf. 7:4) meets its end, because the Davidic monarchy is no longer, Judah has lost its independence as a state, the capital of Jerusalem has been devastated, the elite class has been deported, and—worst of all—God has thrust his people from his presence (52:3) and his own dwelling-place in the temple has been destroyed. The remaining population is scattered among three groups: there is one group in Babylon, another remains behind in Judea, and a last one has gone to

Jeremiah, Prophet of Ultimate Ruin and New Hope

Egypt. Although one would at first not expect it, the future belongs to the first group (24:5-7, 29:10-14).

The threat and terrifying events of those days stand in the background to the entire book of Jeremiah. The prophet's words give a careful analysis of the events, and as their cause he points to the people's apostasy and God's resulting wrath. Theology and politics are closely interrelated in this time of life and death. "The Book of Jeremiah may be understood as a long, sustained act of prophetic imagination whereby theological claim and political reality are shown to be intrinsically related" (Brueggemann, 2007: 77).

Content and Structure of the Book

In the book of Jeremiah one finds a wide variety of literary styles (poetic prophecy, prosaic narrative, speeches), a remarkable number of repetitions (e.g., the temple sermon of 7 and 26, or the announcement of judgment in 6:22-24 and 50:41-43 directed against others) and numerous quotations and allusions to passages from other books of the Bible. A chronological order is largely absent and certain passages appear to conflict with each other (22:30 and 23:5—will there be a descendant of David on the throne, or not? 2:2ff and 7:24—did the sojourn in the wilderness constitute the time of first love, or a period of apostasy?). The reader also meets a variety of voices that switch throughout the chapters without being identified, and the relationship between prophecies is on occasion unclear. A further complication is represented by the Greek text (LXX), which differs considerably from the Hebrew (MT). LXX is 1/7 shorter than MT, and places the prophecies against the nations not at the end of the book as in MT but in the middle (after 25:13). Such considerations have led some readers to call the book of Jeremiah "unreadable."

Upon closer examination, however, Jeremiah turns out to be less chaotically composed than it first appears to be. Of structural importance are, for example, the dates provided in key texts (e.g., "the thirteenth year of Josiah" in 1:2 and 25:13, "the fourth year of Jehoiakim" in 25:1, 36:1, 45:1, and 46:2, "the fourth year of Zedekiah" in 28:1 and in 51:59), the introductory formulas, the repetitions, etc. G. Fischer even speaks of a "deliberate, intentional composition from beginning to end" (Fischer 2007, 114: "eine beabsichtigte, von Anfang bis Ende überlegte Komposition")—a characterization which in spite of its accuracy is nevertheless debatable to the extent that it is embedded in Fischer's hypothesis that Jeremiah was written by a single author living in the fourth century BCE.

In spite of the partially disparity of its material, the book of Jeremiah can be divided into several largely coherent parts. Jeremiah is in a sense a collection of anthologies. Three factors in particular are decisive for the determination of its structure: a) the periodization of Jeremiah's prophetic activity under the reign of Josiah, Jehoiakim, and Zedekiah, respectively (a more precise date for many prophecies cannot be determined), b) the distinction between the words of and reports about Jeremiah, between poetry and prose (largely prose after Jer 33), and c) the content and themes of the passages. The overall structure can thus be rendered as follows:

1		Jeremiah called as a prophet
2–25		*During the time of Josiah and Jehoiakim*
	2–6	Call to repent to God and the announcement of the "enemy from the North"
	7	Temple sermon
	8–20	Final warnings and transition to inevitable judgment; the so-called confessions of Jeremiah
	21–25	*(partly in the time of Zedekiah)* Judgment is coming on kings, prophets, and nations
26–36		*During the time of Jehoiakim and Zedekiah*
	26	Temple sermon and true prophecy
	27–29	True and false prophecy
	30–33	Jeremiah's "Book of Comfort" and promises of salvation
	34–36	Warnings, the burning of the scroll
37–45		Jeremiah and Zedekiah; the fall of Jerusalem; the "postlude" under Gedaliah and the flight to Egypt
46–51		Oracles against the nations, culminating in the great oracle against Babylon
52		Historical conclusion: Jerusalem falls and the temple treasures are carried off; the release of Jehoiachin

Theology of the Book

To summarize the theology of the book of Jeremiah clearly and coherently is just as difficult as to define its structure. From a number of different perspectives, Jeremiah shows the theological struggle over the (continued)

Jeremiah, Prophet of Ultimate Ruin and New Hope

existence of Israel, the people of God, as a direct reaction to and reflection on the religious abuses and drastic political events of those days. The line that runs throughout the message of the book is the preaching about Yhwh, the God of the covenant, who speaks and who acts majestically in the history of Israel and the nations. His word announces both doom and salvation, both judgment and grace; it reveals God's wrath against idolatry and social injustice. We also hear sounds of pain; God's accusation goes together with his complaint. In judgment and downfall, Yhwh nevertheless opens the way to a new future in which the new son of David will reign. Given this central line of the book of Jeremiah, its "theology" can be summarized in the following seven elements: 1) God's word, 2) God's sovereignty, 3) God's judgment and grace, 4) God's wrath, 5) God's complaint, 6) God's future, 7) God's anointed king.

1. The word of God

More than any other prophet, Jeremiah is the prophet of God's powerful word. The *Wortereignisformel* ("The word of the Lord came to me, saying") appears thirty-six times, the *Botenformel* ("This is what the Lord says") 154 times and the *Gottespruchformel* ("declares the Lord") 166 times. The book opens with the heading "the words of Jeremiah" (1:1), which is immediately followed by "the word of the Lord came to him" (1:2). These expressions authorize and legitimate the content of the entire book: Jeremiah does not speak his own words, but stands in the service of the God who speaks. This is stated out emphatically in the vision of his call: "You must say whatever I command you" (1:7; cf. 26:2). God touches Jeremiah's mouth: "Now, I have put my words in your mouth" (1:9). God guarantees that his word will be realized. When Jeremiah watches the branch of an almond tree (*šāqēd*, שָׁקֵד), the Lord says to him: "You have seen correctly, for I am watching [*šoqēd*, שֹׁקֵד] to see that my word is fulfilled" (1:12). God's word is a word laden with power, and he will not turn back from it (4:28). The word is destructive like fire (5:14; 23:29), like a hammer that breaks a rock in pieces (23:29). To stand fully in the service of this divine word means that Jeremiah will speak no worthless words of his own, but worthy words: "you will be my spokesman" (15:19; cf. Rendtorff, 1999: 213).

What does it mean to have to bring the word of God? At times it seems like Jeremiah delights in this task: "When your words came, I ate them; they were my joy and my heart's delight, for I bear your name" (15:16). He continues proclaiming the word of God in dangerous situations, even when it puts his life at stake (26:11–15; 38:1–4). However, more often he groans under the weight of his task, and he expresses this at times with very strong language: "O Lord, you deceived me, and I was deceived, you overpowered me and prevailed." But the prophet absolutely has to speak, for it is impossible for him to keep God's word silent: "But if I say 'I will not mention him or speak any more in his name,' his word is in my heart like a fire, a fire shut up in my bones. I am weary of holding it in; indeed, I cannot" (20:9). The prophet makes full and radical use of the prophetic word spoken from God to Israel and the nations, and cannot himself escape from the power of this word. He is also entirely dependent on it. In an embarrassing situation he stands silent without a word from God (28:10f.), and in critical circumstances he has to wait ten days for the word of the Lord to arrive (42:7)—but he neither will nor can speak words of his own.

This is also illustrative of the big difference between Jeremiah and the other prophets of his days. More than any other prophetic book, Jeremiah gives attention to the struggle for the true word: who is the one that speaks the word of Yhwh? In 23:9–32 a description is given of the "false" prophets (cf. 14:14f.). They are the source of the profanation of the entire land (23:15), lead people to idolatry, speak visions of their own mind and not from the mouth of God (23:16), and bring comforting words of peace (23:17). A recurring key word is שֶׁקֶר "lie": because the false prophets mask and blur the truth, their words are lies (5:31, 23:25, 26, 27:10,14, etc). Typical of the false prophets is that they seek to please the people, fail to address their immorality and idolatry, and reassure them by denying the imminent danger. The source of true prophecy is described as סוֹד יְהוָה "[to stand in] the council of the Lord" (23:18, 22): the image is that of a heavenly council in which God deliberates with his prophets, gives them insight into his plans and commissions them to proclaim his word (cf. Amos 3:7).

In 26–29 the confrontation between true and false prophet is developed extensively. Jeremiah presents himself as a prophet who has been sent by God "in truth." Against his opponent Hananiah, Jeremiah appeals to the *successio prophetarum*, arguing that he stands in the line of the prophets whom God sent to Israel "day after day, again and again" (7:25, 25:4, 29:19), and to whom the people refused to listen: "From early times the prophets who preceded you and me have prophesied war, disaster and plague against many countries and great kingdoms" (28:8; cf.

Jeremiah, Prophet of Ultimate Ruin and New Hope

the recollection of the prophet Micah in 26:16–19). Tradition-historical studies have shown how Jeremiah indeed stands in the line of his predecessors Hosea and Amos (Lalleman, 2000; Lundbom, 1999: 1f.; Fischer 2007: 134–43). In the letter he sent to the exiles in Babylon (29:8ff.), Jeremiah warned them not to listen to such misleading prophets and diviners as Ahab, Zedekiah, and Shemaiah who have not been sent by God. The judgment over Judah will not be overturned in two years (28:3), but will last a full seventy years (29:10). True prophecy rejects "cheap grace" ("*billige Gnade*") and leads through the depths to real freedom.

The prophet Jeremiah is completely taken up in his prophetic task: he is the bearer of the word of God, the mediator between God and his people, the prophet of the new covenant. The biblical portrayal of Jeremiah has several traits from Moses, the great prophet. A number of elements in the account of his call make us think back to Moses' call: the language of 1:7, 9, 17 takes up Deuteronomy 18:18 ("I will raise up for them a prophet like you from among their brothers; I will put my words in his mouth, and he will tell them everything I command him"). Like Moses, Jeremiah prays for God's people—until God forbids it (7:16, 11:14, 14:11). Jeremiah is allowed to proclaim a new exodus (16:15) and to announce a new covenant (31:31–34). "Jeremiah is being presented from the beginning of his career as a prophet after the manner of Moses. ... In fact, Jeremiah is the last of 'his servants the prophets,' bringing to an end a long history of prophetic emissaries beginning with the exodus" (Blenkinsopp, 1996: 137f.; cf. Fischer 2005, 98f.). Here we also find the connection between law and prophets: "What Moses had taught now comes to fruition in the words of Jeremiah" (Brueggemann, 2007: 74).

Jeremiah used different ways to bring God's word: preaching, writing (through Baruch; cf. 36:2, 18) and even sending letters (29; 51:59–64). He further regularly supported his preaching with symbolic acts, such as the sign of the linen belt as a portrayal of Israel's downfall (13:1–11), his visit to the potter who does whatever he wants with his pottery (18:1ff.; Yhwh will do the same with Israel) or the purchase of a field when the enemy had already laid siege to Jerusalem (32:6ff.). Such symbolic acts as the reception of the cup of wrath (25:15ff.) or the carrying of a wooden yoke (27:2ff.) likewise vividly portrayed the prophetic message. Even the prophet's own life was in fact a sign: he was to remain unmarried and have no children, and was not allowed to be present at mourning or feasting (16:1–9). Jeremiah's life symbolized the lot of the word of God that was rejected, and the lot of the people of God who were meeting their downfall (see further below under paragraph 5).

2. The sovereignty of God

As was already explained (see *Historical setting*), Jeremiah lived in turbulent times. The borders of Judah were being broken through, the kingdom of Judah was about to lose its independence, God's people were being decimated, God's temple was destroyed; the gods of Babylon seemed to have the upper hand. Exactly in these times, however, Jeremiah the prophet declared the boundless majesty of Yhwh who continued in absolute sovereignty his royal way with Israel and the nations. Yhwh is the Maker of all things (10:16 = 51:19) in creation as well as in history.

"Ah Sovereign Lord, you have made the heavens and the earth by your great power and outstretched arm," Jeremiah confesses (32:17). The great Creator of all things has made a covenant with day and night (33:20, 25; cf. 31:35). Especially in Jeremiah 10 God's sovereignty is preached: "But God made the earth by his power, he founded the world by his wisdom, and stretched out the heavens by his understanding" (10:12ff = Jer 51:15ff.). At this point the polemic against idol worship also comes up. How foolish it is to make idols and then to bow down to them! The *Verspottung fremder Religionen* (mocking different religions) becomes quite sharp in Jeremiah 10: An idol is nothing but a rigged-up piece of wood fastened with hammer and nails so that it will not totter (10:4), like a scarecrow in a melon patch (10:5). Not these gods, but Yhwh made heaven and earth (10:11)! How could Israel ever have followed such gods, "worthless idols" (2:5, 11, 28), and have traded Yhwh, "the spring of living water," in for "broken cisterns that cannot hold water" (2:13)?

In his judgment of evil, the Creator can also destroy that which he himself has created. Like clay in the hand of the potter, so Israel is in the hand of Yhwh (18:6). Jeremiah indirectly testifies to God's majesty as creator by referring to a return to the pre-creation state (4:23ff.). Where God withdraws his hand from his people, chaos returns: "I looked at the earth, and it was formless and empty; and at the heavens, and their light was gone. I looked at the mountains, and they were quaking; all the hills were swaying . . ." After God's judgment on the land of Judah has passed, nothing will be left but ruin—"Therefore, the earth will mourn, and the heavens above grow dark" (4:28; cf. 12:4).

Jeremiah, Prophet of Ultimate Ruin and New Hope

In the proclamation of God's majesty we hear the "formula of incomparability": Who is like Me? (50:44; cf. 10:6). If people think they can hem God in or claim him, they are utterly mistaken. He is indeed a God nearby, but at the same time a God far away: "Can anyone hide in secret places so that I cannot see him? . . . Do not I fill heaven and earth?"(23:23f). "The God of this text is not a warm, fuzzy God. . . . Rather, this is a God who *stands over* and *apart from*, who has a distinct purpose on the earth, and who will have no one as a permanent ally" (Brueggemann, 2007: 49).

God is not only entirely different from idols, the sovereign Lord of creation, he is also the sovereign King of the nations (10:7). "He is the living God, the eternal King" (10:10). While there is less and less hope for Judah as a nation, wide international perspectives are opened in the book of Jeremiah. The particularity of God's chosen people is connected to the universality of God's rule over all the nations. In the heart of Jeremiah's call lies the awareness of God's kingship over the nations, for he is called to be a "prophet to the nations" (1:5): "See, today I appoint you over nations and kingdoms" (1:10). The word that the prophet must bring from God does not only concern Israel, but the entire web of international power relations of those days.

The world powers of Jeremiah's time are introduced at the beginning of the book: "Now why go to Egypt to drink water from the Shihor? And why go to Assyria to drink water from the River?" (2:18, 36; Assyria is here a symbol for Babylon). Inundated by a flood from Egypt, and later again from Babylon—this was Judah's lot in those days. Jeremiah and Judah lived in a special sense "between the Nile and the Euphrates." Egypt and Babylon thus play a major role in the book of Jeremiah, culminating in the judgments of the oracles against the nations where they come up first (Jer 46) and last (Jer 50–51). Egypt is always portrayed negatively; to seek help from Egypt is a dead end. When after 587 a group of Judeans flees to Egypt, they are handed a crushing prophecy: "I am watching over them for harm, not for good; the Jews in Egypt will perish by sword and famine until they are all destroyed" (44:27). The contours of the "enemy from the North," to whom Jeremiah frequently refers (1:13f.; 4:6; 6:1, etc.), become more and more apparent until it is clear that it stands for Nebuchadnezzar and Babylon (20:5; 24:2; 25:9). This king is God's "servant" (27:7), God's "hammer" (50:23; 51:20) with which YHWH breaks the nations and kingdoms in pieces (51:20ff.; cf. 1:10!). The Subject behind the politics of those days is the divine "I." But Babylon itself will not escape the sword of God which He has called up against all the inhabitants of the earth (25:29). The judgment that was first addressed to Judah/Jerusalem through Babylon (6:22–24) also turns on Babylon with exactly the same words (50:41–43). God is sovereign over the nations; he calls them into his service, uses them as his instrument, and calls them to account—and all shall drink the cup filled with the wine of God's wrath (25:15ff.). The full emphasis is placed on this aspect of wrath, although Jeremiah also has a message of salvation for the nations (12:15f.; 46:26; 48:47, etc.).

This comes out in a remarkable way in the collection of oracles against the nations (seven other nations are sandwiched between Egypt and Babylon, 46–51), which offers a breathtaking message. In the whirlpool of the downfall of Assyria which had terrorized the world for centuries and the emergence of Babylon which takes Assyria's place, Judah sinks into despair. A storm of destruction makes its way throughout all countries. Soon Jerusalem will be taken, the temple will be devastated and the people of Israel will be decimated and dispersed. When everything collapses and all safety falls away, the prophetic finger points to him who sovereignly goes his way in this hectic world. It points to him who is not bound to geographical or ethnic borders. The prophetic word is the scan which shows the world events in the light of God and his deeds. Not politics, but God determines history. At the background of the insanity of those days, it is not fate nor any earthly power but the hand of God that rules. Nebuchadnezzar is only the servant of him who in his majesty calls nations, and governs the progression of times after his will and plan. No injustice will go unpunished: the heathen nations also have to give account to him. Those who try to attain worldwide power are punished by this King. He does not allow the powers of evil to triumph permanently. In the big tangle of history, with all its evil and incomprehensible suffering, it is God who reigns.

In this preaching of God's worldwide sovereign kingship the permanent value of the oracles against the nations is to be found. These passages of Scripture certainly are not the product of a narrow-minded and nationalistic way of thinking. Rather, they offer a universal view of the nations. The centre of history lies in Judah, in Jerusalem—the judgment on the nations is directly related to the judgment on Israel, which has to drink the cup first. But although everything in the Old Testament is centered around Israel, YHWH Zebaoth is concerned with much more: the nations over which he rules. In this way Jeremiah's oracles against the nations witness a *historia salutis* which leads to the One who has accepted the cup of God's wrath from the hand of the Father and has drunk it to the dregs, on whom judgment was exercised fully as a Lamb who died for his own enemies, and who in that way broke down the separating wall, the Lion from Judah's tribe, the King of kings.

3. The judgment and grace of God

Large parts of the book of Jeremiah are dark in color due to the sharp announcement of judgment. It becomes increasingly clear that Israel will not change its rebellion against God, so that judgment has to come. "Can the Ethiopian change his skin or the leopard its spots? Neither can you do good who are accustomed to doing evil. I will scatter you like chaff driven by the desert wind" (13:23). The linen belt, symbol of Israel as God's own precious possession, is ruined and becomes completely useless (13:7). The judgment pronounced is frightening: "I will smash them one against the other, fathers and sons alike, declares the Lord. I will allow no pity or mercy of compassion to keep me from destroying them" (13:14). The end draws unrelentingly near, "for you have kindled my anger, and it will burn forever" (17:4). This is certainly true after Jeremiah 36, the chapter that describes Jehoiakim's burning of Jeremiah's scroll: "All prophecies in the book dated after the event of Jer. 36 regard judgment as an inevitable thing" (Lalleman, 2000: 162).

As serious and comprehensive as the preaching of judgment may be, the book of Jeremiah at the same time contains messages of salvation and hope—even if in number and scope they clearly take a second place. A number of exegetes (e.g., S. Mowinckel, W. Thiel, R. P. Carroll) argue that these words of salvation cannot be from the prophet Jeremiah because they contrast with the preaching of judgment and undermine it to a degree. The majority of scholars correctly maintain, however, that the message of hope cannot be torn away from Jeremiah, and that the contrast between judgment and grace is even fundamental to Jeremiah's message. We also need not propose a periodization for Jeremiah's preaching as if the announcement of salvation must be dated for the most part after 587. The difference between Jeremiah and the "false" prophets is not that he only proclaims judgment while they only announce salvation, but that the message of salvation proclaimed by the false prophets is unconditional while Jeremiah even in his words of salvation continues his persistent call for conversion and repentance. This call to repentance is a constitutive element in Jeremiah's preaching (Rendtorff, 1999: 208).

The words of Jeremiah 3:12 are directed specifically to the former Northern Kingdom of Israel: "Return, faithless Israel, declares the Lord, I will frown on you no longer, for I am merciful, declares the Lord, I will not be angry forever." The judgment will be on Judah, "though I will not destroy it completely" (4:27; cf. 5:10, 18). Exile will come, but is limited to 70 years (25:11, 29:10). In the midst of this judgment, the prophet preaches that the exile will not be the end, but that God will bring his people home (e.g., 12:15; 16:16; 23:8, etc.). Jeremiah 3 contains a moving announcement of God's incomprehensible grace. Because he is merciful, God calls his faithless people—to whom he had already given a certificate of divorce—back so that they might turn back to him (3:1–13); this message refers directly to the provisions of Deuteronomy 24:1–4. The largest concentrations of salvation prophecies can be found in Jeremiah 29 (the letter to the exiles deported to Babylon in 597) and in Jeremiah 30–33 (the Book of Comfort with additional promises). J. G. McConville even argues that the salvation passages, especially in Jeremiah 30f., form the very centre of the book. Remarkable about the preaching of salvation is that it does not come after the downfall and exile, but that it begins in a certain sense in the very middle of the threat and pain (Fischer, 2007: 98). Also in the collected oracles against the nations God's blissful future for his people is accentuated, as the prophecies against Egypt (46:27f.) and Babylon (50:4f.; 19f.) constitute a message of salvation for Israel. The nation of Israel will be saved from the grip of the world powers and return home for good in peace with God.

From the very beginning of the book, there is a tension between judgment and grace, doom and salvation. This is already evident in the commission which Jeremiah receives from God at his call: "See, today I appoint you over nations and kingdoms to uproot and tear down, to destroy and overthrow, to build and to plant" (1:10). The prophetic task is described with six words; four pertain to the coming judgment, two to salvation. This ratio reflects the emphasis on judgment in Jeremiah. The message of these six words runs thematically throughout the entire book (12:14, 17; 18:7–9; 24:6; 31:28; 40; 42:10; 45:4; cf. also 29:6f., for example). Remarkable about these words is that they constantly point to God's work: the mouth of the prophet verbalizes Yhwh's acts. Judgment and grace are not only for Israel/Judah, but also for the nations. Babylon, which at one time was God's instrument together with Nebuchadnezzar as "the servant of the Lord" (27:6), will now fall under the judgment of God because, as a serpent/dragon, it acted wickedly towards Israel (51:34). The changing of the times must be discounted in the interpretation of the texts, because every prophecy in Jeremiah is a "word in season."

The tension between judgment and grace, doom and salvation, remains an important element of the prophet's preaching throughout the book, because his message is deeply rooted in the requirements of the covenant (see also section 6 below). The covenant of YHWH with his people stands under the tension of blessing and curse, corresponding with obedience and disobedience (Deut 27f; Lev 26). When YHWH revealed himself in Exodus 34:6f.—a text which is cited and adapted numerous times in the Old Testament as a kind of "creed"—the same tension between the two sides of God's acts is revealed: "maintaining love to thousands, and forgiving wickedness, rebellion and sin. Yet he does not leave the guilty unpunished; he punishes the children and their children for the sin of the fathers to the third and fourth generation" (Exod 34:7). Similarly, Jeremiah can in a single sentence announce God's acts of judgment and salvation: "He who *scattered* Israel will *gather* them and will watch over his flock like a shepherd" (31:10). This twofold theme of judgment and grace, downfall and hope, is characteristic of the entire book of Jeremiah which struggles to place the horror of Judah's downfall in light of God's righteous judgment and his work of salvation.

4. The wrath of God

The book of Jeremiah speaks regularly of God's fierce anger (4:26; 12:13; 25:37f.; 49:37), that is, God's holy indignation over all the evil which Israel committed and in which it remained unmoved in spite of all prophetic warnings. "My anger will kindle like a fire that will burn against you" (15:14; 17:4). The deepest cause of God's wrath which has been kindled against his people lies in the fact that Israel broke the covenant: "Both the house of Israel and the house of Judah have broken the covenant I made with their forefathers" (11:10). God emphasized this covenant with words of blessing and curse (11:3–5). Israel returned to the sins of their fathers (11:10), but God remained true to his word. In Jeremiah's prophetic activity, the wrath of God becomes concrete: "I am full of the wrath of the Lord, and I cannot hold it in" (6:11). The vehement call for Judah to repent is frequently sounded with the use of the word שׁוּב ("turn back," "repent," e.g., 4:1; 18:11; 25:5; 35:15). With two kinds of evil did Israel break the covenant and earn the wrath of God: socio-ethical sins, and cultic-religious sins.

When Yhwh asks Jeremiah to go and see if there is a single *tsaddiq* ("righteous one") in Jerusalem (cf. Gen 18:16–33!), he comes up empty-handed. At all levels from high to low society, the nation has become corrupt, and this includes prophets, priests and kings. People openly commit adultery and sexual immorality (5:7f.), exercise extortion and are greedy for their own gain (6:6, 13). They deceive each other wherever possible (9:4–8), and do so without shame: "No, they have no shame at all, they do not even know how to blush" (6:15). The prophet's criticism is immediately deflected: "I am innocent" (2:35). Jeremiah preaches sharply against kings such as Jehoiakim who, in contrast to his father Josiah, entirely neglects social justice (22:15–17). God's wrath is particularly aroused because people offend the poor (2:34; 5:26–28). When the rich undo the freeing of the slaves, the God of the covenant intervenes: "The men who have violated my covenant and have not fulfilled the terms of the covenant they made before Me, I will treat like the calf they cut in two and then walked between its pieces" (34:18). In the temple sermon Jeremiah complains against the whole nation because it has oppressed the defenseless, shed innocent blood, and committed theft, murder, and adultery (7:6–9).

In the same temple sermon Jeremiah addresses the cultic-religious sins. On the one side, there is syncretism and idolatry. The people have begun to worship foreign gods: Ashtaroth, the goddess of love (7:16–20; 44:15f.); Moloch, the god to whom children were sacrificed in the valley of Ben Hinnom (7:30ff.); and Baal, the god of fertility (7:9; cf. 2:8, 23; 11:13, 17, etc.). God's people have defiled the land by committing adultery with 'wood and stone' (2:27f.; 3:9). Idols have even been placed in temple (7:30). On the other side, Israel's worship of Yhwh is only outward, without internal piety and observance of the law. They do indeed bring sacrifices, but in such a way that God can only reject them (6:20; 7:21). Instead of these sacrifices, God desires something else: "Obey Me, and I will be your God and you will be my people. Walk in all the ways I command you, that it may go well with you" (7:23). However, the people of Israel abuse the worship of God for their own religious satisfaction, and allow themselves to be deluded by prophets and diviners. The temple's existence is little more than a religious talisman: would Yhwh really come down in judgment on his own temple (7:10)? The prophet criticizes the false trust: "Do not trust in deceptive words and say, 'This is the temple of the Lord, the temple of the Lord, the temple of the Lord!'" (7:4).

In short, because Israel refuses to listen to God's words and rejects his law (6:19), God will in his wrath not listen to Israel's prayers and reject his people (7:16; 11:14; 6:30).

5. The complaint of God

The book of Jeremiah is full of the sound of complaint, more than any other prophetic book of the Old Testament: the people complain, the land complains, the prophet complains, and even God himself complains.

The prophetic task weighs heavily on Jeremiah; after all, his message largely consists in the announcement of doom and destruction. He himself is a symbol of it. He will remain unmarried and have no children, because Israel's children will succumb to the judgment of God (16:2-4). Jeremiah is no longer allowed to participate in the social commemoration of life's low and high points (i.e., mourning and marriage), because on account of God's judgment the dead will remain unburied and the joyous sounds of weddings will be silenced (16:5-9). Jeremiah is threatened with death (Jer 26; 32-38). The words he has to bring are often a heavy burden to him: "My heart is broken within me; all my bones tremble. I am like a drunken man, like a man overcome by wine, because of the Lord and his holy words" (23:9). He is deeply moved by the message of judgment: "Oh, my anguish, my anguish! I writhe in pain. Oh, the agony of my heart! My heart pounds within me, I cannot keep silent" (4:19; cf. 8:21; 10:19). With good reason tradition has given Jeremiah the name of the "weeping prophet": "Oh, that my head were a spring of water and my eyes a fountain of tears! I would weep day and night for the slain of my people" (9:1; 14:17). Jeremiah's path is that of a *via dolorosa*. As the suffering prophet, Jeremiah is a forerunner of the great prophet Jesus Christ. Jeremiah is enlisted with his entire life in the service of Yhwh to bring his word to his people who nevertheless reject it. In this the prophet reveals a two-sided solidarity: he is the mouth of God for the rebellious people, and he brings the complaints and pain of the people before God (intercession). Especially the so-called "confessions of Jeremiah" vividly portray the struggle for the prophetic word.

The confessions of Jeremiah are usually considered to include Jeremiah 11:18-23; 12:1-6; 15:10-21; 17:12/14-18; 18:18-23; and 20:7-18.

The popularly accepted designation "confessions" only partially covers the content, style, and genre of these texts. They are prophetic dialogues with God, or monologues in which the element of complaint and lament predominates. These texts "betray close affinity in style and language with the psalms of individual lamentation" (Blenkinsopp, 1996: 134). The traditional approach saw the confessions as biographical documents of the "Seelenkampf" or "inner life" of Jeremiah. The result was an individualizing and psychological exegesis, which placed the emphasis upon the emotional, tension-filled relationship between Jeremiah's personality and his prophetic office. Scholarship has since shifted, having increasingly recognized the implications entailed in the genre characteristics of the confessions and the use of conventional language in them.

A one-sided form-critical approach went so far as to deny the authorship of Jeremiah in the confessions altogether, attributing these sections instead to a redactional interpolation intended to interpret the character of the prophet. The ensuing result was a collectivistic exegesis which emphasized the paradigmatic function of the prophet as a righteous sufferer. Instead of choosing between the alternative of biography or paradigm, individual or collective interpretation, it is better to do justice to both the authenticity of the confessions as well as to the redactional intentions behind the final formulations of these sections and their order in the context of Jeremiah 11–20. "The most satisfactory understanding is one that allows for the individuality of these poems as really emanating from the prophet's experience, yet also articulating in some sense the situation of the people as a whole" (McConville, 1997: 760). The exegesis of these texts should be theological rather than psychological in nature, which is to say that the focus is not the inner feelings of the *person* Jeremiah but the complaint and prayer of the *prophet* Jeremiah, as a component of his proclamation.

It is no coincidence that the prayer for judgment upon the enemies is the one element that all the confessions have in common (11:20; 12:3; 15:5; 17:18; 18:21–23; 20:12). What takes place in the life of the prophet is, in part, a reflection of the relationship between God and Israel in Jeremiah's day. The people would not listen to Jeremiah because they would not listen to the words of the covenant and to the God of the covenant (6:10, 17, 19; 7:24, 26-28; 11:3, 8, 10). Therefore, God applies the threat of the covenant curse (11:3–8), which is heard in Jeremiah's proclamation of judgment. Those around Jeremiah, even his own house (12:6), make plans against him (11:19; 12:6), just as God's inheritance conspires against God (11:9; 12:7). Jeremiah's *rîb* (lawsuit) is inseparable from God's *rîb* (2:9, 29,

Jeremiah, Prophet of Ultimate Ruin and New Hope

35); God lays charges against his people, as does Jeremiah against his enemies. In the context of God's *rîb*, Jeremiah must see, know and test (3:6; 5:1; 6:9, 27; 7:17; 8:6), just as at Jeremiah's *rîb* God sees, knows and tests (11:18, 20; 17:10; 20:12). The outcome of the *rîb* is absolutely clear. The injustice is not with God (2:4) but with Israel, not with Jeremiah (18:20) but with his enemies. This calls for vengeance and visitation as enactment of the curse and the punishment of the covenant (5:9, 29; 9:8: נקם and פקד). Jeremiah too in his *rîb* calls for נקם—the vengeance of God, which results in a visitation (פקד,11:22f, 15:3).

From the formulation of the announcement of the vengeance of God in 5:9, 29; 9:8 it is evident that God's vengeance is not something that He happily executes (note especially the interrogative form). Nor do Jeremiah's prayers for vengeance arise from a vindictive heart. Just as the prophet weeps over his people, shows solidarity with his people, prays for his people, and remains with his people to the extreme, so too God stays with his beloved people to the end and he passionately calls them to conversion (see the metaphors in Jer 2-3). But the godlessness of the people who obstinately refuse to listen exceeds all bounds, both with respect to Jeremiah (murder plot, 11:19) and with respect to God (breach of the covenant, 11:10). The life of the messenger and the honor of the Sender are at stake. Here the prayer for the people must be brought to an end and make way for the curse upon the people (7:16; 14:11; 15:1). If God did not arise in vengeance on behalf of his prophet, Jeremiah would succumb; if God did not arise in vengeance for his covenant and justice, the honor of his name would be transgressed (cf. 17:15). The urgent call for God's vengeance upon Jeremiah's enemies is closely connected with the prophecy of the inescapable vengeance of God upon the covenant people of God.

Thus, in the complaint of Jeremiah the prophet, God's own complaint is revealed. McConville in this context speaks of "an incarnational aspect": "At times the suffering of the prophet seems to echo that of God himself" (McConville, 1997: 760). In such passages as 8:18—9:9 the prophet's "I" seamlessly transitions into God's "I," and can hardly be distinguished from it (Fischer, 2005: 99: "Jeremia spiegelt Gott"). The same applies to 14:17. God's complaint is concrete in the many painful questions in 2:1—4:4, where God is depicted as a betrayed bridegroom: "What fault did your fathers find in me, that they strayed so far from me?" (2:5). "Have I been a desert to Israel or a land of great darkness?" (2:31). God appeals almost beseechingly to his adulterous bride Israel to return (3:6–15). God's complaint is likewise to be remarked in the word "perhaps" with which Jeremiah sends the people on their way: "*Perhaps they will listen and each will turn from his evil way*" (26:3; 36:3, 7). The prophet's pain of which he complains further reflects something of the pain of God himself who is overcome by the apostasy and downfall of his people (Fischer, 2005: 100). One cannot but be moved by God's pain over and love for his people: "Is not Ephraim my dear son, the child in whom I delight? Though I often speak against him, I still remember him. Therefore my heart yearns for him; I have great compassion for him, declares the Lord" (31:20). God is intensely involved in the lot of his people. The announcement of judgment beats with God's appeal to return to him, and in this his long-suffering love is made manifest.

6. The future that God will bring about

At the very time the judgment has arrived, the first group of Judeans has left for Babylon, and the absolute depths have been reached, Jeremiah writes a letter to the exiles in Babylon with the powerful message that God will give his people a new future. The judgment that appeared to be final now turns to grace. In Jeremiah 29 we hear for the first time the formula שוב שבות ("I will restore your fortunes"), which is then repeated seven times in the section that follows (Jer 30–33). The so-called Book of Comfort (Jer 30–31, see the words "I will give them comfort" in 31:13) is supplemented with the symbolic acts of Jeremiah 32 (the purchase of a field as sign of future land ownership) and a further unfolding of promises of salvation in chapter 33.

The Book of Comfort colorfully portrays the future which God will give to his people. Israel will no longer have to groan under the yoke of foreign rule (30:8), but will serve God under his king (30:9). The exile will come to an end, and God will save Israel from all the countries in which they now live as exiles (30:11). He will "heal their wounds" (as a symbol of general restoration, 30:12–17) and bring joyful feasting (30:19, 31:4f.; 31:13), restoration of honor (30:19) and prosperity (31:12). Israel will not decrease but multiply (30:19; cf. 29:6!), and there will be growth and flourishing all around: God himself will build and plant (31:27f.).

When Jeremiah announces this new future, he draws on representations and images from the past. The new future will be based on and guaranteed by "a new covenant" (31:31–34). The word ברית "covenant" appears twenty-three times in Jeremiah. The theology of the book is also unmistakably colored by the notion of the covenant. Jeremiah's preaching is firmly rooted in the theology of the Sinai-covenant, of Hosea and of Deuteronomy (Brueggemann, 2007: 10-27). Whereas Judah has broken its covenant with God (11:8, 10; 22:9; 31:32), Yhwh maintains his promises even in the very midst of judgment—and he promises a new covenant. This comes to expression in a singular way in 31:31-34.

God will make his covenant of the future with both the house of Judah and of Israel (31:31; cf. 30:3f.): the old division between them will be undone so that the people of God will once again be united in one. This covenant will be rooted in the hearts of the people; God will write the *torah* and the old covenant formula "I will be their God, and they will be my people" (31:33) in their innermost being. There will no longer be a need for mutual correction, exhortation and instruction to maintain God's covenant, "because they will all know me, from the least of them to the greatest" (31:34). This covenant stands by the grace of God: "For I will forgive their wickedness and will remember their sins no more" (31:34). God's new future is as unshakable as the foundations of heaven and earth (31:35-37).

The covenant concept implies that a covenant can be renewed. The covenant of 31:31-34 is likewise not "new" as if it were entirely different from the old covenant, but it is a restored and renewed covenant. There are various points of continuity between old and new: the same law will be in the heart (Deut 6:6f.; 30:6), the same Law-giver binds himself to his people with the same covenant formula, and it is by the same grace of God that his covenant people live (Exod 34:6f.). However, there is also discontinuity between the old and new covenants, and the new covenant radicalizes and deepens the old. Unique to the new covenant is the promise that *all* the people will know God (31:34), that there will be no "remnant" anymore, no distinction between believing and unbelieving Israelites. Likewise unique is God's promise that he will take the initiative for the entire realization of the covenant, as he himself will write the law on the heart (31:33, but also earlier in 24:7). In a sense, this covenant is more unilateral than bilateral. It is for these reasons that a number of scholars speak in this context of a "spiritual metamorphosis" (M. Weinfeld; cf. Fischer, 2005: 119).

Against the background of the history of Jeremiah's time, the prophet's preaching gains great depth. "The seventh century was the greatest moment of impending destruction for the nation; yet in the midst of the faithful warnings of God's servants came one of the most spectacular series of promises and hope" (Kaiser, 2008: 203). Although the term "new covenant" appears in the Old Testament only in Jeremiah 31:31, other prophets likewise spoke of "an everlasting covenant" or "a covenant of peace" which God in the future would make with his people (e.g., Isa 54:10; 55:3; Ezek 37:26), and about the "the new heart" or "the new spirit" which God would give (e.g., Ezek 11:19; 36:26). However, 31:31-34 is and remains the *locus classicus* for the concept of the new covenant. The New Testament would reflect this as well, especially in Hebrews 8:8-12 and 10:16f. Also at the institution of the Lord's Supper and in Paul's preaching do we find references to Jeremiah 31 (cf., e.g., Matt 26:28; 1 Cor 11:25; 2 Cor 3:6). Jeremiah's preaching about the great future which God would bring and realize through his covenant is one of the strongest links between Old and New Testament.

7. The king anointed by God

That which had given Judah and Jerusalem confidence and certainty throughout the ages—i.e., the Zion tradition and the David tradition—was taken away from them in Jeremiah's days. The knowledge that God is enthroned on Zion and protects city and temple (cf., e.g., some Psalms, Isaiah) was used for the benefit of a self-centered religion (7:4). The old promise that God would always have someone sitting on the throne of David (2 Sam. 7:16) was likewise abused by the people in order to cultivate a false sense of security. Jeremiah in contrast preached that the temple would fall as quickly as Shiloh had fallen (7:12), and that there was no future for the current royal house anymore (13:13; 22:5; 29:16; 36:30). The dark words of judgment spoken against the royal house in Jeremiah 22 finish in a dead end with Judah's last but one king, Jehoiachin: "Record this man as if childless, a man who will not prosper in his lifetime, for none of his offspring will prosper, none will sit on the throne of David or rule anymore in Judah" (22:30). Indeed, king Jehoiachin was deported to Babylon by Nebuchadnezzar (in 597), just as Judah's last king Zedekiah (in 587); both of them died there (52:11, 33).

However, the last chapter of Jeremiah is not God's final word regarding Davidic kingship. Even at this point the perspective for the future breaks surprisingly through the clouds formed by the announcement of judgment. Whereas the book of Jeremiah concludes with the end of Jejoiachin and Zedekiah in exile (Jer 52), the salvation oracles of the centre of the book has already provided for another, messianic Davidide. The prophecy concerning the downfall of the Davidic dynasty (22:30) is immediately followed in Jeremiah 23 by a salvation prophecy in which YHWH as the flock's Great Shepherd promises to bring Israel back to its own pasture and to give it new "shepherds." The climax of this announcement is found in the following words: "The days are coming, declares the Lord, when I will raise up to David a righteous Branch, a King who will reign wisely and do what is just and right in the land. In his days Judah will be saved and Israel will live in safety. This is the name by which he will be called: The Lord Our Righteousness" (23:5f.). The names given to the new son of David are remarkable: on the one hand, they connect to the language of Isaiah 11:1, and on the other they draw—ironically?—on the name of the last king who sat on Jerusalem's throne, Zedekiah. The coming King has a special position and has devoted himself entirely to the task which he has received from God: "Their leader will be one of their own; their ruler will arise from among them. I will bring him near and he will come close to me for *who is he who will devote himself to be close to me*? declares the Lord" (30:21; cf. Von Rad, 1961: 231f.).

The messianic expectation of Jeremiah 23 is taken up and developed in the Book of Comfort (30:9, 21), and especially in Jeremiah 31. The words of 23:5f. are (with some variation) cited in 33:15, followed by the promise that "David will never fail to have a man to sit on the throne of the house of Israel" (33:17). God's covenant with David will be without end, so the prophet assures the people with a powerful reference to the covenant with Noah (33:20, 25), Abraham (33:22, 26), and the Levites (33:18, 21; cf. Num 25). Because Jeremiah 33 is omitted in the Septuagint, it has been argued that this is a post-exilic addition. Anyway, it is an undeniable fact that this messianic preaching fits entirely within the tensions typical of the book of Jeremiah (Fischer, 2007: 76, 102).

In Jeremiah the old prophecy of Nathan as found in 2 Samuel 7 is reinterpreted and actualized: God will give his people a *David redivivus*. From a New Testament perspective, we recognize in him the person of Jesus Christ (Luke 1:69f.).

Conclusion

The book of Jeremiah gives evidence of a very dynamic theology which prompted the prophet to action, gave direction to his preaching, and sustained him in the many hours of crisis (Thompson, 1992: 107). For both the distressed people of his own age and future generations up to our own time his prophecies have made a particular contribution, testifying to a sovereign Lord God who through the depths of human failure never abandons the work of his hands.

Bibliography

Blenkinsopp, Joseph. *A History of Prophecy in Israel*. 2nd ed. Louisville, KY: Westminster John Knox, 1996.

Brueggemann, Walter. *The Theology of the Book of Jeremiah*. Cambridge: Cambridge University Press, 2007.

Carroll, R. P. *Jeremiah*. Old Testament Guides. Sheffield, UK: JSOT, 1989.

Fischer, Georg. *Jeremia. Der Stand der theologischen Diskussion*. Darmstadt: Wissenschaftliche Buchgesellschaft, 2007.

———. *Jeremia 1–25*. Herders theologischer Kommentar zum Alten Testament. Freiburg: Herder, 2005.

Hill, John. *Friend or Foe? The Figure of Babylon in the Book of Jeremia MT*. Biblical Interpretation Series 40. Leiden: Brill, 1999.

Kaiser, W. C. *The Promise-Plan of God: A Biblical Theology of the Old and New Testaments*. Grand Rapids: Zondervan, 2008.

Lalleman-de Winkel, H. *Jeremiah in Prophetic Tradition: An Examination of the Book of Jeremiah in the Light of Israel's Prophetic Traditions*. Contributions to Biblical Exegesis & Theology 26. Leuven: Peeters, 2000.

Lundbom, J. R. *Jeremiah 1–20*. The Anchor Bible 21A. New York: Doubleday, 1999.

McConville, J. G. "Jeremiah: Theology of". In *New International Dictionary of Old Testament Theology and Exegesis. Volume 4*, edited by W. A. VanGemeren, 755–67. Grand Rapids: Zondervan, 1997.

———. *Judgment and Promise. An Interpretation of the Book of Jeremiah*. Leicester, UK: Apollos, 1993.

Maier, Michael P. *Ägypten—Israels Herkunft und Geschick. Studie über einen theopolitischen Zentralbegriff im hebräischen Jeremiabuch*. Österreichische Biblische Studien 21. Frankfurt am Main: Lang, 2002.

Rendtorff, Rolf. *Theologie des Alten Testaments. Ein kanonischer Entwurf. Band 12: Kanonische Grundlegung*, Neukirchen-Vluyn: Neukirchener Verlag, 1999.

Seitz, Christopher R. *Theology in Conflict. Reactions to the Exile in the Book of Jeremiah*. Berlin: De Gruyter, 1989.

Thompson, J. A. *The Book of Jeremiah*. The New International Commentary on the Old Testament. Grand Rapids: Eerdmans, 1992.

Von Rad, G. *Theologie des Alten Testaments. Band II : Die Theologie der prophetischen Überlieferungen Israels*, München: Kaiser, 1961.

Chapter 9

Habakkuk, Prophet of Comfort in God Alone

Historical Setting of the Book

THE PROPHET HABAKKUK IS something of an enigma. We are provided no patronymic with which to learn something of his lineage, no specific historical reference by means of which confidently to situate his ministry, and no call narrative that might yield clues to his personal situation. Even the meaning of his name is problematic (*HALOT*, 287).

Nevertheless, the situation Habakkuk describes in 1:6–11 suggests he lived and ministered during the rise of the Neo-Babylonian empire (626–539 BCE), referred to in 1:6 as הכשדים ("the Chaldeans"), a people group who had entered Babylonia between 1000 and 900 BCE and eventually extended their control over the entire region (Millard, 2000: 70). An additional indication of the likely period of Habakkuk's ministry is provided by the societal dysfunction he describes (1:2–4). The social and moral reform imposed by King Josiah (640–609 BCE) apparently had lost its hold over the populace. Moreover, Judah appears to be yet relatively independent of Babylonian control, though the threat from that quarter is imminent and growing. These inferences argue for a probable date for Habakkuk's ministry in the last years of the seventh century; i.e., those years surrounding 605 BCE—the year when Babylonian hegemony over Syria-Palestine was definitively decided at the Battle of Carchemish by Nebuchadnezzar.

Content and Structure of the Book

Unlike most other prophetic books, the book of Habakkuk contains no message explicitly directed to God's people. It is instead presented as a recorded dialogue between Habakkuk and God, in which Habakkuk's theological quandaries, sparked by troubling national and international circumstances, are resolved under divine tutelage. The structure of the book reflects this dialogue.

Following the brief introduction of the "pronouncement" (משא), we are presented with two complaints from Habakkuk (1:2–4; 1:12—2:1) that are each followed by a response from God (1:5–11; 2:2–20). The book ends with what is described as a "prayer" (תפלה)—a general term applied to a wide variety of speech acts, including communal lament, supplication of the king or the people, prayer of repentance and supplication, intercession, and the prayer of the priest in blessing the community (*HALOT*, 1776–77). The prayer (3:2–19) is of a different genre than the rest of the book and includes its own heading (3:1), prompting some to suggest its original independence from chapters 1–2 (Hiebert, 1996: 652–53). However, its continuity of theme and parallel features with the rest of the book argue against concluding that chapter 3 is other than an integral, and even climactic, part of the book (Armerding, 2005: 636–37).

Theology of the Book

Canonically, the book of Habakkuk follows the book of Nahum. It is surely no coincidence that after a book describing God's judgment should come one that points us toward God's comfort. The prophet Habakkuk ministers when Nahum's prophecy was in the process of being fulfilled. God was, in fact, bringing judgment against Assyria by means of the ascendant (Neo-)Babylonian empire. With the threat of external attack removed at least temporarily from immediate concern, Habakkuk turns his attention more inward, to the interrelations of God's people. And he doesn't like what he sees. In this book, Habakkuk voices the concerns of all God's people throughout the ages whose theology is challenged by the continued manifestation of sin in their midst. Habakkuk also learns, as we all have to, that in the midst of these challenges God offers his people a comfort that is not found in the places where the world looks for it.

Habakkuk, Prophet of Comfort in God Alone

1. Habakkuk's first complaint

Like many of us, Habakkuk begins his theological journey with a complaint. In 1:2-4 he describes a situation of societal breakdown characterized by violence (חמס), injustice (און), wrongdoing (עמל), destruction (שד), strife (ריב), and conflict (מדון), that render law and justice not only ineffective (תפוג), but so corrupted that they have become contributors to the problem instead of means for its resolution. Habakkuk had no doubt experienced the great national reforms under King Josiah. But after Josiah's death in 609 BCE, the veneer of moral order quickly wore off under the abradingly corrupt regimes of his successors and sons, King Jehoahaz and King Jehoiakim (2 Kgs 23:31—24:4). It was hard enough for Habakkuk to witness the societal breakdown, but what made the situation even more intolerable for him was God's apparent unwillingness to do anything about it. In the second verse of the book, Habakkuk's frustration boils over in lament: "How long, Lord, must I call for help, but you do not listen!" (1:2). His cry highlights one of the three main theological themes/tensions in the book: the simultaneous existence of a good God and the continuing presence and influence of evil in the world. For Habakkuk, God's seeming inaction and unconcern in the face of such evil were bringing his justice and faithfulness into question.

2. Habakkuk's response to God's first answer

God's answer to Habakkuk's initial complaint (1:5-11) is entirely unsatisfying and troubles Habakkuk even more than the situation he was complaining about. God reveals that, far from being inactive, he is raising up the ruthless (מר) and rash (מהר) Babylonians. By this revelation he is clearly implying that he intends by the agency of this "guilty [אשם] people, whose own strength is their god," to judge his own people—the people of the true God. This divine intention only exacerbates Habakkuk's sense of divine injustice and unfaithfulness and leads to his second complaint (1:12—2:1), the heart of which is found in v. 13: "Why are you silent while the wicked swallow up those more righteous than themselves?" Habakkuk's question introduces the second main theological tension/theme of the book: the question of God's justice and faithfulness toward his people with respect to *the way* he deals with evil in the world.

3. God's second answer to Habakkuk

In God's second, longer response to Habakkuk (2:2–20), he reassures Habakkuk that the Babylonians would receive their own measure of divine judgment, at the appropriate time. In a series of "woe" oracles (Matthews, 2009: 171) presented as a future taunt (משל) in the mouths of the defeated peoples, the Babylonians' lust for plunder (2:6), their self-advancement by means of other-ruination (2:9), their injustice (2:12), their abasement of others (2:15), and their idolatry (2:19) are held up as grounds for their coming divine judgment. Against this blameworthiness is held up the righteous person, who "will live by his faithfulness" (2:4) (אמונה). While the meaning of this final phrase has been much debated (Andersen, 2001: 193–203), the context implies it means, at least, *not* being "puffed up" (עפלה), arrogant, greedy, never satisfied, and never at rest (2:4–5). The verse thus serves as a gentle rebuke by which Habakkuk's perspective is redirected back toward the trustworthiness of his just and faithful God in whom alone his satisfaction and rest are to be found.

4. The resolution of Habakkuk's struggle

The satisfaction or rest that should characterize the righteous person is ultimately realized by Habakkuk at the end of the book. His prayer in chapter 3 represents the *terminus ad quem* of Habakkuk's theological journey and is also the resolution of the two previous theological tensions of the book. Habakkuk resolves to "wait patiently" (אנוח) for God to settle the scores (3:16). In the meantime, after reflecting on how God has consistently acted throughout past history for the good of his people (3:2–15), Habakkuk ultimately comes around to the insight that God wanted him to have, which forms the final and climactic theme of the book. His comfort—physically and theologically—is not to be sought in his own understanding, in behavior of his countrymen that is more agreeable to him, or when circumstances turn out the way or in the manner he would like. In other words, his ultimate comfort and confidence do not come from those things to which the Babylonians looked. His comfort and confidence are to be found instead in the One who can never fail, change, or disappoint—the Sovereign Lord himself (3:17–19).

5. The theme of Habakkuk and Jesus

The sufficiency of this unfailing comfort located in this just and faithful, yet ultimately inscrutable Lord is reiterated centuries later to those who once again found themselves challenged by the injustices and cruelty of others. The people of God in Jesus' day were wrestling with some of the same theological tensions Habakkuk was. They, too, observed injustice coming from inside and outside their community and wondered how this could square with their understanding of God. How could God, for example, allow hypocritical religious leaders to load down his people with burdens that they couldn't possibly carry (Luke 11:46)? Or how could God allow a pagan nation like Rome to subjugate his own people? Like Habakkuk, God's people were jaded, troubled, and confused. They needed to be reminded once again that God alone should be the source and object of their contentment, and not their circumstances. Because, clearly, the outworking of God's mysterious will is often attended by very troubling circumstances. Jesus reminded them that even when circumstances were beyond their ability to understand, their comfort could still (and always) be found in their relationship with their all-powerful God: "In this world you will have trouble. But take heart! I have overcome the world" (John 16:33). The force of these words is multiplied when it is realized that they come from one who would experience the full weight of the presence and effect of sin in the world in the accomplishment of the Father's will.

The Theme of Habakkuk and Us

In words that echo Habakkuk 3:17–19, Jesus invites us also to find that reassuring comfort and rest in him: "Come to me, all you who are weary and burdened, and I will give you rest" (Matt 11:28). He is the good shepherd who leads us beside still waters—even though those waters might very well be flowing in the very presence of our enemies (Ps 23:5).

Sometimes the things we have been leaning on give way. By means of behaviors and events that challenge our faith, God occasionally pushes us, as he did Habakkuk, out of our comfort zones so that we are forced to remember where our true comfort lies. When we, like Habakkuk, get confused or discouraged in the face of seemingly unchecked evil, we may need to reorient our thoughts. Yes, there is evil in the world. But God is engaged in its ultimate eradication, on a timetable that unfortunately sometimes does not agree with the one we would choose. Yes, God apparently uses methods and means to accomplish his evil-eradication program that do not fit nicely into the box we have constructed for him. But it should come as no surprise to us that we cannot plumb the intricacies of the divine plan. We, like Habakkuk, need only look back on God's consistently just and faithful activity on behalf of his people in the past to be reassured of his just and faithful activity toward them in the present and future. Habakkuk was encouraged to have patient hope, patient trust, and patient confidence in God. In any trouble, we too may find comfort in God and in his care for us. As Habakkuk was, we can be reassured as well that our future is as secure as the God who directs it. When we redirect our focus back onto our always reliable, always faithful, and all-powerful God, then we will able to say along with Habakkuk, "Though [all sorts of disturbing things may happen], yet I will rejoice in the Lord, I will be joyful in God my Savior" (3:17–18). Although the disturbing things won't necessarily go away, they will be eclipsed in our field of vision by the only true and abiding source of comfort.

Bibliography

Andersen, Francis I. *Habakkuk: A New Translation with Introduction and Commentary*. Anchor Bible. New York: Doubleday, 2001.

Armerding, Carl E. "Habakkuk." In *The Expositor's Bible Commentary*. Rev. ed. Vol. 8: *Daniel–Malachi*. Edited by Tremper Longman III and David E. Garland, 604–48. Grand Rapids: Zondervan, 2005.

Bruckner, James. *The NIV Application Commentary: Jonah, Nahum, Habakkuk, Zephaniah*. Grand Rapids: Zondervan, 2004.

Hiebert, Theodore. "The Book of Habakkuk." In *The New Interpreter's Bible*. Vol. 7: *Introduction to Apocalyptic Literature, Daniel, the Twelve Prophets*, edited by Leander E. Keck et al., 621–58. Nashville, TN: Abingdon, 1996.

Mason, Rex. *Zephaniah, Habakkuk, Joel*. Sheffield, UK: JSOT, 1994.

Matthews, Victor H. "Habakkuk." In *Zondervan Illustrated Bible Backgrounds Commentary*. Vol. 5: *The Minor Prophets, Job, Psalms, Proverbs, Ecclesiastes, Song of Songs*, edited by John H. Walton, 164–77. Grand Rapids: Zondervan, 2009.

Millard, Alan. "Chaldeans." In *Dictionary of the Ancient Near East*, edited by Piotr Bienkowski and Alan Millard, 70. Philadelphia: University of Pennsylvania Press, 2000.

Patterson, Richard D. *Nahum, Habakkuk, Zephaniah: An Exegetical Commentary*. N.loc.: Biblical Studies Press, 2003.

Sixth-Century Prophets

Chapter 10

Ezekiel, Prophet of the Glory of the Lord

Historical Setting of the Book

IN THE BOOK OF Ezekiel fifteen dates are given for different oracles, visions, or events. In Ezekiel 1:1 it is said that the prophet received his first vision in the thirtieth year. This date has given rise to many different theories. One possible solution is that it refers to the thirtieth year of the prophet's life (Odell, 2005: 16), but other solutions proposed include the thirtieth year from the reform of Josiah or from the ascension of Nabopolassar. Most probably, however, the thirtieth year of the prophet's life is in view (Zimmerli, 1979: 113–14).

The other dates that are given in the book all relate to the exile of King Jehoiachin. In most instances, the exact day is given, but in some only the month. The dates can be tabulated as follows (cf. Hill & Walton, 2000: 446):

Initial vision	1:1–3	June 593 BCE
The watchman	3:16	June 593
First temple vision	8:1	August/September 592
Ezekiel and the elders	20:1	August 591
Siege of Jerusalem	24:1	January 588
Prophecy against Tyre	26:1	March/April 587/6
Prophecy against Egypt	29:1	January 587
Prophecy against Egypt	29:17	April 571
Prophecy against Egypt	30:20	April 587

Prophecy against Egypt	31:1	June 587
Lament over pharaoh	32:1	March 586
Lament over Egypt	32:17	April 586
Fall of Jerusalem	33:21	December/January 586/5
Second temple vision	40:1	April 573

As is clear from this table, the dates occur in all three sections of the book (chs. 1–24, 25–32, 33–48, see below), within which they are in rough chronological order. Only the date in 29:17 is out of sequence—apparently this prophecy against Egypt is placed here because of its thematic agreement with the other prophecies against this nation. In the last part of the book, only two dates occur. The date in 33:21 is found at the beginning of the section where the prophet begins speaking again after the fall of Jerusalem, while the date in 40:1 is found at the beginning of the vision of the new temple.

These dates place the activity of the prophet in the final days of the kingdom of Judah and the beginning of the exile. This last phase in the history of the kingdom of Judah coincided with the fall of the Assyrian Empire and the rise of the Neo-Babylonian Empire. During his reign, king Josiah brought about a final period of reform in the kingdom of Judah. However, after he had died at Megiddo in a battle against pharaoh Neco in 609 BCE, the situation soon became desperate. Jehoahaz was made king by the people of the land. After three months pharaoh Neco deposed him and replaced him with his brother Eljakim, renamed Jehoiakim.

After the battle of Carchemish in 605 BCE, Judah became part of the Neo-Babylonian Empire. Nebuchadnezzar defeated the Egyptians in the same year. He was the son of Nabopolassar, who founded a new dynasty on becoming king in Babylonia in 626, the year in which he warded off an attack by the Assyrians on Babylon. That was the last time the crumbling Assyrian empire tried to subjugate Babylon.

After four or five years, Jehoiakim attempted a revolt against the Babylonians, but it resulted in a siege of Jerusalem in 598–597 BCE. After Jehoiakim's death during the siege, he was succeeded by his son Jehoiachin, who capitulated within three months. According to 2 Kings 24:14, the king, his family and 10,000 of the important people of Jerusalem were taken into exile by the Babylonians (Jer 52:28–30 has lower figures). Zedekiah was installed as the new king of Judah by Nebuchadnezzar.

Ezekiel was one of these exiles. He was settled, together with other exiles, in a Jewish colony close to Nippur on the Chebar canal, one of many canals that were part of an elaborate system of canals bringing water to the city. Ezekiel 3:15 refers to the place where Ezekiel lived as Tel Abib. The exact location of this settlement is unknown. Here Ezekiel was called as prophet in the fifth year of the exile of Jehoiachin. Although Zedekiah was ruling in Jerusalem, the exiles regarded the exiled king Jehoiachin as their legitimate ruler. That is why the prophecies in Ezekiel are still dated according to the years of Jehoiachin's exile. When Zedekiah rebelled against Nebuchadnezzar, Jerusalem was besieged again, which siege lasted eighteen months from the tenth month of the ninth year of Zedekiah's rule, in the year 587 BCE, till the fourth month of Zedekiah's eleventh year. The horror of the capture of the city and its destruction, including that of the temple, is described in 2 Kings 25. Zedekiah was captured and his sons were killed before his eyes. He was then blinded and taken into exile as well.

Although the exiles blended into the Babylonian society, they retained their identity as a distinct group, as can be seen from Psalm 137, which is generally located at the rivers of Babylon (cf. Ps. 137:1). Theologically speaking, however, the exiles were devastated. They had believed their God would protect them. In spite of all warnings by the prophets that they had to repent or suffer the consequences, they had persisted in their evil ways. The exile came as a shock. Initially, they hoped that they would soon return to their own land, and trusted that Egypt would help. Ezekiel had to point out that that was a false trust. In his letter to the exiles, Jeremiah told the people that they would have to remain in exile for a long time (Jer 29:4-23). After the destruction of Jerusalem Ezekiel had to lift their spirits by preaching repentance and the return to their land at a later stage.

Content and Structure of the Book

Different scholars divide the book into sections in different ways, mostly into either three or five sections. Most popular is the division of the book into the following three major sections (cf. Cooke, 1970: xvi; Zimmerli, 1979: 1-2 and Allen, 1994: xxv):

1-24	Prophecies against Israel before the fall of Jerusalem
25-32	Prophecies against the nations
33-48	Prophecies of hope after the fall of Jerusalem

Block (1998: 3) wants to divide the book into two main sections, 1–24 and 25–48, with 25:1 being the important pivot between the two sections. He regards the prophecies against the nations as the beginning of the message of hope for Israel.

Other scholars (e.g., Cooper, 1994: 39; Clements, 1996: 6) divide the book into four sections, regarding the section dealing with the call of the prophet (Ezek 1–3) as a separate section. For a possible division into five parts, 33–39 can be regarded as the fourth section, with prophecies of hope, and 40–48 as the final section, about the restored people of God.

These different views do not have a great impact on the flow of the contents of the book, although the division in three major parts results from placing the prophecies against the nations between the prophecies of doom and the prophecies of hope. The following table gives a more detailed analysis of the structure and contents of the book:

1–24		Prophecies against Israel before the fall of Jerusalem
	1–3	Inaugural vision: chariot vision and the call of the prophet
	4–11	Signs and visions proclaiming judgment on Israel, especially Judah and Jerusalem
	12–24	Prophecies of judgment
25–32		Prophecies against the nations
	25:1–7	Against Ammon
	25:8–11	Against Moab
	25:12–14	Against Edom
	25:15–17	Against Philistia
	26–28	Against Tyre
	29–32	Against Egypt
33–48		Prophecies of hope after the fall of Jerusalem
	33	Introduction to final part of the book
	34–39	Messages of hope
	40–48	The return of the Lord and the restoration of the people, the land and the temple

In Ezekiel 1–3, after the inaugural vision, Ezekiel is sent to a people (the exiles) that will not listen to him. Ezekiel 4–11 ends with the departure of the glory of God (כבוד יהוה) from the temple and Jerusalem. Within Ezekiel 12–24 the oracles against the false prophets in Ezekiel 13–14 are very important, as well as the proclamation of individual responsibility in Ezekiel 18. This section ends with the death of the wife of Ezekiel and the instruction that the prophet must remain silent. At the end of the oracles against the nations, the oracle bearing the latest date occurs in 29:17-24.

Ezekiel 33 serves as a pivot in the book, linking up with Ezekiel 24 and paving the way for the prophecies of hope to follow. Ezekiel receives the message of the fall of Jerusalem and begins to speak again. In Ezekiel 34-39 the exiles receive a message of hope proclaiming that the Lord will bring about the restoration and salvation of his people. This message is proclaimed in various ways, the vision of the dry bones coming alive in Ezekiel 37:1-14 and the prophecy against Gog in Ezekiel 38-39 being especially noteworthy.

The book concludes with the vision of the return of the Lord and the restoration of the people, the land and the temple in Ezekiel 40-48. The return of the glory of God is described in Ezekiel 43, with the resulting restoration of the land finding a climax in the vision of the river flowing from the temple in Ezekiel 47.

Theology of the Book

1. Ezekiel and the prophetic calling

The book of Ezekiel places special emphasis on the calling of the prophet and the task God gave him. Block (1997: 78) distinguishes two kinds of callings of prophets, one where the prophet protests against his calling and one where he is overwhelmed by his calling without protesting. Ezekiel's call seems to be of the latter kind and is described in detail in the first three chapters of the book. In this kind of call the prophet sees an overwhelming vision of God, such as the vision Ezekiel saw according to chapter 1. He fell with his face on the ground and then the Lord began speaking to him (Ezek 1:28).

Subsequently, he was prepared and equipped for his task and given a special commission, being instructed to go to the house of Israel and proclaim the word of the Lord to them (Ezek 2-3). He has to do this expecting them to refuse to listen to his message. While eating the scroll as instructed in Ezekiel 3, the Spirit came into him to equip him for his task. In this call narrative there are also indications of Ezekiel resisting the call. He is warned in 2:8 not to be rebellious like the rebellious house of Israel to whom he has to proclaim the word of the Lord. After receiving his calling, the prophet goes away in bitterness in 3:14-15, and then he sits silent for seven days before beginning to speak. In 3:16 the Lord comes again to him to tell him that he has made him a watchman for the house of Israel. He has to warn them about the impending doom. If he warns them and they do not listen, they will die for their own sins, but the prophet will save himself. However, if he does not warn them, they will still die on account of their sins, but the Lord will hold the prophet accountable. Furthermore, he has to bring the Lord's words to the people, not his own words.

The prophet remains a mere human being, "son of man," as he is frequently called in the book. At the same time, he is the instrument of God. He is a prophet, and he will be recognized as such. That will be the case when his prophecies become true, as stated in Ezekiel 2:5: "And whether they listen or fail to listen—for they are a rebellious house—they will know that a prophet has been among them." In Ezekiel 33 the prophet is again commanded to be a watchman for the people of Israel, and at the end of the chapter (33:33) the Lord affirms the statement of 2:5: "When all this comes true—and it surely will—then they will know that a prophet has been among them."

Time and again it is stated that the prophet receives the word of the Lord, for example in Ezekiel 6:1: "The word of the Lord came to me." The prophet often says that the Spirit of the Lord came into him or upon him (e.g., 2:2; 11:5). Frequently, the Lord says to Ezekiel that he must tell his audience: "This is what the Lord says," or: "Hear the word of the Lord." He is the messenger bringing the message of the Lord to the people of the Lord. He also has to perform sign acts, such as in Ezekiel 12, to get the attention of the people and then bring the word of the Lord to them. In 12:6, 11 it is said explicitly that the Lord will make him a sign for the people of Israel (cf. also 24:2, 27). These sign acts include the prohibition to mourn his wife when she died (24:15–18).

As a prophet Ezekiel must recognize that his call comes from the Lord alone. God is the one who calls and he gives his instructions regarding the message the prophet must proclaim. To deliver this message, the called one is equipped by the Spirit. The prophet must persevere in his preaching, even when he knows that the people will not listen, as Ezekiel is told in 2:5, 7. He will suffer rejection from the people who reject God, but if he remains true to his calling, the people will realize, though at a late stage, that he is indeed a prophet of the Lord.

Ezekiel, Prophet of the Glory of the Lord

2. The crisis of God's presence

In the history of Israel, the crisis of 587/6 BCE, caused by the destruction of Jerusalem and the temple, and the disappearance of the Davidic dynasty, had a profound impact on the redaction history of the books of the three Major Prophets. Isaiah (especially in the second part of the book), Jeremiah and Ezekiel each had to come to terms with this crisis, each in his own place and time. The messages of these books, proclaimed in this time of crisis, have in common that judgment and hope are connected to each other. Judgment was brought about by the sins of the people, and hope of forgiveness, restoration and return were brought about by the covenant love and fidelity of God. In the book of Ezekiel, the crisis can be described as a crisis of God's presence (Brueggemann, 2003: 190). The presence of the Lord is often described by the phrase "the glory of the Lord" (כבוד יהוה). It points to the glory of the Lord who revealed himself to his people, who elected them but who would judge them on account of their sins. At the beginning of the book, Ezekiel very carefully describes the Lord who appeared to him in a vision. In 1:28 he says: "Like the appearance of a rainbow in the clouds on a rainy day, so was the radiance around him. This was the appearance of the likeness of the glory of the Lord." He saw the glory of God more than once in different visions, as in 3:23, 10:15-19, and 43:1-5. In Ezekiel 10 the prophet describes the departure of the Lord from the temple by using the above mentioned phrase. The glory of the Lord departed from the temple, indicating that the Lord himself has departed from his people on account of their sins. This departure is described in Ezekiel 9:3. Ezekiel says the glory of the Lord went up from above the cherubim and moved to the threshold of the temple. Because of the defilement of the temple caused by the unclean acts and sacrifices of the priests and the people of Israel, it would no longer be a symbol of the presence of the Lord. Therefore, if the Lord departs from the temple, the temple loses its function. However, linked to the final departure of the glory of the Lord from the temple, are the promises of the Lord that Israel will return and that their stubborn hearts, their hearts of stone, will be replaced by hearts of flesh (11:16-20). Those amongst the people who do not repent and persist in serving idols, the abominations of the nations, will suffer the consequences of their deeds (11:21). After these prophecies of judgment and salvation, the glory of the Lord departs entirely from the temple and stops above the mountain east of Jerusalem (11:22-23).

In the vision of the restoration in chapters 40–48, the glory of the Lord appeared again. It is described in Ezekiel 43:1–5:

> Then the man brought me to the gate facing east, ² and I saw the glory of the God of Israel coming from the east. His voice was like the roar of rushing waters, and the land was radiant with his glory. ³ The vision I saw was like the vision I had seen when he came to destroy the city and like the visions I had seen by the Kebar River, and I fell facedown. ⁴ The glory of the Lord entered the temple through the gate facing east. ⁵ Then the Spirit lifted me up and brought me into the inner court, and the glory of the Lord filled the temple.

This return of the glory of the Lord brought the resolution of the crisis of God's presence. As has been indicated, in the visions at the beginning of the book, the glory of the Lord departed from the temple and from Jerusalem. The visions are followed by prophecies of judgment, and finally by the destruction of Jerusalem and the temple of Yhwh. The judgment thus being completed, the prophet began to preach to the exiles about the salvation that the Lord would bring about for them. In the great vision at the end of the book, in Ezekiel 40–48, the prophet saw the people returning to the land, Jerusalem being rebuilt and inhabited, and also the temple being rebuilt. However, with the Lord having departed from his people the restoration would not be complete without his return. Ezekiel saw that He would return, as described in the passage quoted above. Thereafter, the prophet also heard a voice speaking, the voice of the Lord telling the prophet that the Lord would again live in the temple, amongst his people. When Ezekiel was brought to the north gate of the temple, he could see the glory of the Lord filling the temple (44:4).

In this way, the crisis of the Lord's presence was resolved. The glory of the Lord departed from the temple, proclaiming judgment on the people in the first part of the book. This judgment being executed, however, the Lord became gracious again and showed mercy to his people. The change in the situation was affirmed by the return of the glory of the Lord to the temple, which in turn symbolized the abiding presence of the Lord among his people—in a new temple, in a rebuilt city and in the midst of the Lord's people resettled in their land.

3. A radical theocentricity

The book of Ezekiel uses a number of formulae and set expressions. Foremost amongst them is the so-called "recognition formula" or "proof-saying." The first occurrence of this formula in its standard form is found in Ezekiel 6:7: "you will know that I am the Lord." Zimmerli has made an extensive study of this formula and indicates that while this formula has often been regarded as an editorial addition to the book, it must rather be seen as a characteristic element of the book of Ezekiel (Zimmerli, 1979: 36–37; cf. also Joyce, 2009: 27–31). The formula occurs fifty-four times in its standard form in the book, and with minor variations in a further twenty instances. When the Lord speaks to Ezekiel, the phrase constituting the formula usually follows a statement that he will do something, such as punishing the people of Israel or their enemies, or delivering his people. It is then followed by the statement that the result of his actions will be that either the people or their enemies will recognize the power of the Lord, that he is the true God who is in command of the events.

In the first occurrence of this formula (6:7) the prophet is commanded to prophesy against the mountains of Israel (6:2). He has to say that the altars will be destroyed, the people killed and their cities destroyed, which is a summary of the judgment on the people of Israel that the Lord will execute. When these things happen, the people of the Lord will recognize his power. They will acknowledge him and realize that his judgments are just. Moreover, these judgments will result in the exile of the people who remained behind in Jerusalem when Jehoiachin was carried into exile. Then the people going into exile will recognize the Lord (Ezek 12:15), as will the people that are already in exile.

The formula occurs regularly in the prophecies against the nations in Ezekiel 25–32, many times at the end of the pronouncement of judgment on the different nations. Ezekiel has to tell these nations that they also will recognize the Lord. Examples are found at the end of the prophecies against Ammon, Moab, Edom, and Philistia in Ezekiel 25. However, in the case of Moab, the Lord states that Moab will know the Lord's vengeance (25:14), thereby presenting a deviation from the standard formula. In the prophecy against Philistia the Lord adds that they will know him when he takes vengeance. In Ezekiel 29:6 the Lord says that all who live in Egypt will recognize him, which allows for another variation of the formula.

This formula is not only used in connection with the judgment of the Lord, but also with regard to the salvation He will bring about. This is stated very clearly in Ezekiel 34:27: "They will know that I am the Lord, when I break the bars of their yoke and rescue them from the hands of those who enslaved them." At the end of the chapter, it is used in reaffirmation of the special bond between the Lord and his people (34:30–31): "Then they will know that I, the Lord their God, am with them, and that they are my people, the house of Israel, declares the sovereign Lord. And you, my sheep, the sheep of my pasture, are my people, and I am your God, declares the sovereign Lord." The final instance of the formula in the book is used to put the exile and restoration in perspective (39:28): "Then they will know that I am the Lord their God, for though I sent them into exile among the nations, I will gather them to their own land, not leaving any behind."

Related to this formula are the statements that the Lord did not act for the sake of Israel, but for the sake of his name. In Ezekiel 20 the Lord says that he brought Israel out of Egypt for the sake of his name (20:9) and that he did not destroy them in the desert, once again for the sake of his name (20:14, 22). Likewise, for the sake of his name he is about to punish them for their evil ways and deeds (20:44). However, after punishing them, he is going to deliver them, but again for the sake of his name, not for their sake (36:22, 32). Salvation and punishment are closely connected to the glory of his name.

The punishment Israel receives is also connected to the profanation of his name. In the same two chapters where the Lord says that he will act for the sake of his name; he also refers to the profanation of his name. Three times Ezekiel tells the elders in chapter 20 (20:9, 14, 22) that the Lord says he spared his people so that his name will not be profaned in the eyes of the nations. In 20:39 he says that the punishment will bring the people to their senses so that they will no longer profane his name among the nations. Ezekiel reports in 36:20, 21, 22, and 23 that the Lord accuses the people of profaning his name wherever they went amongst the nations, but he will bring them back in spite of what they did, for the sake of his name. When he brings the people back to their land, he will not allow them to profane his name any longer (39:7).

The motivation for God's actions is the holiness of his name. In 20:39 the holiness of God's name is contrasted with the profanation of his name by his people when they serve their idols. When God brings his people back to their land, he will demonstrate his holiness before the eyes of the nations (20:41). The holiness of the name of the Lord is also stressed in Ezekiel 36:20–23. The uniqueness of God is especially demonstrated in the chariot vision of Ezekiel 1–3. The prophet is very circumspect in the description of what he saw. This can be seen in the summary at the end of Ezekiel 1, referred to above. The radiant glory of God is such that no mortal man can comprehend him in his splendor. However, this incomprehensible God is the one revealing himself to his prophet and making the prophet his instrument to proclaim his word to his people. He is the God who rules the whole earth, but his chosen residence is in Jerusalem, in the midst of his people. He made his covenant with his people, and he will maintain it in spite of the faithlessness of his people. The book proclaims God as being holy and in command of the whole creation.

4. Judgment and restoration

In general terms, the contents of the book of Ezekiel can be summarized by the phrase "judgment and restoration." It indicates the basic pattern of the book, which starts with oracles proclaiming judgment and ends with the vision of the restored community, city, and temple. The judgments pronounced in Ezekiel 1–24 are some of the harshest judgments to be found in the entire Old Testament (Joyce, 2009: 17). Ezekiel makes it clear, however, that the downfall of Judah and the judgment pronounced on the people are consequences of their own sins. It is not that the Lord is not capable of saving his people; on the contrary, he has decided to deliver them to their enemies so that they will recognize their evil ways and come to repentance. On the other hand, their repentance will not be the key to their future salvation. That will only come about through God's love and faithfulness, and for the sake of his name.

A very clear proclamation of the impending doom is contained in Ezekiel 7:1–4:

> The word of the Lord came to me: [2] "Son of man, this is what the Sovereign Lord says to the land of Israel: The end! The end has come upon the four corners of the land. [3] The end is now upon you and I will unleash my anger against you. I will judge you according to your conduct and repay you for all your detestable practices. [4] I will not look on you with pity or spare you; I will surely repay you for your conduct and the detestable practices among you. Then you will know that I am the Lord."

The people living in Jerusalem have already experienced the beginning of this judgment, but it will come again, and then much worse, as is stated in Ezekiel 15. The people of the city that survive the destruction of the city will be taken into exile. Ezekiel had to demonstrate the truth of this prophecy by the sign-act in Ezekiel 12, where the Lord commands him to pack his belongings, dig a hole in the wall and depart in the evening. He has to carry his belongings on his shoulder. This will be the fate of the ruler in Jerusalem (Zedekiah). It is interesting to note that a large number of such sign-acts occur in the books of Jeremiah and Ezekiel (see Friebel, 1999). Sign-acts are nonverbal means of communicating the prophet's message (Friebel, 1999: 14). Friebel divides the passage in Ezekiel 12:1–16 in three parts: the command to perform the sign-act (1–6), the prophet's performing of the sign-act (7) and the verbalized interpretation of the sign-act (8–16; Friebel, 1999: 261–67). This is typical of the sign-acts in the book of Ezekiel.

However, after the destruction of Jerusalem, the prophet begins to proclaim a message of hope, of future salvation. In Ezekiel 34 the Lord promises that he will be the people's shepherd who cares for them. The message of hope is especially clear in the vision of the dry bones in Ezekiel 37. In this chapter, as elsewhere in the book, the words of the people are quoted (37:11): "Our bones are dried up and our hope is gone; we are cut off." They have now suffered because of the judgment of the Lord and are despondent. The complaint of the people is answered by a proclamation of salvation (37:12–14):

> This is what the Sovereign Lord says: "O my people, I am going to open your graves and bring you up from them; I will bring you back to the land of Israel. [13] Then you, my people, will know that I am the Lord, when I open your graves and bring you up from them. [14] I will put my Spirit in you and you will live, and I will settle you in your own land. Then you will know that I the Lord have spoken, and I have done it, declares the Lord."

The salvation will take place not on account of the deeds or repentance of the people, but because of the faithfulness of the Lord, as can be seen from the words in 37:14. The Lord promises that he will show mercy and will return his people to their land. He will do what he promised. This is a manifestation of how judgment and restoration are linked in the book. It can also be seen in a statement that occurs frequently in the book. In the first section of the book, God already promises a return of the nation

Ezekiel, Prophet of the Glory of the Lord

scattered into exile, for example in Ezekiel 11:17: "This is what the Sovereign Lord says: 'I will gather you from the nations and bring you back from the countries where you have been scattered, and I will give you back the land of Israel again.'"

Ezekiel's view of the nation of God can be linked to the theme of judgment and restoration. Block (1998: 51–57) discusses the past, present and future of God's people in this regard. Especially in Ezekiel 16 and 20, the people's past is pictured by using vivid images in an allegory. Jerusalem is compared to an abandoned child that God rescued and cared for. The daughter grew up and became a prostitute, following in the footsteps of her sister Samaria. Her behavior will bring about punishment and judgment, as is clearly stated in 16:43: "Because you did not remember the days of your youth but enraged me with all these things, I will surely bring down on your head what you have done, declares the Sovereign Lord. Did you not add lewdness to all your other detestable practices?" However, this retaliation will not be the end of the way for God and his people, as he will remember his covenant, and re-establish it with them in order to be their God again.

Ezekiel 20 summarizes the history of the people, starting with the exodus from Egypt. They received the land from God, but he warned them not to defile themselves with idols. However, the history of the people since that time has been characterized by rebellion, both in the desert and in the promised land. Again and again the people sinned against the Lord, and yet he made a new beginning with them every time. However, they persisted in doing what was wrong, so that the Lord's judgment on the people of Ezekiel's time became unavoidable. God chose the people without any special merit on their side, but they had to obey him. When they persisted in disobedience, judgment became inevitable.

As far as the people of the time of the prophet are concerned, they are regarded as a people in revolt. This is made clear by God to the prophet when He called Ezekiel (2:3–4): "Son of man, I am sending you to the Israelites, to a rebellious nation that has rebelled against me; they and their fathers have been in revolt against me to this very day. The people to whom I am sending you are obstinate and stubborn." The exiles whom Ezekiel is addressing cannot claim immunity from judgment on account of God's special relationship with them or because they have suffered through God's judgment. Moreover, though they represent the future of God's people, it will only come to pass when they live in obedience.

As far as the future is concerned, Ezekiel can look beyond the present and imminent judgment to a better future built on God's promises. The Lord will gather the exiles and bring them back to the land of Israel. They are and will remain God's people, and once they will again live in the land of Israel with God dwelling in their midst in the restored temple.

Part of the judgment pronounced in the book of Ezekiel is directed against the foreign nations. It is found in the middle section of the book (Ezek 25–32), where seven nations are mentioned. It is worth mentioning that half of the prophecies are directed against Egypt. Most of the prophecies are dated at the time of the siege and fall of Jerusalem in 586 BCE. This event may have occasioned these prophecies, as nothing is mentioned about the nations in the call of the prophet. The prophecies against the nations were traditionally regarded as bringing a message of hope to Israel. However, it is not the case with the prophecies against Egypt. Egypt enticed Judah to break their oath of allegiance to Babylon, thus causing greater problems to Judah. The false hope on Egypt had to be exposed. This issue is raised in Ezekiel 17, where it is made clear that collaboration with Egypt against Babylon equaled rebellion and breaking an oath of loyalty (17:12–15):

> The king of Babylon went to Jerusalem and carried off her king and her nobles, bringing them back with him to Babylon. [13] Then he took a member of the royal family and made a treaty with him, putting him under oath. He also carried away the leading men of the land, [14] so that the kingdom would be brought low, unable to rise again, surviving only by keeping his treaty. [15] But the king rebelled against him by sending his envoys to Egypt to get horses and a large army. Will he succeed? Will he who does such things escape? Will he break the treaty and yet escape?

These actions are echoed in Ezekiel 29, where Egypt is called a "staff of reed" (29:6). Ezekiel 29:16 makes this very clear: "Egypt will no longer be a source of confidence for the people of Israel but will be a reminder of their sin in turning to her for help. Then they will know that I am the Sovereign Lord." However, even for the nations a return is envisaged, such as a return from exile for Egypt in 29:13.

5. Repentance

In the books of the prophets, the notion of repentance plays an important role. Three texts are often mentioned in this regard, namely Amos 4:6–14, Hosea 5:15—6:5, and Jeremiah 3:12–24 (*ABD* 5: 671). In the case of Amos, the lack of repentance is bemoaned. In Hosea, the possibility of repentance is stated. Jeremiah refers to a new heart as the context for repentance. In Ezekiel, repentance is explicitly mentioned in three passages, namely in Ezekiel 14, 18, and 33. In Ezekiel 14:6 the Lord commands the people to repent and turn away from their idols: "Therefore say to the house of Israel, 'This is what the Sovereign Lord says: Repent! Turn from your idols and renounce all your detestable practices!'" This chapter describes how the elders came to Ezekiel to consult the Lord. The Lord says that they have set up idols in their hearts. How could they then come to consult him? Anyone who did that would be destroyed.

The second chapter where repentance is mentioned is Ezekiel 18, which will be discussed in more detail below. However, at the end of that chapter, repentance is mentioned twice in the conclusion to the section that deals with personal responsibility (Ezek 18:30–32):

> "Therefore, O house of Israel, I will judge you, each one according to his ways," declares the Sovereign Lord. "Repent! Turn away from all your offenses; then sin will not be your downfall. [31] Rid yourselves of all the offenses you have committed, and get a new heart and a new spirit. Why will you die, O house of Israel? [32] For I take no pleasure in the death of anyone," declares the Sovereign Lord. "Repent and live!"

In this passage, an urgent call to repent is made on every individual; each has to turn away from his idols. However, repentance is never mentioned as a prerequisite for restoration and salvation. The salvation of the people depends solely on the actions of the Lord. The people are expected to recognize the correctness of the Lord's judgment on them and they have to acknowledge his glory and power. Nevertheless, the restoration still depends on the decision and actions of the Lord, not on anything that they can do. The people have to break with their sinful past and then they have to wait on the Lord to bring about a reversal in their fortunes. They have to acknowledge that they have broken the covenant, that they have been disobedient and that they have exchanged the Lord for worthless idols.

The same line of thought is expressed in the message of Ezekiel 33, which is partially related to portions of chapters 3 and 18. The prophet's role is that of a lookout warning his people, the aim of his prophecy being to encourage a change of heart and habit, in order that divine punishment might be averted.

6. Individual responsibility

In the study of the message of Ezekiel the idea of individual responsibility, especially as revealed in Ezekiel 18, has received much attention. Ezekiel's contribution in this regard is seen as a major innovation in the development of the theology of the Old Testament. It is, for example, the view of Von Rad (1962: 394) that in Ezekiel 18 the prophet breaks with the old concept of collective responsibility. The problem with the collective concept was, according to Von Rad, that the individual could hide behind this concept, while Ezekiel gives prominence to the actions of the individual who has to carry the responsibility for his own actions. However, the former consensus on a development from collective to personal responsibility has been challenged lately, especially by Joyce in his seminal work on this topic (1989) and in a summary in his commentary on Ezekiel (Joyce, 2009: 23–26; cf. also Block, 1997: 556–57). The main reason for this challenge is the fact that Ezekiel is attempting, especially in the first part of the book, to convince the exiles that God's judgment on them and on the people who remained behind in Jerusalem, is just. In this sense the disaster of the downfall of the Kingdom of Judah is first and foremost a national, and thus collective, disaster. Joyce (2009: 23) states that the issue of the responsibility of the individual, as moral independence, should be distinguished from the issue of the moral independence of successive generations.

The issue of corporate responsibility has been studied in detail by Kaminsky (1995) as well. He presents a very good history of research in this regard (Kaminsky, 1995: 16–29). As far as Ezekiel 18 is concerned, he states that Ezekiel is trying to convince the generation of his time that the exile was the result of their own deeds, and not the misdeeds of previous generations (Kaminsky, 1995: 166). In his emphasis on individual responsibility, Ezekiel appeals to the individual members, making up the community, to recognize their sins and to repent (cf. Kaminsky, 1995: 177).

For this understanding of Ezekiel 18, one must look closely at the introduction of the chapter. It consists of a question about a proverb the people use, followed by the response of the Lord (Ezek 18:1–4):

> The word of the Lord came to me: ² "What do you people mean by quoting this proverb about the land of Israel: 'The fathers eat sour grapes, and the children's teeth are set on edge?' ³As surely as I live," declares the Sovereign Lord, "you will no longer quote this proverb in Israel. ⁴ For every living soul belongs to me, the father as well as the son—both alike belong to me. The soul who sins is the one who will die."

The question of the Lord is addressed to the collective: "you people." The context of this chapter is the national calamity, of which the exiles say that it was not their fault. They complain that they are being punished not for the sins of their generation, but for the sins of the previous generations. Subsequently, this complaint is refuted by three case studies. The first (18:5–9) states that a righteous man will be rewarded for his righteousness. The second (18:10–13) deals with the evil son of a righteous man. On account of his evil deeds the son himself will be punished. His actions will not be condoned because of the righteousness of his father. The third (18:14–17) deals with the righteous son of an evil father. He will not die for the sins of his father. Ezekiel uses individuals in his examples, linking up with priestly case law, but each individual stands for a generation. In this way, the principle of divine righteousness and just retribution is explained to the people who wanted to shirk their own responsibility. Ezekiel wants to bring the exiles to a corporate transformation. They must admit their own sins and return to the Lord. The final example is about a righteous third generation that would not suffer because of the sins of the previous unrighteous generation. The complaint of the exiles is that they are suffering for the sins of the previous generation. However, if they had lived according to the law of the Lord as a righteous generation, they would not have been punished for the sins of their fathers. The final call to repentance at the end of the chapter is also directed to the nation as a whole. Instead of thinking about the unjust judgment of the Lord, they should focus on their own lives and repent.

On the other hand, the idea of individual responsibility should not be underestimated. Ezekiel attempts to strike a balance between the individual and the community. The individual members of the community are called upon to take responsibility for the community, for the state of the nation. The emphasis on the individual can be seen in Ezekiel 9, where guards are commanded to go through the city and put a mark on the foreheads of the individuals who are lamenting over the detestable things done in the city (9:4). They will be spared. Although the collective is emphasized, one person will not take the blame for the sins of another person. An individual's fate, whether it is salvation or damnation, is not predetermined by the actions of a previous generation. God's judgment on a nation and on individuals remains just. The conclusion of Ezekiel 18 states that God is not bent on judgment and destruction. He wants the people to live, and thus calls for repentance.

This was the call that the exiles had to hear, that they should turn away from idols and live according to God's commandments. This was not the message of unconditional hope they wanted to hear, but it was the message they should have heard.

7. The future of the house of David

The destruction of Jerusalem and the temple brought about the end of the Kingdom of Judah, but not an end to the promises of the Lord, or his covenant with David. This is stated very clearly in Ezekiel 34 and 37. When the people will be gathered to their own land, David will be their shepherd and he will tend them (Ezek 34:23). He will be the prince among the people of the Lord (34:24; 37:25). In the restored kingdom that is envisaged, a shoot from the house of David will be king, and the people will live in the land forever, under the rule of David (37:25). The future of the House of David will entail a reversal of the prophecies against that house. Ezekiel sees a prince coming from that house. He is called David to make it clear that he is heir to the promises made to the House of David. The Lord calls him "my servant" to emphasize the special relationship between the Lord and this future ruler.

Ezekiel 40–48 refers to a future prince (נשיא), but his task is quite restricted. He is not explicitly linked to the House of David and described in the same lofty style as the future leader in Ezekiel 34 and 37. In the final vision of the book he does not have a political role, but rather a cultic one. He has to promote the true worship of the Lord and lead the people in their celebration of the presence of the true God in their midst.

8. The use of formulas and the theology of Ezekiel

Different formulas occur relatively frequently in the book of Ezekiel and are used to highlight important aspects of his words and message. Three of them especially concern the relationship between God, Ezekiel, and Ezekiel's message (cf. Block, 1997: 32–34). The first is the well-known word-event formula "The word of the Lord came to me" (ויהי דבר־יהוה אלי לאמר). This formula occurs more than fifty times in the book. The message that the prophet has to proclaim is not his own message, but the word of God that is given to him and which he has to bring to his audience. The word-event formula is frequently followed by the citation formula that occurs about 120 times: "Thus says the Lord Yhwh" (כה אמר אדני יהוה). This formula is then followed by the words of the Lord, usually spoken in the first person. The signatory formula occurs eighty-five times in Ezekiel: "Utterance of the Lord Yhwh" (נאם יהוה). This formula can occur at the end of a paragraph or an oracle, but also in the middle of a verse. It functions almost like a signature, signaling that the message the prophet is bringing comes directly from the Lord, not from the prophet. These three formulas thus serve to emphasize the fact that the Lord is using the prophet as his messenger to bring his divine word to the people. It places the task of the prophet in perspective, but also emphasizes the authority of the word proclaimed by the prophet. The people must listen to this word, and refusing to listen to the word will have dire consequences. On the other hand, that Ezekiel's words are the words of God also emphasizes the certainty of restoration in the prophecies of hope and salvation.

In addition to these formulas, there are several verses that further articulate that it is the Lord who speaks. A typical example is found in Ezekiel 5:13: "Then my anger will cease and my wrath against them will subside, and I will be avenged. And when I have spent my wrath upon them, they will know that I the Lord have spoken [כי־אני יהוה דברתי] in my zeal." This phrase often occurs without a connecting particle (e.g., in 5:15). In the first part of the book (Ezek 1–24), the phrase affirms the proclamation of judgment. With the same function it occurs once in the prophecies against the nations (30:12). It is also used in prophecies of salvation, for example in 34:24 and 36:6 in the third part of the book (Ezek 33–48).

Five times the Lord says that he has spoken and that he will do as he spoke. The first example is in 17:24: "I, the Lord, have spoken and

I will do it" (אני יהוה דברתי ועשיתי). It is found at the end of the chapter with the parable of the two eagles and the vine, about the exile of Jehoiachin, his replacement by Zedekiah and the latter's shifting of his allegiance to Egypt. Zedekiah's actions would result in the destruction of Jerusalem, but the Lord also promises a new shoot (from the line of David). At the end of this section, the Lord affirms that he will do what he said. In 22:14 the same words are used in relation to the Lord's judgment on Jerusalem. He will bring that to fulfillment as well. The same is said in 24:14, although here the verb "to come" stands between the two verbs of the normal phrase. In 36:36, the phrase affirms that the nations will recognize the Lord when he restores his people in their land and cities. The last instance of this phrase is found at the end of the vision of the dry bones in Ezekiel 37:14, where the Lord affirms the salvation that he will bring about.

The two verbs "to speak" (דבר) and "to do" (עשה) are used in different forms in Ezekiel 12:25 and 28. Ezekiel 12:25 reads as follows:

כי אני יהוה אדבר את אשר אדבר דבר ויעשה לא תמשך עוד כי בימיכם
בית המרי אדבר דבר ועשיתיו נאם אדני יהוה:

("'But I the Lord will speak what I will, and it shall be fulfilled without delay. For in your days, you rebellious house, I will fulfill whatever I say,' declares the Sovereign Lord.")

The verb "I will speak" (אדבר) at the beginning of the verse is in the imperfect, followed by "and it will happen" (ויעשה), a niph'al imperfect: "I, the Lord will speak and that what I say, will happen." The same verb "I will speak" (אדבר) occurs at the end of the verse and it is followed by a qal perfect with waw consecutive, stating exactly the same as in the previous five examples: The Lord will do what he has promised. The example in verse 28 agrees with the first example in verse 25, affirming that the Lord will bring his judgment to fulfillment. These examples, where the Lord states that his words will become true, testify to the way in which the Lord affirms the threats and promises spoken by his prophet in his name. The prophet is frequently commanded to speak, either by אמר ("say") or by דבר ("speak"). Both these words are used in 12:23, just before the Lord affirms his judgment by the two phrases discussed above. In the context of the Lord giving the prophet his instructions, it is often said that the hand of the Lord was on the prophet (as in 1:3), or that the Spirit fell upon the prophet, or came into him (11:5 and 2:2). All these statements make it quite clear that the prophet was called by God, he was

Ezekiel, Prophet of the Glory of the Lord

sent to proclaim the word of God and that proclamation was affirmed by God himself. In the end, the prophet can only prophesy, but the Lord will bring those prophecies to fulfillment.

Finally, it is interesting to give some attention to the terms used almost exclusively by Ezekiel for the exile and restoration of the people of Israel. Ezekiel 20 is of special importance with regard to the exile of the people of Judah. This chapter, up to verse 44, is a recapitulation of the history of the people since the exodus from Egypt up to the time of the prophet. It starts with the exodus and tells how the Lord warned the people against apostasy. However, the people forsook the Lord and worshipped the idols of the nations. It started already in the desert, but the Lord had pity on them and led them into the promised land. The same happened there. From verse 30 onwards the Lord gives them a promise of restoration, that He will have pity on them again. They are scattered amongst the nations (the verb פוץ), but the Lord will gather them from the nations (the verb קבץ). The same two verbs are used again in verse 41. Of the total of thirty-four occurrences of the two verbs in Ezekiel, twenty-four instances are found where the two verbs occur in close proximity, in Ezekiel 11, 20, 22, 28, 29, 34, and 36. In many of these instances the two words are used together, i.e. where the Lord says that he has scattered the people but that he will bring them back to their land. Ezekiel 11:16 and 17 can serve as a good example of this practice:

> Therefore say: "This is what the Sovereign Lord says: Although I sent them far away among the nations and scattered them among the countries, yet for a little while I have been a sanctuary for them in the countries where they have gone." [17] Therefore say: "This is what the Sovereign Lord says: I will gather you from the nations and bring you back from the countries where you have been scattered, and I will give you back the land of Israel again."

Another, very typical example of how these words are used is found in Ezekiel 20:34: "I will bring you from the nations and gather you from the countries where you have been scattered" (וקבצתי אתכם מן־הארצות אשר נפוצתם בם). In the majority of instances, the two verbs are used in Ezekiel to denote the scattering of God's people as judgment and their gathering (back to their land) as an act of compassion. Exile and restoration play a prominent role in the theology of Ezekiel. The Lord scattered his people as punishment on their sins, but He will gather them back when He shows mercy, mercy they do not deserve.

9. Conclusion

The book of Ezekiel deals with the crisis of God's presence. The book begins with a vision in which the prophet saw an appearance of God and in which he was called to be the mouthpiece of the Lord. He saw the glory of the Lord departing from Jerusalem and the temple, which articulates the crisis. But after the judgment on the people and the proclamation of judgment on the nations, the prophet saw at the end of the book a glorious vision of the presence of the Lord returning to Jerusalem and the temple, and the temple and the people restored.

Bibliography

Allen, Leslie C. *Ezekiel 1–19*. Word Biblical Commentary 28. Dallas: Word, 1994.

Block, Daniel I. *The Book of Ezekiel Chapters 1–24*. New International Commentary on the Old Testament. Grand Rapids: Eerdmans, 1997.

———. *The Book of Ezekiel Chapters 25–48*. New International Commentary on the Old Testament. Grand Rapids: Eerdmans, 1998.

Brueggemann, Walter. *An Introduction to the Old Testament. The Canon and Christian Imagination*. Louisville, KY: Westminster John Knox, 2003.

Clements, Ronald E. *Ezekiel*. Westminster Bible Companion. Louisville, KY: Westminster John Knox, 1996.

Cooke, G. A. *A Critical and Exegetical Commentary on the Book of Ezekiel*. International Critical Commentary. Edinburgh: T. & T. Clark, 1970.

Cooper, Lamar Eugene. *Ezekiel*. The New American Commentary. Nashville, TN: Broadman & Holman, 1994.

Freedman, David Noel, editor. *The Anchor Bible Dictionary*. 6 vols. New York: Doubleday, 1992.

Friebel, Kelvin G. *Jeremiah's and Ezekiel's Sign-Acts: Rhetorical Nonverbal Communication*. JSOT Supplement 283. Sheffield, UK: Sheffield Academic Press, 1999.

Hill, Andrew E., and John H. Walton. *A Survey of the Old Testament*. Grand Rapids: Zondervan, 2000.

Joyce, Paul M. *Divine Initiative and Human Response in Ezekiel*. JSOT Supplement 51. Sheffield: JSOT, 1989.

———. *Ezekiel: A Commentary*. Library of Hebrew Bible Old Testament 482. London: T. & T. Clark, 2009.

Kaminsky, Joel S. *Corporate Responsibility in the Hebrew Bible*. JSOT Supplement 196. Sheffield, UK: Sheffield Academic Press, 1995.

Odell, Margaret S. *Ezekiel*. Smyth & Helwys Bible Commentary. Macon, GA: Smyth & Helwys, 2005.

Von Rad, Gerhard. *Old Testament Theology 1*. Edinburgh: Oliver and Boyd, 1962.

Zimmerli, Walther. *Ezekiel 1*. Hermeneia. Philadelphia: Fortress, 1979.

Chapter 11

Obadiah, Prophet of Retribution and Restoration

Historical Setting of the Book

A NUMBER OF PEOPLE mentioned in the Old Testament are named Obadiah (1 Chr 3:21; 7:3; 8:38; 9:16, 44; 12:10; 2 Chr 17:7; Ezra 8:9; Neh 10:6; 12:25), but it is almost certain that none of these may be identified with the prophet who received the vision recorded in the book that bears his name. The book itself gives virtually no clues to the prophet's identity. While the absence of this information might indicate that Obadiah was well known to the original readers (Longman and Dillard, 2006: 436), to modern readers he remains a "shadowy figure" (Baker, 2006: 146), unknown beyond the twenty-one verses that comprise the book.

We can, however, be somewhat more confident about the historical context that generated Obadiah's vision. In vv. 10–14, the prophet brings a series of increasingly serious accusations against the people of Edom for the "violence" they did against their "brother" nation, Israel (v. 10): (a) they "stood aloof" when "foreigners" attacked Jerusalem and carried off its "wealth," a reference to either people or property (Baker, 2006: 180) (v. 11), (b) they joyfully mocked Judah "in the day of their destruction" (v. 12), (c) they actively participated in that destruction by joining the foreign conquerors in plundering Jerusalem (v. 13) and (d) finally, they either killed or handed over to the attackers any who escaped the sack of the city (v. 14).

Although some commentators argue that Obadiah describes events occurring as early as the ninth century BCE (for a summary, see Raabe, 1996: 49–50), most agree that he has in view Edom's active participation in the destruction of Jerusalem at the hands of the Babylonian army in 587 BCE (see also Ps 137:7; Ezek 25:12; 35:5) (Longman and Dillard, 2006: 438). Accordingly, the majority of scholars date the book of Obadiah to the first half of the exilic period, from 585 to 555 BCE, just before Nabonidus's campaign against Edom in 553 BCE (Raabe, 1996: 51; Patterson, 2008: 231). Others discern a longer redactional history, taking the final verses of the book to have been added much later, perhaps as late as the middle of the fifth century BCE (Wolff, 1986: 19; Nogalski, 2011: 368).

One of the more complex issues concerning the formation of Obadiah is its relationship to the book of Jeremiah. In particular, the many verbal and thematic similarities between Obadiah 1–9 and Jeremiah 49:7–16 suggest that there is a literary connection between the two passages (for a summary, see Raabe, 1996: 22–31). The majority position in recent scholarship is that both Obadiah and Jeremiah are dependent on a third unknown text (Sweeney, 2000: 282), although the view that Obadiah adapted Jeremiah also has significant support (Raabe, 1996: 22–23).

Whenever Obadiah was written, it appears that it was incorporated into a larger work, often referred as the Book of the Twelve (i.e., the Minor Prophets), no earlier than the time of Ezra-Nehemiah (Redditt, 2001: 66), when Edom had ceased to exist as a national entity. In that new historical context, the oracle against Edom and the promise of restoration for Judah may have been interpreted in an eschatological direction, with the destruction of Edom serving as a foreshadowing of the punishment of the wicked on a final day of judgment.

Reading Obadiah as part of the Book of the Twelve might explain, at least in part, the book's location immediately after Amos. With its focus on Edom's fraternal treachery, Obadiah picks up on the oracle in Amos 1:11–12, where Edom is condemned "because he pursued his brother with a sword." There are also a number of structural and thematic parallels between Amos 9 and Obadiah (Nogalski, 2011: 372), with the most obvious connection being that both books climax with the restoration of Jerusalem and Israel's possession of Edom (Amos 9:12; Obad 21). While Obadiah makes no mention of David and expresses no specifically messianic hope, the redactional connection to Amos 9:12 ("In that day I will restore David's fallen tent") invites readers of the Book of the Twelve to expect that the renewed Israel of Obadiah 17–21 will be ruled by a descendant of David (Nogalski, 2011: 392).

Content and Structure of the Book

The literary structure of Obadiah is much debated (Jenson, 2008: 5–6) and many scholars argue that the book has a long redactional history that raises doubts about its unity (Wolff, 1986: 17–18). Nevertheless, irrespective of when it reached its final canonical form, Obadiah has a rhetorical coherence that allows it to be read as a literary unity.

The most straightforward approach to the literary structure divides Obadiah into three parts—vv. 1–9, 10–14, and 15–21 (Patterson, 2008: 21; Armerding, 2008: 425)—that set out a coherent and gradual progression from the proclamation of judgment against Edom to the reasons for this judgment and finally to a prediction of the coming of the Day of Yhwh with its reversal of the fortunes of Edom and Israel (Pagán, 1996: 439).

Theology of the Book

1. The day of the Lord

Obadiah locates the destruction of Edom within the context of Yhwh's wider judgment of the Gentile nations. While vv. 5–14 enumerate specific ways in which Edom would be punished, v. 15 declares, "The day of the Lord is near for all nations." Edom's destiny is now connected to a great day of reckoning for all the gentile nations—a time when Yhwh will punish the wicked, vindicate the righteous, and establish his kingdom (Isa 13:6–11; 34:1–15; Ezek 30:3; Joel 1:15; 2:1, 11, 31 [3:4]; 3:14 [4:14]; Amos 5:18–20; Joel 1:15; 3:14; Zeph 1:7, 14). It is also likely that for Obadiah, Edom functions as a representative of all the gentile nations opposed to God (Stuart, 1987: 421; Patterson, 2008: 232). Along these lines, it should be noted that the word "Edom" in Hebrew is based on the same three consonants (אדם) as the word for "humanity" (Baker, 2006: 183) and this linguistic connection might reinforce the idea that Edom represents all the wicked nations that will be destroyed in this great judgment day.

By tying Edom's punishment to the Day of Yhwh, Obadiah's prophecy takes on an eschatological dimension. Edom's destruction and Israel's subsequent rise are not to be interpreted as events of mere regional political significance. Verses 15–21 are ultimately to be understood in the context of God's history-climaxing judgment of the world and the inauguration of the age to come when Israel would finally fulfill its destiny as Yhwh's chosen people.

2. The restoration of Jerusalem

While the destruction of Jerusalem at the hands of the Babylonians was fitting punishment for Judah's covenantal unfaithfulness, her final destiny would be the polar opposite of Edom's. The underlying reason for the different fates of the two nations can be found in the fact that Yhwh calls Judah, "my people" (v. 13). His commitment to the promises of his covenant with Abraham ensured that utter destruction could not be the final chapter in Judah's story. To be sure, the people of Judah were sent into exile but Yhwh's fidelity to his promise to Abraham to make him into "a great nation" (Gen 12:2) and more specifically, his solemn oath that his descendants would "take possession of the cities of their enemies" (Gen 22:17) guaranteed Judah's eventual return to the promised land, the rebuilding of the temple on Mount Zion (v. 17), and the restoration of Jerusalem's dominion over the old territory of Edom (vv. 19–21).

3. A renewed and reunited Israel

Verse 17 introduces the picture of a restored and purified Israel. "It will be holy" (or, "a holy place") suggests that Mount Zion will be cleansed of the defilement caused by the profane presence of Edom and the other nations (v. 16) and that a rebuilt temple will stand on the site (Raabe, 1996: 242–43; Baker, 2006: 191). Yhwh's presence with his people also implies that the restored Israel will be purified and made into the holy people they were intended to be (Patterson, 2008: 233; Armerding, 2008: 445).

Furthermore, the boundaries of the restored community—from Zarephath in the north and the Negev in the south (v. 20)—and the inclusion of territory formerly occupied by the old Northern Kingdom of Israel—Ephraim, Samaria, and Gilead—suggest that the Israel that emerges from the Day of Yhwh will possess the land originally allotted to the twelve tribes, not just the Southern Kingdom of Judah. In v. 17, Obadiah refers to restored Israel both as "the house of Jacob" and "the house of Joseph." Joseph was, of course, the father of the two tribes that dominated the Northern Kingdom—Ephraim and Manasseh—and so Obadiah envisages a future reunification of all twelve tribes (Renkema, 2003: 205; Armerding, 2008: 446) and this implies the almost unimaginable prospect of a re-gathering of the ten scattered tribes of the Northern Kingdom.

The new Israel will also be the instrument by which Yhwh ultimately destroys Edom (v. 18): Israel will be a fire—a manifestation of Yhwh's burning wrath (Allen, 1976: 167; Pagán, 1996: 455)—that burns off the chaff to prepare the land of Edom for the new growth of Israelite occupation (Jenson, 2008: 24). Thus Israel will not only occupy the territory of the original twelve tribes but will also take possession of Edom's territory (vv. 19-21). In so doing, Israel will fulfill Balaam's ancient prophecy that Jacob would one day destroy Edom and take possession of its lands (Num 24:18-19). In fact, restored Israel will repossess territory once stolen by the Philistines (v. 19), a further hint that the victory over Edom will be part of a wider judgment of the nations.

4. The centrality of Zion and the kingdom of God

The final verse (v. 21) articulates the prophet's sweeping vision of the climax of Israel's history—indeed, the history of the world. The deliverance of Israel from its enemies and its subsequent rule over them is not an end in itself. The ultimate goal of both creation and redemption is the establishment of Yhwh's kingship over the whole world. God's plan from the beginning was that he would rule over creation through his representative people (Gen 1:26-28). With the election of Abraham, that royal calling devolved to his descendants and now at last in Obadiah's eschatological vision, we see Israel, restored from exile, reunified and spiritually transformed, ruling over the nations (represented by Edom). In this way, Israel will exercise dominion on Yhwh's behalf and God's kingship over creation—mediated through the rule of his obedient people—will be established. Mount Zion will not only be made holy again (v. 17); it will once again be the capital city of Yhwh's kingdom, but this time all nations will acknowledge his kingship.

5. A brother's betrayal

One of the most striking features of Obadiah's oracle against Edom is the accusation of fraternal betrayal: "Because of the violence against your brother Jacob, you will be covered with shame" (v. 10) and "You should not look down on your brother in the day of his misfortune" (v. 12). In fact, it is this aspect of Edom's crimes against Judah that Obadiah seems to find most offensive. The neighboring kingdoms were brother nations—twin brothers, in fact (Gen 25) (Allen, 1976: 154)—and this dimension of their relationship is reinforced by the fact that while Obadiah does refer to Edom (vv. 1, 8) and Judah (v. 12), more often he identifies the two kingdoms by the names of their patriarchal ancestors, Esau (vv. 6, 8, 9, 18, 19, 21) and Jacob (vv. 10, 17, 18). While the troubled relationship between the two nations was foreshadowed by the story of Jacob and Esau struggling together in the womb (Gen 25:22), even when the Edomites treated Israel poorly, as they did when they blocked their path to the promised land (Num 20:14–21), Israel respected the filial relationship, and chose not to wage war against them (Deut 2:4, 8). Furthermore, if the climax of the story of Jacob and Esau (Gen 33:4) was any guide, reconciliation between the two nations was the ultimate goal of their interlocking histories. This fraternal connection further intensifies Edom's "violence" against their neighbors. It was bad enough that the Edomites did not come to Jerusalem's aid and then followed Babylon in attacking the city. It was worse that they handed over the refugees from the destruction. But that they did all this to their "brother" was especially perverse (Allen, 1976: 155; Patterson, 2008: 217).

6. An eye for an eye

The message is clear: Yhwh will not ignore Edom's crimes, but will punish her, measure for measure: "As you have done, it will be done to you; your deeds will return upon your own head" (v. 15). This principle of an eye for an eye (the *lex talionis*) is given concrete expression through the image of drinking. The opening words of v. 16 ("Just as you drank on my holy hill") most probably refer to Edom's revelry on Mount Zion after the Babylonians destroyed Jerusalem (Watts, 1969: 58; Stuart, 1987: 420; Niehaus, 1993: 535–36). Accordingly, Edom will be punished for the profane drinking by being forced to "drink continually," this time not from a cup of celebration but from the cup of Yhwh's wrath, until it ceases to exist as a nation (Raabe, 1996: 233; Baker, 2006: 191) and its identity forgotten (Jenson, 2008: 24) (v. 16). The same thought is repeated elsewhere in Obadiah: Edom will be "destroyed [lit. 'cut off'] forever" (v. 10) and left without survivors (v. 18), with a restored Israel playing the primary role in Edom's demise (v. 18).

Bibliography

Allen, Leslie C. *The Books of Joel, Micah, Jonah and Micah*. New International Commentary on the Old Testament. Grand Rapids: Eerdmans, 1976.

Armerding, Carl E. "Obadiah." In *The Expositor's Bible Commentary. Volume 8*. Revised edition, edited by Tremper Longman III and David E. Garland, 422–49. Grand Rapids: Zondervan, 2008.

Baker, David W. *Joel, Obadiah, Malachi*. NIV Application Commentary. Grand Rapids: Zondervan, 2006.

Jenson, Philip P. *Obadiah, Jonah, Micah: A Theological Commentary*. Library of Hebrew Bible/Old Testament Studies 496. London: T. & T. Clark, 2008.

Longman III, Tremper, and Raymond B. Dillard. *An Introduction to the Old Testament*. 2nd ed. Grand Rapids: Zondervan, 2006.

Niehaus, Jeffrey. "Obadiah." In *The Minor Prophets: An Exegetical and Expository Commentary. Volume 2*, edited by Thomas E. McComiskey, 495–541. Grand Rapids: Baker, 1993.

Nogalski, James D. *The Book of the Twelve: Hosea-Jonah*. Smyth & Helwys Bible Commentary. Macon, GA: Smyth & Helwys, 2011.

Pagán, Samuel. "The Book of Obadiah." In *The New Interpreter's Bible*, Volume VII, 434–59. Nashville, TN: Abingdon, 1996.

Patterson, Richard D. "Obadiah." In *Minor Prophets: Hosea-Malachi*. Cornerstone Biblical Commentary 10, 213–40. Carol Stream, IL: Tyndale, 2008.

Raabe, Paul R. *Obadiah: A New Translation with Introduction and Commentary*. Anchor Bible 24D. New York: Doubleday, 1996.

Redditt, Paul L. "Recent Research on the Book of the Twelve as One Book." *Currents in Research: Biblical Studies* 9 (2001) 47–80.

Renkema, Johan. *Obadiah*. Historical Commentary on the Old Testament. Leuven: Peeters, 2003.

Stuart, Douglas. *Hosea-Jonah*. Word Biblical Commentary 31. Nashville, TN: Thomas Nelson, 1987.

Sweeney, Marvin A. *The Twelve Prophets. Volume 1*. Berit Olam. Collegeville, MN: Liturgical, 2000.

Watts, John D. W. *Obadiah: A Critical Exegetical Commentary*. Grand Rapids: Eerdmans, 1969.

Wolff, Hans W. *Obadiah and Jonah: A Commentary*. Minneapolis: Augsburg, 1986. Translation of *Obadja und Jona*. Neukirchen-Vluyn: Neukirchener, 1977.

Chapter 12

Isaiah, Prophet of the Lord Who Heals His People and Restores Their Land (Isa 40–66)

Historical Setting of the Book

TRADITIONALLY SCHOLARS HAVE ALIGNED the book of Isaiah with three historical periods. To highlight this division an overall view of the information is presented in a diagram:

Chapters	1–39	40–55	56–66
Name	Proto- (first)	Deutero- (second)	Trito- (third) Isaiah
World power	Assyria	Babylonia	Persia
Period	Before exile	During exile	After exile
Age	Eighth century BCE	Sixth century BCE	Late sixth century BCE

The subdivision of Isaiah into three distinct historical periods as shown in the diagram indicates that Isaiah 40–66 was written against the background of the Babylonian exile and its aftermath. For this reason, both Isaiah 40–55 and Isaiah 56–66 are dealt with in this one chapter. The country, temple, and city of Jerusalem were destroyed by the Babylonians ca. 587/6 BCE. Many Israelites were forced to leave their country and settle in Babylonia (cf. 43:14; 47:1; 48:14, 20). This disaster which struck Judah/Israel did not develop overnight. It took several decades to reach its lowest point. The exile also represents the climax of the disintegration of Israel's relationship with its Lord, the Holy One of Israel. Several inscriptions and stone carvings depicting the horrors accompanying the habit of forcing people into exile were found by archaeologists. Examples include the decapitation, impalement of soldiers, as well as the amputation of opponents' hands and feet, while women and others were driven from their homes (e.g., Rizza, 2007: 150–51, 158–59). These artifacts underline the fact that the biblical narratives were not written in a vacuum.

At the beginning of the second major part of Isaiah (Isa 40–66) the exiles were informed that the God of their fathers had forgiven their sins and that they were to be set free and return to their own country. This took place against the background of developments on the international scene. The reality of these events can be traced back to the time of Cyrus the Persian emperor. This ruler came to power in the middle of the sixth century BCE. After his conquest of Babylon (fall of Babylon in 539 BCE), he promulgated a decree (in 538 BCE) which made provision for exiles to gain their freedom and return to their country of birth. For Judah/Israel this meant that they were released from Babylonian oppression and were permitted to live as free citizens in their country of origin. The order given by the emperor is engraved on the Cyrus Cylinder (Edwards & Anderson, 2008: 56; cf. 2 Chr 36:22–23; Ezra 1:1–4).

Isaiah 40–66 does not describe the disaster of the exile which struck God's people, but instead focuses on God's exoneration of Israel's guilt. For them this marked the end of the Babylonian exile (40:1–11). The book opens with words of consolation for Israel. God's people are commanded to rise and leave the country of their oppression. They are given the opportunity and urged to return to their homeland (e.g., 43:2, 5, 6, 8; 45:13; 48:20; 49:8–13, 17, 18, 22; 51:10, 11; 52:7, 11, 12, etc.). According to ancient inscriptions the god Marduk empowered the Persian emperor to take control of most countries in the Near East. But in prophetic light YHWH is the One who enabled the emperor and delivered Judah/Israel (and the nations for that matter) from exilic bondage and encouraged them to participate in the exodus from Babylonia (41:2, 25; 44:28; 45:1). In contrast to the claim that Marduk was behind the freeing of nations, Isaiah reassured God's people that YHWH is the One who took action. As an incompetent idol, no god had any part in this process (cf. 46:1–13).

Content and Structure of the Book

Judging from recent literature on Isaiah it seems clear that new approaches tend to emphasize (overall) literary structures, particularly the phenomenon of parallelism. Authors have pointed out that literary structures determine the way the content of biblical books were put together and how they should be interpreted (e.g., Sweeney & Ben Zvi, 2003: 15–84; 269–75). However, the idea is not to superimpose or force a foreign grip on the content and message of the book. Recently the historical-critical approach has been overshadowed by these literary approaches, the latter of which are intimately related to the theological ideas set forth in the prophecy. In a variety of ways, these observations provide keys to unlock and interpret the book. Reading Isaiah with this in mind makes it clear that theological dimensions impacted decisively on the contents of the document (see, e.g., Melugin & Sweeney, 1996: 32–186; Broyles & Evans, 1997: 3–474).

Readers may analyze the book of Isaiah in different ways. The approach of Sweeney (2005: 51–52) is appealing since in a way he provides a breakdown of the contents of the book on the basis of a single and central concept. This idea is expressed in the phrase regarding the contention (dispute) of Yhwh with his people. The concept of God's dispute with Israel deals with everything stated in the entire book of Isaiah, even more so in Isaiah 40–66. Part of this exposition is inserted here.

A. Prophetic instruction that Yhwh is maintaining his covenant and restoring Zion: 40:1—54:17

   a. renewed prophetic commission to announce Yhwh's restoration of Zion 40:1-11

   b. contention: Yhwh is master of creation: 40:12-31

   c. contention: Yhwh is master of human events: 41:1—42:13

   d. contention: Yhwh is redeemer of Israel: 42:14—44:23

   e. contention: Yhwh will use Cyrus for the restoration of Zion 44:24—48:22

   f. contention: Yhwh is restoring Zion: 49:1—54:17

B. Prophetic exhortation to adhere to Yhwh's covenant: 55:1—66:24

   a. exhortation proper to adhere to Yhwh: 55:1-13

   b. substantiation: prophetic instruction concerning reconstituted people in Jerusalem: 56:1—66:24

      1. prophetic instruction concerning proper observance of Yhwh's covenant: 56:1—59:21

> 2. prophetic announcement of restoration for the people: 60:1—62:12
>
> 3. prophetic instruction concerning the process of restoration for the people: 63:1—66:24

The opening passage of Isaiah 40-66 presents Yhwh as encouraging his people to accept his invitation and depart from Babylonia. Isaiah 40:1-10 provides consolation for God's people that they will be released from exile and allowed to go home. They are also reminded that they will be set free only because God is the sole Ruler of the world (40:12-31). Chapter 41 announces that God will appoint an individual to set them free, namely Cyrus the Persian emperor (41:1-7, 21-29; 44:24—45:8).

However, the messenger who brought the good news is confronted by a rebellious people who blamed God for their hardship and argued that Yhwh was not that all-powerful Deity he claimed to be. Israel, instead of being content with their acquittal and accepting the forgiveness granted by Yhwh, rebelled again as in the past forcing the prophet to confront them with God's reaction and purpose (49:14—50:3). Not convinced that God is able to and will take them back to their homeland, Israel taunts its God as being unable to overcome the gods of Babylon. How will he then be able to rescue them from the oppression of the Babylonians? God's answer to this inexplicable reaction of his people (40:27-31) is to claim that he is the unique God, the only true God and that the gods of the nations are nothing in comparison to him (44:6-23; 46:1-13).

Thus Israel's position over against and their attitude towards Yhwh during the Babylonian exile plays an important part in Isaiah 40-66. Israel's (mostly reactionary) attitude towards Yhwh, his threats of judgment and offer of salvation, the destruction of the wicked and restoration of the pious, the devastation and renewal of the land and the recreation of heaven and earth are the issues and promises constantly referred to.

An important issue which often comes up is that God demands righteousness and rejects unrighteousness. But in spite of God's requirement, Israel continues to sin (Isa 56). Nevertheless, the humble will be consoled (Isa 57). The ineluctable demand of God is to distinguish between true and false religion (Isa 58). In spite of Israel's interest in God's offer (Isa 59), they persist in their folly and sinful lifestyles (59:1-19). But the possibility that God will redeem them was still in place (59:20-21).

In the new dispensation, Jerusalem/Zion will be the focal point of the nations (Isa 60), sharing in the benefits offered by the Servant

(61:1–11). This is followed by another reference to Jerusalem as the centre of the nations/the world (62). Since Israel's neighbors (Edom) also ignore the prophetic demand to repent, Yhwh will attack them as well (63). However, Israel still judges the situation as unsatisfactory, complaining about God's action (63–64). Eventually, the difference between habitual sinners (Isa 65), and the offspring of the Servant of the Lord, namely his servants (65:13, etc.) will become clear. The end of it all culminates in God creating a new heaven and a new earth (65:17ff.). Eventually Zion will be glorified, but sinners will perish (Isa 66).

In addition to the usual practice of dealing with subjects in prose style, that is, in straightforward descriptive language, Isaiah 40–66 also utilizes literary structures to enhance the meaning of words and ideas. Thus, Isaiah 40–66 may also be viewed as a literary unit on a different level presented from a different angle with among others its own internal tripartite subdivision. A statement on the absence of peace apparently divides the twenty-seven chapters in this part of the book into three equal subunits of nine chapters each (Olley, 1999: 351–70). Chapters 40–48, 49–57 and 58–66 represent the different blocks of content respectively (Banwell, 1964–65: 166). The following table demonstrates the set-up:

First part	Second part	Third part
Isaiah 40–48 (nine chapters)	Isaiah 49–57 (nine chapters)	Isaiah 58–66
Key text = Isaiah 48:22	Key text = Isaiah 57:21	Conclusion
"There is no peace," says the Lord, "for the wicked."	"There is no peace," says my God, "for the wicked"	No statement

The absence of peace signaled in this tripartite division carries a serious warning for the godless, those who neglect God's injunctions as set out in the rest of the unit and book. This pronouncement of judgment is also related to an utterance at the beginning and end of the book of Isaiah (1:31 and 66:24; Blenkinsopp, 2000: 369). The message is clear: there will be no peace for those who rebel against God, only punishment awaits them.

Theology of the Book

God's intention in connection with Israel's rejection and salvation represents a theme which dominates the entire book of Isaiah 40–66. Earlier in the book it was indicated that God called Isaiah to a prophetic task (1:1; 2:1; 6:1–13; 20:2–3). The opening chapter of Isaiah 40–66 refers to the calling of a prophet who had to announce God's command to prepare a way for him in the wilderness (40:3, 6). The latter texts most probably refer to the return of the exiles from Babylonia. Some understand the two references as calls pertaining to the eighth-century "Isaiah of Jerusalem" (Proto-Isaiah) and to the sixth-century "Isaiah of Babylon" (Deutero-Isaiah) respectively. Others reckon that the book accommodates three prophetic calls, adding the summons of the Servant of the Lord (49:1–7) to the first two (Lind, 1997: 317). Thus three prophetic calls were recorded: Isaiah of Jerusalem (6:1–13; 20:2–3), Isaiah of the Exile (40:3, 6), and the Servant of the Lord (49:1–7). According to Lind (1997: 317–38), this arrangement of the texts can be considered as "centers" for the entire book. These references to prophetic calls underpin and qualify the content of the book as coming from the unique God of Israel.

Theological dimensions represent basic tenets in Isaiah. Yhwh, the unique God, takes centre stage in Isaiah 40–66. Whatever the mode, genre or intention of the statements and other utterances in the prophecy may be, all bear witness to the fact that God's revelation is written large in the book. Isaiah 43:15 brings together in a cluster of terms some of the main conceptions of God as depicted in Isaiah 40–66. Thus this text identifies him as Lord, King, Creator, and the Holy One. These constitute the first four paragraphs (1–4) to be dealt with in this theological outline; three other paragraphs are added: God and the gods (5), the Servant of the Lord (6), and eschatology (7).

1. God is Lord

God's covenant name Yhwh dominates the introduction of Isaiah 40–66 to a certain extent, supported by a literary design (40:2, 3, 5 [2x], 7, 10, 13). It is important to realize that the phrases "*our* God" (40:3, 8) and "*your* God" (40:1, 9), express the kernel of the covenant (forming part of the so-called "covenant formula"). The latter expression ("*your* God") frames the greater part of the passage concerned (40:1, 9, cf. 1–11). The counterpart of the latter covenant component, namely "*our* God" is inserted within this frame (1, [3+8], 9). References to the covenant formula were cast in a chiastic (cross-wise) pattern, namely A-B-B-A. Thus, Isaiah 40:1–10 displays the following structure:

A	v. 1 – "*Your* God"
B	v. 3 – "*Our* God"
B'	v. 8 – "*Our* God"
A'	v. 9 – "*Your* God"

The notion of "covenant" defines the relationship between God and Israel and appears throughout the book (cf. 24:5; 28:15, 18; 33:8; 42:6; 49:8; 54:10; 55:3; 56:4, 6; 59:21; 61:8). O'Connell (1994: 20), pointed out that the literary structure of Isaiah as a whole is aligned with the covenant concept. According to him the book includes an exordium, which appeals for covenant reconciliation (1:1—2:5), followed by two structurally analogous accusatory threats of judgment (2:6a-21: denouncing cultic sins; 3:1—4:1: denouncing social crimes); two structurally analogous schemes for the punishment and restoration of Zion and the nations (4:2—11:16; 13:1—39:8); an exoneration by Yhwh (40:1—54:17), and a final ultimatum, which again appeals for covenant reconciliation (55:1—66:24).

The arrangement of the prophetic pronouncements focuses on God and his covenant promises. God comforts his people and reassures them that their hard service has been completed, their sins have been paid for and they have received from the Lord's hand double for all their sins (40:1-2). The introduction (40:1-11) opens a perspective on Isaiah 40-66. The God of the covenant occupies the centre.

Israel's attitude towards the covenant shows a positive and negative outcome. In the earlier part of the book those who abandoned the covenant of Yhwh are depicted as having made a covenant with death (28:15, 18), hoping that they will be safe during the onslaught of enemies attacking from the North. In contrast to the latter, in the second part of Isaiah (42:6; cf. Matt 12:18-20) the speaker announces that the Servant of the Lord is destined to represent the covenant between God and his people worldwide.

2. God's kingship and throne

Isaiah 40-66 proclaims Yhwh as the only true God. He is depicted as the King of the universe and all humankind, especially his people Israel. Prophetic statements in the entire book of Isaiah are dominated by references to God as King (6:1, 5; 24:23; 33:22; 41:21; 43:15; 44:6; 52:7) and to

Isaiah, Prophet of the Lord Who Heals His People and Restores Their Land

his throne (6:1; 9:6; 14:9; 14:13; 16:5; 22:22-23; 47:1; 66:1). Both groups of references are arranged in chiastic patterns.

It is difficult to grasp the meaning of the different texts in Isaiah 40-66 without a comprehensive view of the literary structure of the whole book and an investigation into the relationship between its different parts. To demonstrate the importance of this phenomenon, two literary structures which dominate the entire book of Isaiah will be discussed (Kruger, 2008: 519-21). These structures (discussed in the following subparagraphs) highlight the main motif of the prophecy, namely the kingship of the God of Israel.

God as King

Firstly, Y<small>HWH</small> is depicted as *King*. This motif can be presented as follows:
Pivotal axis: 6:1, 5 The *King*, Lord Almighty

A1	24:23	The Lord Almighty is *King* (reigns)
B1	33:22	The Lord, Judge, Leader, *our King*
C1	41:21	The Lord, *King of Jacob*
B2	43:15	The Lord, Holy One, Creator, *your King*
C2	44:6	The Lord, *King of Israel*, Savior, Lord Almighty
A2	52:7	Your God is *King* (reigns)

This exposition confirms that the notion of the kingship of God dominates the book to a large extent. The first two references (6:1, cf. 5) introduce a series of keywords in connection with the subject concerned. This is followed by three pairs of references each of which includes two terms which are in balance with one another in a reciprocal manner. Indicators A1 and A2 frame the whole book, while the other two pairs B1 and B2 as well as C1 and C2 inserted between A1 and A2 frame the remaining keywords. A1 and A2 belong together, B1 and B2, as well as C1 and C2.

This emphasis on the status of God as King is reinforced by another name of him, which pervades the book of Isaiah (sixty-two times; Lind, 1997: 319): Y<small>HWH</small> *ṣěbā'ôt*, "the Lord Almighty" or "Lord of Hosts." This name is linked to the messenger formula (Isa 10:24; 22:15; 44:6; cf. 39:5; 47:4; 48:2; 51:15; 54:5) and emphasizes the undisputable power of God. The name "the Holy One of Israel" identifies Y<small>HWH</small> as the unique God (see below) and the notion "King" depicts him as the omnipotent God. The name "Lord of Hosts" ties the two aspects of God's holiness and kingship together (holiness: 6:5, cf. also 1:24; 5:16, 24; 10:20; 21:10; 37:16; kingship: 1:24; 3:1; 10:16; 19:4, cf. 3:15). Together the two expressions (King and Holy One) express God's action in connection with Israel's demise and salvation (44:6; 47:4; 54:5). The name "Lord of Hosts" thus represents the former two expressions (the Holy One and the King) in their quality and functions against the background of the One who accomplishes Israel's salvation (47:4a; 54:5c).

In addition, Mettinger (1997: 144-52) indicated that God became King on the basis of his acting as the Divine Warrior. This idea stems from a model of the ancient Near East whereby the individual involved first had to conquer his enemies before he could qualify to become king. Mettinger singles out Isaiah 51:9—52:12 as the passage which has a direct bearing on the subject of the Warrior. This passage encloses the focus text of Isaiah 52:7-10 (cf. 40:9-11). Having conquered his enemies, the king proceeded to build a temple for his god. At least part of this idea seems to lie behind the occurrences in Isaiah of the actions of Yhwh as the Almighty King. The multiple actions consisted of chaos–battle–kingship–palace–(temple) (Isa 52:7-10; 40:9-11). Naturally Isaiah does not compare Yhwh with any earthly king. He merely states that the God of Israel overcame all his enemies (cf. also the Warrior-God's revenge and salvation (59:15b-21; 61:1, 2; 63:1-6) and the Warrior's outfit (59:17-18; 61:10-11; 63:1, 2, 3).

The throne of God

Secondly, the kingship of God finds expression in the *throne* concept. Isaiah refers to different thrones which are set in opposition to one another. The throne of God supports or opposes the thrones of human kings. However, the throne of God dominates all other thrones and thus takes pride of place in the prophecy. In this way God's throne surpasses all other thrones. The importance of God's throne is emphasized by its being situated in the first part (6:1) as well as at the end of the book (66:1).

O'Connell (1994: 15-30; 236) identified more than thirty cases of a particular pattern related to this idea in different parts of the book, namely a 2-1 - 1-2 pattern, called the triadic, and 2-2, indicated as the quadratic pattern. The latter accommodates four phrases which are kept in balance. However, further investigation brought to light that the first arrangement with a slight adjustment thereof actually covers the whole book of Isaiah in a single grand design (Kruger 2009a: 120-28; 2009b: 427-33).

Applying the triadic pattern to the whole book, it becomes clear that a 1-2 structure represents David's throne (9:6; 16:5; 22:22-23) and a 2-1 structure the throne of the king of Babylonia/the nations (14:9; 14:13; 47:1). These two arrangements form a chiastic pattern. However, all the thrones are hedged in by God's throne which is referred to at the beginning and end of the book (6:1; 66:1). The diagram below illustrates the arrangement and position of the throne concept. Similarities and differences between the concepts are underlined using different styles:

A1	6:1	Throne of the *King, the Lord*
B1	9:6	Throne of king *David*
C1	14:9	Thrones of kings of the *earth*
C2	14:13	Throne of *Babylon*
B2	16:5	Throne of king *David*
B3	22:22-23	Throne of king *David*
C3	47:1	Throne of king of *Babylon*
A2	66:1	Throne of the *King, the Lord*

In this diagram the letters and numbers concerned (i.e., A1, A2; B1, B2, B3; C1, C2, C3) all carry the keyword "throne" which indicates the royal motif behind the structure. The most important throne belongs to Yhwh, the great King of heaven and earth. In literary terms the whole book is constructed on the basis of his throne (A1 and A2). The throne of David is presented as a combination of three references one near to the beginning of the book (B1) followed by two other references later on (B2 and B3). Adjoining these, the thrones of the Babylonian king and the nations are presented in the same way but in an inverted manner (C1, C2 and C3) in comparison with David's throne (cf. Kruger, 2008: 519-22). The two sets of keywords constitute a crosswise arrangement (a chiastic pattern).

According to some the term "king" is used sparingly in Isaiah with reference to Yhwh (cf. Lind, 1997: 319). In contradistinction to this view the presentation of God as King seated on his throne as indicated above actually reinforces the idea that this depiction of him dominates the book. Yhwh is the unique King and sole Ruler. He controls everything and everyone. The fact that the throne reference was inserted at the beginning (6:1) and end (66:1) of the book means that everything originates before his throne and everything ends there. Everything in heaven and on earth is subject to the throne of the King.

In addition, a related but slightly different arrangement—a tripartite structure—also reinforces the centrality of God's throne in Isaiah 40–66. According to 40:22 the Lord "resides," that is, "sits enthroned above the circle" of the earth. In 44:13 this word is translated as "compass" (NIV). Thus both cases refer to something with a circular or disk-like shape. This tripartite arrangement is based on three references to God's throne which indicate a step-like ascending line. The position of God's throne is thus enhanced in terms of a staircase as the book unfolds. At the beginning of the book the throne appears in the temple in Jerusalem (6:1). Subsequently the throne is situated above the circle of the earth (40:22; cf. Exod 24:10). Finally the heavens serve as God's throne, and the earth as his footstool (66:1). This arrangement may be presented as ascending steps:

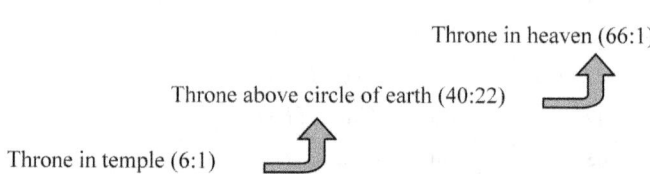

Another possibility which may support the literary arrangement of enhancing the throne of God consists of three other references which function together. According to Isaiah 6:1 God occupies his throne which is qualified as "high and lifted up." The same expression appears in 53:13 and 57:15. In the former case, the Servant of the Lord is described thus, while in the latter the phrase describes Yhwh. The possibility that the phrase, "high and lifted up" in 57:15 may refer to the throne of Yhwh, can be deduced from the fact that the same double-term which describes the throne of Yhwh in 6:1, is applied to the Lord's person in 57:15. Thus, the expression, "high and lifted up" apparently serves as a three-pronged anchor of the book, emphasizing the prominence of God, his throne and his Servant:

6:1	The throne of God high and lifted up
53:13	Servant of the Lord high and lifted up
57:15	The Lord high and lifted up

3. Yhwh the Creator

Isaiah 40–66 often refers to God as Creator. The following phrases and texts describe this God: Who created everything? Who can be compared to this God? (40:26); Creator of the world, incomprehensible (40:28); he created for all to see and acknowledge him (41:20); he calls his Servant for the salvation of people (42:5); as Creator, God saves his people (43:1); as Creator, he also gathers his own (43:7); he creates opposite realities, engaging both to reach his goal (45:7 [2x]; he creates salvation to pour forth like rain (45:8); he created heaven and earth (45:12); he created the universe and the earth to be inhabited (45:18 [2x]); new things are/were created by him (48:7). He is the Creator of the blacksmith, and that which hampers his work (54:16 [2x]); he is the Creator of those who pursue peace (57:19); the Creator of a new heaven and a new earth (65:17), evoking joy over God's creation, creating Jerusalem to rejoice and its inhabitants to be glad (65:18 [2x]).

4. The Holy One of Israel

The identification of Yhwh as "the Holy One of Israel" (*qĕdôš yiśrā'ēl*) represents the most intriguing notion of God in the prophecy of Isaiah. Leaving aside variations for the moment, it is striking that the full name, "the Holy One of Israel" appears twelve times in both Isaiah 1–39 and 40–66 (1:4; [4:3] remnant will be called: "holy"; 5:19; 5:24; 10:20; 12:6; 17:7; [29:23] the Holy One of Jacob; 30:11, 12, 15; 31:1; 37:23; [40:25] the Holy One; 41:14; 41:20; 43:3, 14; 45:11; 47:4; 48:17; 49:7; 54:5; 60:9; 60:14).

The expression "Holy One" as applied to Yhwh does not in the first place imply that in comparison to humankind God is by far morally *superior*. In fact, as the Holy One of Israel God thinks and acts completely *different* when compared to the thoughts and acts of human beings. One example will suffice. Israel's God claimed to be the Creator of everything (cf. section 3), as the One who pronounces the end from the beginning (46:10). He removed his people Israel from their country casting them into the abyss of the Babylonian exile, and inversely rescued them as well. This action demonstrates God's holiness. It implies a complete otherness, the reverse of the holiness sometimes understood as a moral requirement only.

5. Yhwh and the gods

Yhwh's command to reject the gods is addressed in Isaiah 40–48 (cf. 21:9) and especially chapters 46–48. The book refers to the gods of Babylon in general (e.g., 44:28; 45:13), but also singles out two of them, namely Bel and Nebo (46:1). The Old Testament condemns idolatry (e.g., Exod 20:3–6). Isaiah links up with this reality and ridicules the gods since they are worthless, good for nothing, static, that is immobile. They are blind and dumb images carved out of wood, stone or metal (46:1–13). In addition, they had to be carried around during festivals. The author uses a term related to picking up, load and carry, several times (vss. 1, 2, 3, 4, 7). Compare the way they were tilted over (46:1) when their worshippers had to remove them from their temples to prevent invading enemies from destroying them.

The latter indicator represents the main differences between Yhwh and the idols: to carry or to be carried. Yhwh carried Israel since the beginning of time (1:2; 46:3b–4); the gods were carried by those who venerated them (46:1, 2, 5–7). Isaiah 46 provides a challenging argument in connection with the difference between Yhwh and the idols. However, the verdict is given: God is the all-powerful; the idols are incompetent.

6. The Servant of the Lord

Traditionally four passages in Isaiah 40–55 were isolated and identified as "songs" of the (anonymous) Servant of the Lord (the 'ebed Yhwh, 42:1–9; 49:1–7; 50:4–11; 52:13—53:12). However, since Isaiah 56–66 links up with chapter 40–55, Isaiah 61:1–11 must be considered as belonging to this group of songs as well, even to the point of forming its climax. Among other things, this is clear from the fact that the figure in chapter 61:1 is anointed with God's Spirit, just as the Servant of the Lord in 42:1. The plural form of the word concerned appears thirty-two times in Isaiah 40–66 (over against nine times in Isaiah 1–39). In Isaiah 56–66, the term appears ten times (56:6; 63:17; 65:8, 9, 13 [3x]; 14, 15, 66:14) but in the plural form. The presentation of the plural form of the substantive "servants" indicates that God has granted a new status to his followers.

The book of Isaiah seems to identify certain historical personalities as the Servant, namely Isaiah (of Jerusalem: 20:3), Jacob (Judah/Israel: 44:1–2, 5; cf. 63:11, 12: Moses), and Cyrus, the Persian emperor (44:28; 45:1). Yhwh designated Cyrus as his "anointed" (45:1), a term which indicated a particular task given to a person. In the book of Isaiah the term is never applied to a king of Judah or Israel. Thus Yhwh designated a foreigner to deal with his people's problems. In this connection it must be noted that the figures of Cyrus and the enigmatic "Servant of the Lord" partly overlap.

The Servant-figure dominates this part of Isaiah to a great extent, not in textual reference but in terms of his action on behalf of God. While describing the involvement of Cyrus in God's plan (44:24–28; 45:1–8; 9–16; 48:1ff), the emphasis eventually shifts from Cyrus to the Servant's action regarding the establishment of God's rule. Constantly the reader learns about the prophetic word emphasizing God's promise to help (42:8ff.; 18ff.; 43), taunting the idols and their worshippers (Isa 44; 46). Israel will be restored, but must heed God's call (51:1–16); indeed the wake-up call resounds (51:17–23): Israel must rise and return to Palestine (52:1–12). The Servant of the Lord suffers on behalf of Israel (52:13—53:12), thus Israel's future is assured (54). They are encouraged to drink from God's fountain of life (Isa 55). Among these chapters the reader will find references to the Servant of the Lord and what his involvement with Israel's position entails (42:1ff.; 49:1ff.; 50:4–11; 52:13—53:12; 61:1–11).

Some scholars view the Servant as a composite personality. The songs of the Servant appear in the vicinity of the new exodus described in Isaiah 40–66. Thus Moses could have served as a model for the anonymous Servant (63:11–14), although the Davidic figure also played a role in the establishment of a figure of salvation (Isa. 9:5–6; 11:1; 55:3). In addition, these depictions also appear intertwined with the triple office of king (42:1), priest (53:7–8), and prophet (61:1). Two facets of the personality are highlighted: he is anointed with God's Spirit (42:1b; 61:1ff.) and he will lead God's people back to him (49:5–6) through suffering (53:6b, 8b).

Literary strategy also highlights the figure of the Servant of the Lord emphasizing his importance. The last part of Isaiah (Isa 56–66, traditionally indicated as Trito-Isaiah), comprises a typical form of parallelism, or a kind of palindrome. A palindrome starts from a marked point, moves through a series of subjects, and reaches a climax, and returns to the original starter subject. Thus an arrangement of texts placed in a conical and chiastic shape. The two groups of subjects (Servant, Zion, Warrior, etc.) as displayed in the pattern are in harmony, to the point that they represent duplicates of each other. This literary structure, like most of the other devices discussed, serve to emphasize certain ideas. It is obvious that the main character stands at the head of the arrangement, at the climax or turning-point, in this case chapter 61 (Kruger 1984: 156; cf. Gileadi, 1994: 242 fn. 13). In the present case the Servant of the Lord occupies the peak of the structure. Placing the Servant in this position, confirms his high status. The pattern speaks for itself:

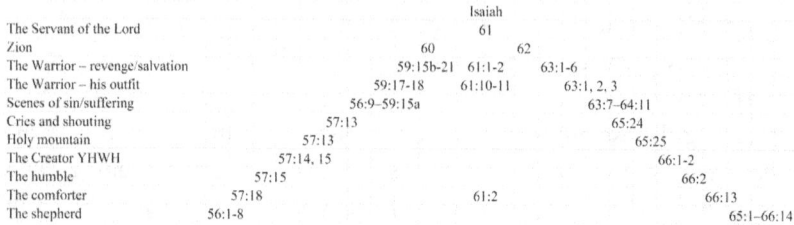

		Isaiah		
The Servant of the Lord		61		
Zion		60		62
The Warrior – revenge/salvation		59:15b-21	61:1-2	63:1-6
The Warrior – his outfit		59:17-18	61:10-11	63:1, 2, 3
Scenes of sin/suffering		56:9–59:15a		63:7–64:11
Cries and shouting		57:13		65:24
Holy mountain		57:13		65:25
The Creator YHWH	57:14, 15			66:1-2
The humble	57:15			66:2
The comforter	57:18		61:2	66:13
The shepherd	56:1-8			65:1–66:14

This emphasis on the position of the Servant as illustrated inspired Luke to cite from Isaiah 61 when he highlighted the person and work of Jesus Christ (Luke 4:18–21).

7. Eschatology

All the actions of God are based on his "plan/counsel/advice" (5:19; 11:2; 14:24, 26–27; 19:17; 25:1; 28:29; 30:1; 40:13; 44:26; 46:10, 11). God's plan will be realized through his eschatological acts. The concept of eschatology comes from the Greek words *eschatos* "last" and *logos* "word." Generally speaking the concept refers to events under God's guidance that are taking place and others that will take place sometime in the future, usually at a time unknown to the prophets. The emphasis is not so much on a particular moment to be determined with the aid of a calendar. Rather it deals with God's intention of shaping and preparing his people and their land to represent the unfolding of his kingdom at a time when he will do away with everything that undermines the coming of that kingdom. The message of the prophets is directed towards reaching this goal. Eschatology embodies new things that will take place during the life of a prophet, either soon after his announcement or some other time.

A crucial aspect of this phenomenon finds expression in a text like Isaiah 46:10. God controls the past, present and future: "I make known the end from the beginning." This is the all-encompassing ability of God over against the gods. None of the idols can imitate him in any way. But the realization of God's will for his people requires time to take shape;

the reason being that Israel continues to rebel against its Maker. Thus the eschatological outlook of the book may be summed up with the phrase: "in spite of." In spite of God's attempt to bring Israel to their senses, his people persist in unbelief. And vice versa, in spite of Israel's abandoning its Creator, God remains the trustworthy One. One day there will be a new people and a new land.

Eschatological perspectives are marked by the custom of seizing high-pitched moments in Israel's history and apply them to the present and future. These moments in Israel's past serve as framework, models, or examples for expected victory/success in future. When traditions were applied to contemporary events, previous happenings displayed new and more intense levels of meaning.

Reference to a new creation features prominently in Isaiah's prophecies. The God of Israel is proclaimed as the Creator of heaven and earth (40:12–26). Isaiah engages the (first) creation to reveal God's plan, namely his undertaking not only to restore, but to recreate heaven and earth. The new heaven and earth will far exceed the existing reality (51:9–11; 65:17–25). The surface of the earth will be changed (40:4; 45:2a); the desert will become a fertile garden, like Eden (51:3; 65:25). Jerusalem will be restored (65:18–19). New things will be at the order of the day (41:15; 42:9; 43:18–19; 48:6; 62:2; 65:7).

A new exodus is also in prospect. Isaiah revives this tradition (of the tribes' exodus from Egypt) adding a new dimension regarding the future (cf. 40:3–5, 9–11; 52:11–12). On this basis an idealistic situation is depicted of Israel being released from the Babylonian oppression. A colorful return from exile is pictured (51:10–11; 51:17—52:3; 52:11–12; 40:2–5, 10–11; cf. 10:24–27; 11:15–16; 43:16ff.); the journey through the desert (48:21); the restoration of paradise (51:3); universal peace (2:2–4; 9:1–7), even among animals (11:6–8), and the renewal of the covenant with king David (55:3; cf. Jer 31:31–34). Idolatry will be destroyed (Isa 46; 47). In addition, the author gives fresh impetus to Israel's custom of going up to Jerusalem/the Temple Mount for the annual festivals. However, he opens a new dimension on future pilgrimages when he announces that henceforth these movements will include individuals from all nations.

A typical characteristic of the eschatological expectation finds expression in the phrase, "the Day of the Lord"/"that Day" (2:12; 13:9; 34:8; 61:2). The word/phrase often appears in Isaiah (125 times). According to Isaiah 61:2 (cf. 63:4) the Day of the Lord is the time of his vengeance against his enemies. God will be extolled; Israel and the nations will be humiliated. Thus the agenda for that Day is God's action against anything that is not according to his will.

The names: "David" and "Zion" feature prominent in this perspective. God's future action regarding Israel is based on his covenant with David, henceforth it will hold good (55:3). The name of David is also intimately related to Zion. The latter is designated as the abode of David (14:32). Yhwh will protect this city under all circumstances (Isa 17; 36–39). It serves as the place where God will meet the returning exiles (Isa 49; 51). At the end of time the nations will come to Zion to learn and obey God's Word (Isa 2).

God's enemies will be judged and salvation extended to his people within the boundaries of history (10:24–27) and in creation at large (27:1). The announcement in connection with the emperor of Persia (Cyrus) is preceded by the promise that God's judgment is over (40:1–2; 51:17–20), salvation is on its way (40:3ff.; 51:21–23; 57:14–19; 60–62; 65:15–25; 66:5–24). The Lord comes with might to save his people (40:10), because they were elected by him (41:8–10); mercy will characterize God's actions (54:7–8). His people's salvation is not based on anything contributed by Israel. It is solely the work of God (6:3, 5; 43:28). The reader also notices that the righteous will rise from their graves (26:19); death will be destroyed (25:8). However, in the meantime and sadly, God's people continue their sinful lifestyles (65:1–16; 66:1–3). The prophet requests God to reveal himself to his people and to take action (63:15—64:12). The Lord will come in fire (66:15–16, 24).

Although the idea of "the remnant" or "the rest" (šĕ'ērît) appears mostly in the first part of Isaiah, a text like Isaiah 46:3 goes to the heart of the matter when God expresses his unfailing loyalty towards his own. This expression adds profile to judgment and salvation within the eschatological sphere. The term fits in where there is speech of threat and promise in connection with the coming of the Lord.

8. Conclusion

Summarizing, the message of Isaiah 40–66 breaks surface with reference to the way God is depicted in the book. He is the Creator of the Universe, the great King, Controller of humanity, expecting all to pursue justice and righteousness, realizing his plan through the remnant who survived the exile. He is also depicted as the Holy One of Israel, namely the controversial God, who acts contrary to everything that was expected of gods in the ancient world. He is the Lord Almighty, rising above all superpowers, and the Divine Warrior, who destroys everything opposing his will.

The Servant of the Lord serves as God's agent in this work of restoration. Reference to the Servant touches the heart of God's intention on how he planned to redeem his people. Israel/Judah expected God to intervene by simply destroying their enemies without them having to bear any pain and suffering at all. In contradistinction to this expectation, or false hope, God used their enemies to put tremendous pressure on his people, so much so that Israel/Judah perished in the struggle. Israel was ruined. The God of Isaiah acts differently, but consistently. Thus he picked up his people from the ashes and restored (some of) them (at least) as his representatives among the nations. "Going under" is the keyword which describes the route God follows to redeem. Israel went under, never really comprehending the mind of God. This incomprehensible act of God was transferred to the Servant, who went under by bearing the sins of many.

Bibliography

Banwell, B. O. "A Suggested Analysis of Isaiah xl–lxvi." *Expository Times* 76 (1964–65) 166.

Blenkinsopp, J. *Isaiah 1–39*. Anchor Bible. New York: Doubleday, 2000.

Broyles, C. C., and C. A. Evans, editors. *Writing and Reading the Scroll of Isaiah: Studies of an Interpretive Tradition*. 2 vols. Leiden: Brill, 1997.

Edwards, B., and C. Anderson, C. *Through the British Museum with the Bible*. Leominster, UK: Day One, 2008.

Gileadi, A. *The Literary Message of Isaiah*. New York: Hebraeus, 1994.

Kruger, H. A. J. "The Book of Isaiah: Patchwork of Literary Fragments Versus Predetermined Literary Structure? Part I." *Nederduitse gereformeerde teologiese tydskrif* 50.1/2 (2009a) 120–34.

———. "The Book of Isaiah: Patchwork of Literary Fragments Versus Predetermined Literary Structure? Part II." *Nederduitse gereformeerde teologiese tydskrif* 50.3/4 (2009b) 427–33.

———. "Jesaja." In *Christelike Kernensiklopedie*, edited by F. Gaum et al., 519–21. Cape Town: Lux Verbi BM, 2008.

———. *Verbond en apokaliptiek in Jesaja 56 tot 66*. PhD diss., University of Stellenbosch, 1984.

Lind, M. C. "Political Implications of Isaiah 6." In *Writing and Reading the Scroll of Isaiah: Studies of an Interpretive Tradition*, Vol. 1, edited by C. C. Broyles, and C. A. Evans, 317–38. Leiden: Brill, 1997.

Melugin, R. F., and M. A. Sweeney, editors. *New Visions of Isaiah*. JSOT Supp. Series 214. Sheffield, UK: Sheffield Academic Press, 1996.

Mettinger, T. N. D. "In Search of the Hidden Structure: Yhwh as King in Isaiah 40–55." In *Writing and Reading the Scroll of Isaiah: Studies of an Interpretive Tradition*, Vol. 1, edited by C. C. Broyles, and C. A. Evans, 144–52. Leiden: Brill, 1997.

O'Connell, R. H. *Concentricity and Continuity. The Literary Structure of Isaiah.* JSOT Supp. Series 188. Sheffield, UK: Sheffield Academic Press, 1994.

Olley, J. W. "'No Peace' in a Book of Consolation. A Framework for the Book of Isaiah?" *Vetus Testamentum* 19 (1999) 351–70.

Rizza, A. *The Assyrians and the Babylonians: History and Treasures of an Ancient Civilization.* Novara, Italy: White Star, 2007.

Sweeney, M. A., and E. Ben Zvi, editors. *The Changing Face of Form Criticism for the Twenty-First Century.* Grand Rapids: Eerdmans, 2003.

Sweeney, M. A. *The Prophetic Literature.* Nashville, TN: Abingdon, 2005.

Chapter 13

Haggai, Prophet of the New Temple

Historical Setting of the Book

JEWS TYPICALLY REFER TO the post-exilic period as the Second Temple period. The construction of this second temple is directly connected with the activity of the prophet Haggai. Although Haggai is one of the very short prophetic books, the role that the prophet played in the beginning phase of this project was highly significant. Of the four months in which Haggai was active, the book mentions four prophetic appearances, all of which are dated to the second year of the reign of the Persian king Darius. The majority of scholars interpret the dates as follows:

1:1	Year 2, month 6, day 1	29th August 520
1:15	Day 24, month 6, year 2	21st September 520
2:1	Month 7, day 21	17th October 520
2:10	Day 24, month 9, year 2	18th December 520
2:20	Day 24, (month 9)	18th December 520

Similar overlapping dates can be found in Zechariah:

1:1	Month 9, year 2	10th August 520
1:10	Day 24, month 11, year 2	15th September 519
7:1	Year 4, day 4, month 9	7th October 518

The close historical connection between these two prophets coincides with the mention they receive in Ezra-Nehemiah. Their appearance led to the resumption of the rebuilding of the temple (Ezra 5:1; 6:14). This was not a joint operation, however. Rather, each prophet provided his own independent witness. By means of this prophetic verification, a task that had been contested by certain segments of the population was once again set in motion. Haggai's identity remains hidden. His name (derived from the Hebrew word "festival") may be due to his birth during a particular festival, yet no mention is made of either his occupation or the role he played within the Israelite community.

The edict of Cyrus (538 BCE) had called upon the exiled community to rebuild the Jerusalem temple that had been destroyed by Nebuchadnezzar (cf. Ezra 1:2–4; 2 Chr 36:23). To this end, those items of the temple's equipment that could still be found in Babylonian depots were entrusted to Sheshbazzar and the other returnees (Ezra 1:8–11).

The book of Ezra-Nehemiah makes clear that the returnee exiles first of all renewed the cult of burnt offerings and the regular sacrificial system (Ezra 3). The activities of those who had returned home created tensions with segments of the local population. These tensions had various sociological causes and are hardly surprising if, as is reported, a group of newcomers suddenly arrived in the area making claims to the land and transforming the political order. After all, the land was not unoccupied when they arrived. In the texts of Ezra-Nehemiah the conflicts are primarily connected with the project of reconstructing the temple. This led to a suspension of the construction work. The political situation was probably more complex, but its exact details remain unclear. It is probable that when the returnees arrived the administrative structures were just as they had been during the decades of the Babylonian period before being adopted by the Persian regime. It is clear that the newcomers would have received little political support from this element of the local administration. The first time they are mentioned in Ezra-Nehemiah they are called "enemies of Judah and Benjamin" (Ezra 4:1). This is then followed by a list of their hostile activities (Ezra 4). From the narrative perspective of the author, which reflects the entire epoch from Zerubbabel to Nehemiah (Neh 12:47), these activities constitute a coherent picture. Chronologically, however, they do not belong in the period before the construction of the temple. The problems that were to continue for decades began with an attempt to interrupt early plans for rebuilding the temple. The indigenous provincial governors evidently had enough political influence during the time of Cyrus and his son Cambyses to significantly impede construction work (Ezra 4:4—5:24). Cyrus was primarily interested in

Haggai, Prophet of the New Temple

ensuring political continuity and peace whereas Cambyses desired to conquer Egypt. Their political loyalties, therefore, were directed towards regional representatives and not the small and economically weak district of Judah with its religious concerns.

The second year of Darius marks a turning point, though we can only speculate as to its exact causes. The sudden death of Cambyses was followed by conflicts for the succession to the throne, for he had no direct heir. After roughly one year Darius proved to be the victor, having "overcome seven fraudulent kings" (cf. Willi-Plein, 2007: 11–16). In the center of the conflict was above all Gaumata, who portrayed himself as prince Smerdis. One of the first measures that Darius took was a comprehensive administrative reform. His second year is characterized by the fact that he successfully managed to establish his claims to power and bring peace to the country. The old ruling elite in the satrapy of Trans-Euphrates, an administrative unit containing the small province Judah, had evidently tended to sympathize with Darius' opponents, so that after the establishment of his authority these posts needed to be refilled. This is the context in which to understand the journey of Tattenai to the land for an inspection in Ezra 5. He toured the land as a high official commissioned by the satrap Ushtannu, himself installed by Darius. In this political context, Haggai called for the construction of the temple.

That project was not a purely religious matter. The expansion of Jerusalem, a former royal city, along with its national shrine, was also of high political significance. This explains Tattenai's critical queries. He demanded a list of those participating in the construction of the temple. He further provided security for his decision as to whether the building project should take place or not by inquiring directly to the great king. In the meantime, the construction work continued. Tattenai evidently did not consider it to be an expression of political rebellion. The inquiry to Darius met with a positive answer so that the Jerusalem temple could be further expanded under the authority of the Persian king. The building operations lasted from 21st September 520 (Hag 1:15) until its inauguration on 12th March 515 (Ezra 6:15).

Content and Structure of the Book

The book of Haggai reports four appearances of the prophet. They are narratively connected with each other by means of chronological data.

The narrative frame begins with the report that the word of Yhwh came by Haggai the prophet. The outline of the story of Haggai reveals the following structure of the book:

1:1–25	Call to rebuild the temple	
	2–11	First prophetic oracle: The temple must now be rebuilt
	12	Narrative: Haggai's words are effective
	13	The prophet's promise
	14–15	Narrative: God creates the willingness to start construction
2:1–9	Promise of the future greatness of the temple	
	1	Narrative introduction
	2–9	An encouraging prophetic oracle
2:10–19	Promise of blessing despite the impurity of the nation	
	10–11	Narrative introduction
	12–13	The prophet's question and the priests' answer (*torah*)
	14–19	Prophetic oracle to encourage the builders
2:20–21	Divine legitimation of Zerubbabel to build the temple	
	20	Narrative introduction
	21	Prophetic oracle for Zerubbabel

Theology of the Book

1. The rebuilding of the temple

The addressees of Haggai's message are Zerubbabel, who is introduced as an official of the Persian empire (title פֶּחָה), and the high priest Joshua. As in Ezra-Nehemiah, Zerubbabel is here called the son of Shealtiel, whereas in 1 Chronicles 3:19 he is called the son of Pedaiah. Both were sons of Jehoiachin, the last legitimate king upon the Davidic throne. The relation of these two fathers remains a mystery. It is possible that one of them was a foster-father after the early death of the natural father. It is more likely, however, that Shealtiel was the more important ancestor, whereas Pedaiah was the immediate natural father. In any case, Zerubbabel was both the official governor of the small Persian province of Judah as well as a descendant of David. The first status was important for the political legitimation within the Persian empire of the construction of the temple, the second was necessary for it to gain religious recognition among the

Israelites. Theologically speaking only a son of David was authorized to build the temple (cf. 2 Sam 7:12–13; the laying of the foundation stone in Zech 4:7). As a son of Jehozadak (1 Chr 5:40–41; 2 Kgs 25:18–21), the high priest Joshua stands in the succession of the last high priests of the temple of Solomon. For Haggai, Zerubbabel seems to have been the more important person, for he is always named first (Hag 1:1, 12, 14; 2:2, 4) and the final oracle in 2:20–23 is directed solely to him. This is in contrast to Zech 3, in which Joshua receives his own oracle.

Both leaders are addressed with a message that also applies to the entire nation: The time has come to build the temple (1:3–11). A narrative note follows this saying, that the message was positively received by all three addressees (1:11). In light of the economically tense situation such a reception is by no means self-evident. This is followed by the prophet's assurance that God is with them (1:12) and the concluding remark by the narrator that Yhwh was the one who generated the willingness of the addressees, with the result that the work was begun on 21st September 520.

A little less than four weeks later, on 17th October, Haggai offers another encouraging speech to those involved in the construction work. The prophet asks whether any of the builders can still remember the former glory of the temple. Just as in Ezra 3:12, there are some individuals who had seen the first temple (before 586). The comparison puts the newly begun building in a wretched light, but Haggai promises nevertheless that the final product will be even more significant than the older one ever was.

Once again four weeks pass and on 18th December the prophet appears twice on the same day. First of all he turns to the priests with a request for *torah*, instruction, concerning a cultic question: Can something that is pure, purify something that is impure, or is it rather the other way round? To aid the contemporary reader, Ina Willi-Plein compares this with the following question: Does illness infect that which is healthy, or does that which is healthy infect illness? The priests answer: What is impure pollutes what is pure and not the other way round. The answer is immediately clear. As a reply to this *torah* of the priests, Haggai then announces that although the nation is impure and therefore incapable of creating anything that is good, they will nevertheless discover that with the commencement of the building work they will experience blessing. The second message on the same day is directed to Zerubbabel, who is designated as Yhwh's signet ring. Although his grandfather Jehoiachin was rejected as a signet ring (Jer 22:24), Zerubbabel receives direct authorization from the God of Israel to rebuild the temple. Beyond this, the promise does not contain any political connotations.

2. Theocentric orientation

In addition to the rebuilding of the Temple, a primary theme of the book is the efficacy of the "word from Yhwh." Before people take the initiative, Yhwh sends his word. It is communicated via the prophets. The personality of the prophet recedes completely into the background, not even the name of his father is mentioned. In this short book he is named nine times, five times with the addition of the title נָבִיא prophet (1:1, 3, 12; 2:1, 10). In 1:13 he is called the messenger of Yhwh (מַלְאַךְ יהוה), an expression that further underscores the identity of his message with that of the God of Israel. In comparison with other prophetic books the messenger formula "thus says Yhwh" and "saying of Yhwh" is used often and densely. It is not the prophet who is persuasive by means of his dedication to the cause, it is the word of God that is mediated through the prophet—בְּיַד־חַגַּי הַנָּבִיא. God himself is the one who arouses the spirit of those he addresses so that they would take up the task (1:14). He also promises that "his spirit will remain among them." This theocentric orientation determines all four sections. God has the power to hold back the dew of heaven, to withhold the fruitfulness of the earth (1:10–11), to shake heaven and earth, sea and dry land (2:6), to overthrow nations and kingdoms (2:22). Now he turns to his people through the prophet. And whereas other prophets often had to work in vain (Zech. 1:4), with for Haggai things are different: The word of Yhwh is immediately followed (1:12).

3. The right time

Not only is historical time precisely dated, there is a theological emphasis on the question of the right time. The formula "and now," is positioned at important junctures that indicate a change (1:5; 2:4, 15). *Now* is the time to take responsibility. The prophet is engaged in dialogue with the nation and makes use of contrasts: once—now—in the future. He looks at the meager economic situation and inquires into their causes in order to immediately name them in the name of Yhwh: "Because my house is lying desolate, and everyone is only concerned about his own house"

(1:9). The construction site in the ruins of the old temple looks depressingly wretched, not only when compared with the glory of the old temple, but probably also in comparison with the temples experienced by the returnees when they were in Babylon. The temple of Yhwh (2:15, 18), the house of Yhwh (1:2), the house of Yhwh Tsebaoth (1:14) represents the presence of God in the midst of his people. God calls it "my house" (1:9). "But *now*" it is time to be hopeful (2:4). The reminder of the exodus shows the might of God over cosmic powers, and his spirit—just like his presence *then* in the pillars of cloud and fire—will *now* accompany their work. As their goal the construction workers are promised a future *kābôd* ("glory"), one greater than that was ever possessed by the earlier temple. In 2:15 the contrast consists in the impurity of the nation. They will experience how their work on the house of God will be transformed into economic blessing (2:19).

4. A glorious future

As the connection with the exodus demonstrates, that which is new, the future, will come as a restoration of the people of God who will naturally orient themselves towards the Torah. The construction of the temple is compared with its predecessor. And just as temple construction and the promise of a dynasty had always been connected from the start (2 Sam 7:12–13), the book ends with a message to Zerubbabel. He is the elected son of David—whereby he is only tasked with the building of the temple, political perspectives remaining unexpressed. The book does not mention any particular burden that the Persians may have imposed upon the people. Nevertheless, there remains the hope that the nation would experience a total liberation, just as they once did during the exodus, and that instead of Judah bringing gifts to the great kings, the nations would bring their gifts to the house of Yhwh (2:7). And finally, the perspective is demonstrated whereby the power of the nations will be broken and Israel will no longer be under their yoke (2:22). Thus anchored in the period between September and December of the year 520, the book points us beyond the immediate concerns of the construction of the temple towards an eschatological future.

Bibliography

Baldwin, Joyce G. *Haggai, Zechariah, Malachi*. Tyndale Old Testament Commentaries. Leicester, UK: InterVarsity, 1972.

Boda, Mark J. "Haggai: Master Rhetorian." *Tyndale Bulletin* 51 (2000) 295–304.

Deissler, Alfons. *Zwölfpropheten III. Zefanja, Haggai, Sacharja, Maleachi*. Neue Echter Bibel. Würzburg: Echter, 1988.

Kessler, John. *The Book of Haggai. Prophecy and Society in Early Persian Yehud*. Vetus Testamentum Supplements 91. Leiden: Brill, 2002.

Klement, Herbert H. "Rhetorical, Theological and Chronological Features of Ezra–Nehemiah." In *A God of Faithfulness: Essays in Honour of J. Gordon McConville on his 60th Birthday*, edited by Jamie A. Grant, Alison Lo, Gordon J. Wenham, 61–78. London: T. & T. Clark, 2011.

Mason, Rex A. "The Purpose of the 'Editorial Framework' of the book of Haggai." *Vetus Testamentum* 27 (1977) 413–21.

Merrill, Eugene H. *Haggai, Zechariah, Malachi: An Exegetical Commentary*. Chicago: Moody, 1994.

Meyers, Carol L., and Eric M. Meyers. *Haggai, Zechariah 1–8*. Anchor Bible. Garden City, NY: Doubleday, 1987.

Taylor, Richard A., and E. Ray Clendenen. *Haggai, Malachi*. New American Commentary. Nashville, TN: Broadman & Holman, 2004.

Verhoef, Pieter A. *The Books of Haggai and Malachi*. The New International Commentary of the Old Testament. Grand Rapids: Eerdmans, 1987.

Willi-Plein, Ina. *Haggai, Sacharja, Maleachi*. Zürcher Bibelkommentare. Zürich: TVZ, 2007.

Yamauchi, Edwin M. *Persia and the Bible*. 1990. Reprint. Grand Rapids: Baker, 1996.

Chapter 14

Zechariah, Prophet of the King of Jerusalem and All the Earth

Historical Setting of the Book

THE PRESENCE OF DATING formulas in the book of Zechariah (1:1, 7; 7:1) allows for anchoring different parts of the book in the history of Israel and of the world. Major sections of the book are dated to various moments during the early years of the reign of Darius (522–486 BCE), the third king of the Persian empire (ca. 550–330 BCE). These dating formulas reflect the very different political situation after the exile: in the absence of a king in Jerusalem a foreign king establishes the frame of reference for the history of the people of God.

Sources for this period include the biblical books of Ezra and Haggai. After Cyrus (559–530) had allowed subject peoples, including Jewish exiles, to return to their land of origin and rebuild their sanctuaries (Ezra: 1:1–4; 6:1–5; cf. the so-called Cyrus Cylinder [*ANET* 315–16; *COS* 2.124]), a number of exiles of the former kingdom of Judah, but by no means all of them, returned in waves (539, and then the early years of Darius, and also much later, around 458) to Jerusalem and what was now called Yehud, a province of the Persian satrapy comprising Babylonia and Beyond-the-River (the area to the West of the Euphrates river).

An early attempt to rebuild the temple had come to a standstill, but in the year 520 the rebuilding project was taken up again. This second effort also suffered a number of difficulties, due to pressure from outside (Ezra 4:1–5, 24) and lack of priorities on the side of the residents of

Jerusalem (Hag 1:2-4), but the project was finished in the year 515 (Ezra 6:15). The eight visions in the first part of the book of Zechariah are dated to 15 February 519 (Zech 1:7), just under two months after the new start of the rebuilding of the temple (18 December 520, Hag 2:10, 18). Two historical individuals figure in the visions: Joshua, the high priest (chapters 3 and 6) and Zerubbabel, the governor (chapter 4). They are both mentioned in the book of Ezra as leaders of the temple building project, supported by the prophets Haggai and Zechariah (Ezra 5:1-2).

The two directives which form the bulk of the second part of the book (9-11 and 12-14, each introduced by the word מַשָּׂא, "directive," traditionally translated "burdens") have a distinct style and lack detail of a nature which would have enabled us to situate them with any certainty in what is known of the history of the people of Israel. However, there are unmistakable thematic connections between the directives and the visions (see below). In recent scholarship a trend can be observed to date these two directives to a time relatively close to the dates found in the first panel of the book, and not—as was common in earlier scholarship—to hundreds of years later (or, as some have argued, in pre-exilic times).

Content and Structure of the Book

The book of Zechariah is usually divided in two: chapters 1-8 and 9-14. According to this arrangement, the first part of the book, situated in the early years of Darius, contains eight vision reports (1:7—6:15), sandwiched between two sections (1:1-6; 7-8) dealing with the transition from the past experience of living under God's anger to a promised future of living under God's blessing. The second part, which (original) historical background is harder to determine, describes the ups and downs of the (briefly) united tribes of Israel.

Alternatively, however, the close thematic agreement between 1:1-6 and 7-8 can be understood otherwise, namely as the introductions of two panels of a dyptych (chs. 1-6 and 7-14), not as the two sides of a sandwich. Also the striking similarity in content between 2:10[14] and 9:9 points to such an understanding of the structure of the book. Hence, the book of Zechariah can be outlined as follows:

1:1–6	A NEW GENERATION, A NEW BEGINNING		7–8
1:7–6:15	Yhwh *of hosts is Lord of the whole earth*	*The battle is of the Lord, the king over all the earth*	9–14
	Eight visions	Two directives	
1:7–2:17	"Sing for joy and be glad, O daughter of Zion; for behold I am coming and I will dwell in your midst" (2:10[14])	"Rejoice greatly, O daughter of Zion! Shout in triumph, O daughter of Jerusalem! Behold, your king is coming to you" (9:9)	9
3	Leadership (1) priests	Leadership (1) shepherds	10–11
4	Leadership (2) governor	Leadership (2) house of David	12
5	Judgment and cleansing	Cleansing and judgment	13
6	"The Lord of all the earth" and the future ruler	"The Lord will be king over all the earth"	14

Theology of the Book

1. A new generation, a new beginning

The opening sections of the two panels of the book have a common theme. At the beginning (1:1–6) of the first panel the transition from living in exile to returning to Jerusalem and its surroundings is portrayed as presenting a unique opportunity to bring one chapter of the history of the people of God to a close and turn a new leaf. The unwillingness of previous generations to pay serious attention to the prophetic word of Yhwh had resulted in the anger of Yhwh coming down on them. That terrifying experience can remain something of the past if the present generation complements their physical return from exile to Jerusalem with a realignment of their heart to Yhwh of hosts. He will be glad to reciprocate.

The introduction (ch. 7–8) of the second panel covers the same ground. It begins with a question put to the prophet about the continuation of a liturgical practice of fasting (the date, "the fifth month," suggests a link with events marking the beginning of the exile: the destruction of the temple, the palace, and the house of Jerusalem in 586). The men who ask the question have to wait until the end of the next chapter before they receive an answer to their questions.

Prompted by Yhwh of hosts the prophet seizes the opportunity to first ask some probing questions that move beyond practical issues to deep level motives underlying not only religious practice but also social behavior. He reminds his listeners once again of the heart problem of previous generations that surfaced in their refusal to pay serious attention to the prophetic word of Yhwh resulting in an experience of the anger of Yhwh of hosts.

That past experience of Yhwh's anger is contrasted with an alluring picture of a very different but as always passionate future relationship between Yhwh and his people with blessings beyond imagination. In those circumstances fasting (the topic of the original question) will be replaced by "joy, gladness, and cheerful feasts" (8:19). The key issue that will make a difference between anger and blessing is listening to the prophetic word of Yhwh and behavior that demonstrates a shared passion for "truth and peace" (8:19).

2. Yhwh of hosts is Lord of the whole earth (the eight visions)

Zechariah's preferred title for God is "Yhwh of hosts" (NASB: "the Lord of hosts"). This observation is not merely meant as a comment of a statistical nature, it is also an apt summary of a notion that permeates the book. The name inspires trust, something needed particularly when facing invincible old enemies (2:1–4), overwhelming opposition (4:6–7) or a desperate battle situation (9:14–17; 14:3–5). Yhwh is in control, he rules the universe.

The concept behind the name Yhwh *of hosts* is articulated with particular force in the eight visions in the first panel of the book. A closer look at the first and the last vision enables the reader to distinguish different regiments of the hosts of Yhwh. In the first vision the prophet sees a reconnaissance unit composed of horse riders returning and reporting to their commander (1:10–11). Their report is summarized in the words "all the earth is peaceful and quiet" (1:11). The angel to whom they report then becomes the guide of the prophet in the strange world of the visions (the three designations "the man who was standing among the myrtles," "the angel of the Lord" and "the angel who was speaking with me" in 1:8–14 are most likely different ways of referring to one and the same person).

In the eighth vision the prophet witnesses how another regiment is about to be sent out. The four horse-drawn chariots figuring in this vision are identified as "the four spirits of heaven, going forth after standing

Zechariah, Prophet of the King of Jerusalem and All the Earth

before the Lord of all the earth" (6:5). The angelic guide directs the attention of the prophet to one of them in particular, the chariot on a northbound mission. Mentioned before in the visions, the north country is a reference to the area where the agents of God's judgment are located and where the exiled people have just now been urgently called to flee from (2:6–7[10–11]; it seems the call was heeded by the three individuals mentioned in 6:10).

The final words of the angelic guide indicate that the mission of the chariot is not limited to reconnaissance (6:7) but at an earlier occasion included action as well: they "have appeased my wrath in the land of the north" (6:8; probably referring to completing the execution of Yhwh's anger towards Babylon, 1:21[2:4]).

The focus on different regiments in the hosts commanded by Yhwh in the first and last of the visions provides a dramatic envelope or *inclusio* structure bracketing the vision reports. It offers an unambiguous demonstration of the sovereignty of Yhwh over the world. Yhwh of hosts rightly bears the title *Lord* [אָדוֹן] *of all the earth*, in the eighth and final vision (6:5), and already in the fifth vision (4:14).

The mention of the title *the Lord of the whole earth* at the end of the fifth vision (Zech 4) provides the connection between the global scope of the sovereignty of Yhwh and his special interest and concern for the community of one particular people and their locality. A lampstand fuelled directly by two olive trees on its right and on its left (bypassing the normal need of human hands for tending a lampstand) provides an illustration of Yhwh's direct involvement with the work of rebuilding the temple (4:6). Yhwh of hosts promises to exercise his spirit, contrasted with (human) might or power. He will be able to confront any possible opposition which might frustrate the rebuilding of the temple (4:7). And so, its completion is guaranteed (4:9).

The two olive trees are identified towards the end of the vision report as "the two anointed ones who are standing by the Lord of the whole earth" (4:14; NASB adds in a footnote: "Lit. *sons of fresh oil*"). Establishing the precise identity of these two figures is extremely difficult. They are called "sons of the oil" (בְּנֵי־הַיִּצְהָר), which seems to exclude the usual translation *the anointed ones*. The use of the verb עָמַד in combination with the preposition עַל points to a heavenly council setting where the "sons of the oil" belong to the attendants of the Lord of the whole earth and would make them belong to one of the regiments under the command of Yhwh of hosts.

The presence of Yhwh of hosts on earth will be concentrated once more in one particular city: Jerusalem. Decades earlier the prophet Ezekiel had described how the glory of Yhwh left the city (Ezek 11:23) when Yhwh had executed his judgment on it and the population had gone into exile. Now Zechariah is told by the angelic guide to proclaim Yhwh's resolve (1:16): "'I will return to Jerusalem with compassion; My house will be built in it,' declares the Lord of hosts, 'and a measuring line will be stretched over Jerusalem.'"

The promise contains two closely related matters: the return of Yhwh and the rebuilding of the city. The third vision shows in more detail how both will be accomplished. Yhwh's glory will dominate life in the city while at the same time he himself will provide security for her unusually large population by being a wall of fire around her. This will allow for a ground-breaking architectural design of a city without walls (2:4–5[8–9]).

Finally, Yhwh of hosts is mentioned four times as the person behind the mission of one of the speakers in the visions. The authority of this speaker is made dependent on the fulfillment of specific elements pictured in the visions: first, the reversal of the fate of those who plundered the people of Yhwh but who in turn "will be plunder for their slaves" (2:9[13]), next, the addition of many nations to the people of Yhwh and the presence of Yhwh among his people (2:11[15]), then, the completion of the rebuilding of the temple (4:9) and, finally, the return of exiles and their participation in the building of the temple under the direction of the future ruler Zemah (6:15). Usually the prophet Zechariah is identified as the one speaking the authenticating formula "Then you will know that Yhwh of hosts has sent me." However, given the close association between the angelic guide and the hosts of Yhwh it seems more likely that it is the mission of this angel which will be proven true when these things reach their fulfillment.

3. The battle is of the Lord, the king over all the earth (the two directives)

It is more difficult to discover the flow of the two directives in chapters 9–14. One way to look at these chapters is to see chapter 9 as an overview, the overall thrust of which is then spelled out in greater detail in the following chapters. This way of reading makes sense of the fact that different

Zechariah, Prophet of the King of Jerusalem and All the Earth

stages of the sequence battle—intervention—bliss in 9:9–17 are found in the following chapters culminating in the last battle in the final chapter. It seems that some linear development can be traced in these chapters, particularly with respect to deteriorating relationships between shepherds and their flock (an image of leadership both on national and international levels), even in the case of a committed shepherd, and the announcement and then execution of judgment on a dysfunctional shepherd.

On a number of occasions in the second panel of the book the reader is confronted with battle scenes (9:13–15; 10:4–5; 12:1–9; 14:1–5, 12–15). Eventually, Jerusalem will be safe (14:11), but only after much fighting which will result in a considerable number of casualties. The most alarming details are found in the description of the last battle and include the rape of women of Jerusalem (14:2).

The turn of events that will lead to the defeat of the enemies of Jerusalem ("all the nations," 12:2–3, 9; 14:2) is attributed to interventions by Yhwh (9:14–17; 10:5; 12:4–9; 14:3, 12–15). The timing of these interventions may raise questions: in the last battle Yhwh arrives only after women have been raped and half of the city has gone into exile (which is a lower number than the two-thirds that will not survive Yhwh's judgment announced in the preceding chapter, 13:8–9).

The battle will be severe, but in the end there will be victory for the people loyal to Yhwh which will be an evident result of the intervention of their God (12:6). A variety of imagery is used to describe the surprising way in which things will turn out in the end, e.g. Yhwh making "the clans of Judah like a firepot among pieces of wood and a flaming torch among sheaves, so they will consume on the right hand and on the left all the surrounding peoples" (12:6).

Measures will be taken to keep the house of David and the inhabitants of Jerusalem in their proper place in relation to what are called "the tents of Judah" (12:7). At the same time, a leading role is given to the house of David, and it is even said that "the house of David *will be* like God, like the angel of the Lord before them" (12:8). Immediately following this provoking statement the house of David and the inhabitants of Jerusalem are portrayed as recipients of a spirit of grace and supplication (12:10) that will make them look on the mysterious "pierced one" and mourn for him in a communal ceremony of monumental proportions (12:10–14).

The bliss which ensues eventually marks the end of the world as people have always known it. A cosmic climax has the Mount of Olives

189

as the epicenter, when the feet of the Lord will have touched down on it (14:4). The landscape of Jerusalem and its surroundings will change beyond recognition, and the universe as a whole will be transformed in such a manner that the words *day* and *light* will receive a new meaning altogether (14:6–7).

The enemy nations will suffer a horrific judgment which is described in gruesome detail (14:12–13). At the same time, strikingly, the survivors of the nations (with Egypt mentioned by name) are welcome to join the celebration of the Festival of Booths, under the threat of punishment in the form of absence of rain for those of the families of the earth who refuse to "go up to Jerusalem to worship the King, the Lord of hosts" (14:17).

4. The inclusivity of the exclusive people of God

Yhwh has an exclusive relationship with one special people. Over its long history covering several centuries, the relationship has suffered a number of crises, but Yhwh is willing once again to make a new beginning (1:1–6; 7–8). However, the composition of the special people of God is about to undergo remarkable change.

The third vision (2:1–13[5–17]) in its portrayal of the new Jerusalem introduces bold innovations in urban planning in order to meet the challenge of rising population numbers: a city without walls (2:4[8]), protected by Yhwh himself who will simultaneously be a wall of fire around it and the glory inside it (2:5[9]). The growth explosion is caused by an influx of "many nations" into what Yhwh using traditional (and exclusive) language calls "my people" (2:11[15]; cf. the exclusive "Judah" and "Jerusalem" in the next verse.

A similar picture emerges in the response of the nations to the transformation of society which occurs when God's plans for a community marked by truthful communication, justice in the courts and loving relationships between citizens (8:16, 19) materialize. Outsiders of different national and linguistic backgrounds will interpret those features as evidence of the presence of God and sense a strong attraction to join in (8:20–23).

Zechariah, Prophet of the King of Jerusalem and All the Earth

5. The ambiguity of kingship

The institution of kingship dominates the book of Zechariah, both by its presence and by its absence. Kingship was one of the three pillars (with land and temple) on which the society of the people of Israel had been built since the times of David and Solomon. The three dating formulas in the book (1:1, 7; 7:1) all refer to a distant and foreign king, Darius. They are a painful reminder of the absence of a king in Jerusalem.

No king is mentioned in the visions. In the fourth vision (3:1–10) Joshua the high priest is given responsibilities that once were the privilege of the king, possibly preparing for a situation where there is no king present. Similarly in the fifth vision not a king, but the acting governor, Zerubbabel, is responsible for the rebuilding of the temple (4:6–10; interestingly, Zerubbabel's Davidic ancestry, 1 Chr 3:17–19, is passed over in silence by Zechariah, Haggai, and Ezra).

Only in the symbolic action report which concludes the vision reports do we hear about someone "who will bear the honor and sit and rule on his throne" (6:13). The report narrates how Joshua, the high priest, receives a royal crown on his head. However, the symbolic action does not imply a royal coronation of the high priest: the crown is to be deposited in the temple as a sign (cf. 3:8) guaranteeing the future fulfillment of the detailed promise concerning someone else: the royal figure.

Strikingly, this ruler is not given the title "king." But he does have a name: צֶמַח, "Zemah" (probably a proper name, like "Florian"; the meaning of the related noun is "vegetation, greenery," not "branch" or "sprout"!). The background for the imagery suggested by the name is to be found in Jeremiah 23:1–6 (not Isa 11:1–10, which uses different imagery). The provision by YHWH of future growth (צֶמַח) for (לְ) David in 23:5 is contrasted with the dead end of the House of David in its present condition announced in the verses immediately preceding (22:24–30), culminating in the words "For no man of his descendants [זֶרַע] will prosper / Sitting on the throne of David / Or ruling again in Judah" (Jer. 22:30). The imagery, the use of future verbal forms and the details describing the nature of his rule (6:12–15) suggest that this is a future model ruler (and so a "messianic" figure).

Coming after the symbolic action in which a royal figure is presented, it would not be unreasonable to expect a king to be included in the profile of a society living under the blessing of God (chapters 7–8) which opens the second panel of the book. However, the blueprint demonstrates that such a society can be envisaged without a king (actually, there is a king in these chapters: he appears in the dating formula in 7:1, the only time in the book of Zechariah that Darius is mentioned with a title: מֶלֶךְ, "king").

Finally the king of Jerusalem arrives (9:9–10). He is a somewhat unusual king in a number of ways: humbly riding on a donkey, destroying conventional weaponry, ruling a global empire. But who is he? The reader who has started reading from the beginning of chapter 9 may wonder about the relationship between Yhwh marching down like a king in a military campaign from the North to set up a camp in Jerusalem as presented in the verses immediately preceding (9:1–8) and the king arriving in Jerusalem in the next verse: could they be one and the same person?

This identification finds confirmation in another reference to global kingship, with Yhwh as king, in the final chapter of the book (14:9). The most prominent piece of confirmation, however, is the close correspondence between 9:9 and a verse in a similar location in the first panel of the book: Zechariah 2:10[14]. The two verses have three constituents in common: (1) a call to rejoice, (2) addressed to the city of Zion/Jerusalem, (3) on the occasion of the arrival of a special person. In the presence of so much commonality, the precise identity of the one to arrive becomes a matter of interest: in 2:10[14] the person to be honored is Yhwh, in 9:9 he is the king of Jerusalem.

The suggestion of the divine identity of the king in 9:9 would fit well with the discouraging picture of human leadership in later chapters (10–13). They are presented as dysfunctional shepherds, contrasting sharply with Yhwh's care for his flock (9:16). The last time we hear about shepherds is when the sword of Yhwh is called to execute Yhwh's deserved judgment (cf. 11:17) on a failing shepherd (13:7–9).

In this context the House of David is mentioned, once in a position of leadership (12:8) but, remarkably, four times positioned side by side with the rest of the population (12:7, 10, 12–14; 13:1), including one occasion where together they receive cleansing (13:1) after the event where the house of David and the inhabitants of Jerusalem mourn for a pierced one (12:10; unfortunately there are few clues to establish the identity of the victim).

If Zechariah 9:9 is about a king entering Jerusalem who is Yhwh himself, the choice by Jesus of precisely this prophecy in an episode in the final week before his arrest, trial, and execution may have played an important role in the development of what has been called "divine identity Christology" (Bauckham, 2009: 172). By orchestrating a ride on a donkey for his entry into Jerusalem Jesus operates simultaneously as director and principal character staging the fulfillment of Zechariah's prophecy (all four Gospel writers record the event and Matthew and John quote the prophecy of Zechariah; Matt 21:5; John 12:15; cf. Mark 11:9; Luke 19:29-40).

As further quotations and allusions in the four Gospels and other books in the New Testament make clear, Zechariah 9-14 plays an important role in establishing the meaning of significant moments in the public life of Jesus. The bold orchestration of the prophecy of the (in the reading I have proposed: possibly divine) king entering Jerusalem riding on a donkey is without doubt one of the most thought-provoking ways in which these chapters are used, putting Jesus' messianic claims in an even larger perspective. Could this king of Jerusalem be the king of all the earth?

Bibliography

Bauckham, Richard J. *Jesus and the God of Israel: God Crucified and Other Studies on the New Testament's Christology of Divine Identity*. Milton Keynes, UK: Paternoster, 2009.
Boda, Mark J. *Haggai and Zechariah Research: A Bibliographic Survey*. Tools for Biblical Study 5. Leiden: Deo, 2003.
———. *Haggai, Zechariah*. NIV Application Commentary. Grand Rapids: Zondervan, 2004.
Boda, Mark J., and Michael H. Floyd, editors. *Bringing out the Treasure: Inner Biblical Allusion and Zechariah 9-14*. Journal for the Study of the Old Testament Supplement Series 370. Sheffield, UK: Sheffield Academic Press, 2003.
———, editors. *Tradition in Transition: Haggai and Zechariah 1-8 in the Trajectory of Hebrew Theology*. New York: Continuum, 2008.
Curtis, Byron G. *Up the Steep and Stony Road: The Book of Zechariah in Social Location Trajectory Analysis*. Academia Biblica 25. Atlanta: Society of Biblical Literature, 2006.
Meyers, Carol L. and Eric M. Meyers. *Haggai, Zechariah 1-8*. Anchor Bible 25B. Garden City, NY: Doubleday, 1987.
———. *Zechariah 9-14*. Anchor Bible 25C. Garden City, NY: Doubleday, 1993.
O'Kennedy, Danie F. "The Use of the Epithet יהוה צבאות in Haggai, Zechariah and Malachi." *Journal of Northwest Semitic Languages* 33.1 (2007) 77-99.
Reventlow, Henning. *Die Propheten Haggai, Sacharja und Maleachi*. Das Alte Testament Deutsch 25.2. Göttingen: Vandenhoeck & Ruprecht, 1993.
Rose, Wolter H. "Zacharia." In *Daniël-Ezra-Haggai-Zacharia-Esther-Nehemia-Maleachi: Zeven bijbelboeken uit de Perzische periode*, edited by G. W. Lorein and W. H. Rose, 247-329. De Brug 11. Heerenveen, the Netherlands: Groen, 2010.
———. "Zechariah and the Ambiguity of Kingship in Postexilic Israel." in *Let us Go up to Zion. Essays in Honour of H.G.M. Williamson on the Occasion of his Sixty-Fifth*

Birthday, edited by Iain Provan and Mark J. Boda, 219–31. Leiden; Boston: Brill 2012.

———. *Zemah and Zerubbabel: Messianic Expectations in the Early Postexilic Period.* Journal for the Study of the Old Testament Supplement Series 304. Sheffield, UK: Sheffield Academic Press, 2000.

Van der Woude, Adam S. *Zacharia.* Prediking van het Oude Testament. Nijkerk, the Netherlands: Callenbach, 1984.

Williamson, H. G. M. *Studies in Persian Period History and Historiography.* Forschungen zum Alten Testament 38. Tübingen: Mohr Siebeck, 2004.

Wolters, Al. *Zechariah.* Historical Commentary on the Old Testament. Leuven: Peeters, [forthcoming].

"Zechariah and the Ambiguity of Kingship in Postexilic Israel." in *Let us Go up to Zion. Essays in Honour of H.G.M. Williamson on the Occasion of his Sixty-Fifth Birthday*, edited by Iain Provan and Mark J. Boda, 219–31. Leiden; Boston: Brill 2012.

Fifth- to Second-Century (?) Prophets

Chapter 15

Malachi, Prophet Proclaiming the Lord in the Present, Past, and Future

Historical setting of the book

THE BOOK OF MALACHI can be placed in the years between 460–450 BCE, thereby situating the book within the Persian Empire. The Persian rulers up to the time of the proposed and presumed date of the book of Malachi can be summarized as follows: Cyrus the Great 550–530 BCE; Cambyses 530–522 BCE; Darius I 521–486 BCE; Xerxes 486–465 BCE; Artaxerxes I 464–424 BCE.

Artaxerxes I became ruler of the Persian empire after he assassinated his elder brother Darius and so at the age of eighteen years he became king. As was always the case when a new king ascended the throne there was a couple of rebellions he had to deal with, but he swiftly gained control of the empire as a whole. It was the Egyptian and Greek forces that Artaxerxes I had to cope with throughout the larger part of his reign. Egypt and Greece united their armies and by 460–459 BCE regained Memphis. Artaxerxes I responded with an alliance with Sparta negotiated by Megabyzus, one of Artaxerxes' generals, and succeeded to gain a victory over Greece (458–457 BCE). But in 451–450 BCE Sparta entered into an alliance with Athens and declared war against the Persian Empire. The Persians were able to withstand this onslaught and Athens entered into negotiations that resulted in the peace of Callais (449 BCE). This brought an end to hostilities for the next thirty years between Greece and the Persian Empire. When

Artaxerxes I died in 424 BCE he was eventually succeeded by Darius II Ochus who reigned from 424–404 BCE.

It seems strange that there is no mention whatsoever of the movements that took place on the scene of world politics in the book of Malachi. This is in stark contrast with other books from the Persian Period (Deutero-Isaiah, Nehemiah, Ezra) which do mention foreign rulers. The interest the book of Malachi has was more focused on the internal conditions within the province of Yehud and its inhabitants. It is also interesting to note the total lack of references to the dynasty of the House of David or to a regaining of Judah's political independence, even though the Persians had to cope with upheavals from both Egypt and Greece. From the side of the Persian Empire there was also perhaps little interest in either Yehud or even the satrapy of Beyond-the-River (Eber-Nahara) because of the threat Greece and Egypt held for the empire. The only possible interest Persia could have had in Yehud was to see them and the surrounding provinces as buffers against military actions from the side of either Egypt or Greece (Berquist, 1995: 108).

Content and Structure of the Book

The question of whether the book displays an inner structure of coherence is a matter of dispute in the research history of the book. Also those scholars who believe the book to have a certain coherent structure, take widely different views with regard to this topic (Van Selms, Clendenen, Floyd, Assis). The content of the book displays the following structure:

- A Mal 1:1—Superscription
    - B Mal 1:2–5—A view from the past to the future
        - C Mal 1:6—2:9—Malpractices in the worship of Yhwh by the priests and the people
            - D Mal 2:10–16—The issue of mixed marriages
            - D' Mal 2:17—3:7a—Addressing the issue of the God of justice
        - C' Mal 3:7b–12—Tithing as a cultic malpractice and the blessing to come
    - B' Mal 3:13—4:3[3:3–21]—A view from the present time to the future
- A' Mal 4:4–6[3:22–24]—Postscript: two additions regarding Moses and Elijah

Malachi, Prophet Proclaiming the Lord in the Present, Past, and Future

Theology of the Book

The theology of the book can be described in terms of the present, past, and future. The emphasis is first of all on the present time where current conditions are addressed. There is also a move to the past where Yhwh's redemptive acts are re-called. Finally, the book opens up a vision of times to come where justice and righteousness will prevail.

1. God is the God of the present time

The first thing that strikes one when reading the book is the frequent use of the well-known prophetic messenger formula "Thus speaks the Lord, the Almighty," amounting to a number of no less than twenty-four times. That God speaks to his people is the first theological claim the book makes. In a time when there was little to be excited about, no major international events and no sign of God's active and dramatic intervention in the present plight of his people, it is important to be reminded that God still speaks to his people through his prophet. Malachi's message was that even though his people are still subjected to the Persian rule, it is God who is the almighty God. Twice in the book it is said that Yhwh is God beyond the borders of Israel (1:5) and that his name is honored among the nations "from where the sun rises to where the sun sets" (1:11).

The very first statement made by God to the people is also astonishing: God loves his people (1:2). In a time when the people have their doubts about God (they question his love, they do not worship him in a proper way, they question his justice, they are skeptical of how meaningful it is to keep on serving God), he declares his love for his people. His love is demonstrated when the twin brothers Jacob and Esau are compared. In a series of chiasms God's love for his people is demonstrated in what happened to Esau/Edom (1:3-4).

It has been stated (Baldwin, Verhoef, Redditt) that the covenant between God and his people is an important concept in this book (2:5-7; 2:10; 3:1). Not only is God revealed to his people by his covenant name, the term "covenant" (ברית) occurs no less than six times in the book and there are other allusions to the covenant as well. The covenant is still intact, in spite of the questions and doubts the people may have. The close relationship between God and his people suggested by the covenant is also accentuated by the metaphor of God as Father which occurs three times (1:6; 2:10; 3:17).

God is also revealed as the graceful God. In spite of the many wrongdoings of his people, he still wants to live in a covenantal and loving relationship with them. Therefore, rather than to judge them for questioning his love, his justice, and his active involvement in what happens to them, the Lord enters into a dialogue with his people, patiently answering the questions of his people.

The Lord Almighty demands to be worshipped in the right way

God is worshipped by bringing sacrifices to the temple sanctuary as was prescribed in the Torah of Moses. The purpose of the sacrifices was to honor God (1:6) and to make atonement for sins committed. But this is not what happened during the ministry of Malachi. A list of animals unfit to sacrifice is made: blind, crippled, and diseased animals may not be offered. The reason for bringing animals without blemish or defect is to offer Yhwh the best of the herd. He deserved to be offered with the best available livestock there is. Offerings described as defiled are unacceptable, not fit for a proper offer dedicated to Yhwh. The prophet makes clear that practicing no worship at all is better than the kind of worship they practice (1:10). It would therefore be better to close the door of the temple so that there will be no one to kindle a fire for the burnt offerings to be sacrificed. Yhwh denounces these malpractices of the sacrificial system in saying that he has no pleasure in them nor is he pleased with an offering from them. Both the priests and the sacrifices they bring are denounced. The concern of the prophet is not only about the sacrifices as such; ultimately it is about the attitude of the priests—an attitude of disrespect for and ignorance of the way in which Yhwh is to be worshipped. This, in fact, amounts to ignorance of Yhwh himself.

Closely related to the malpractices in the sacrificial worship of Yhwh is the issue of robbing God of what is due to him (3:7b–12). In an innovative, if not shocking way, the metaphor of robbing God by withholding tithes is used to point out a wrong doing of the people. Tithing is a religious custom well-known in the ancient Near East (Mesopotamia, Ugarit, Egypt, southern parts of Arabia; Meinhold, 2006) and from the Pentateuch (Deut 14:22–29; 26:12–15) it appears as something that was practiced also in the community of Judah. In Deut 14:22 the people are admonished to "set aside a tenth of all that your fields produce each year." The one who brings the tithe to the temple must then enjoy the tithe "in the presence of the Lord" (Deut 22:23). The people are also reminded not to neglect the Levites "for they have no allotment or inheritance of their own" (Deut 22:27). It seems that every third year there was also a tithe to be given to the Levites, the strangers, orphans and widows living in the towns so that they can have something to eat (Deut 22:28–29; 26:12). The system of tithing does therefore not only point to a religious duty of serving God in a very direct way, tithing has also a social, human dimension of sharing with the poor and the landless. This will result in the blessing of the people by Yhwh. In Leviticus 27:30 it is stipulated that "a tithe of everything from the land belongs to the Lord." It is further stipulated that "every tenth animal will be holy to the Lord" (Lev 27:32). Numbers 18:21–31 deals also extensively with the issue of tithes and offerings entitled to and brought by the Levites. From Numbers 18:25–29 it seems that the Levites must present a tithe from the tithe they received from the people to Yhwh. This tithe of the tithe is regarded as the offering the Levites must bring. Tithing as a religious custom combined with a social dimension was important. To neglect that amounts to a disruption of the people's relationship with God and their fellow human beings.

When proper worship fails, Yhwh must act with a curse pronounced upon especially the priests for it is primarily their duty to oversee the bringing of sacrifices (2:1–9). At the same time Yhwh is also ready to shower his people with blessings in abundance when they worship him in sincerity (3:10–12).

The Lord Almighty demands an ethical correct way of living

Yhwh does not only require proper worship, he is also concerned with the way in which his people conduct their lives. In the fourth unit (2:17—3:7a) the people questioned God on exactly this matter. According to them, "Yhwh delights in those who do evil." Hence they ask: "where is the God of justice?" or, to put it in other words: where is the justice of God? To this accusation God answers that he will certainly come to exercise justice and that when doing so he will come to cleanse the temple from unworthy worship. This is a surprising way to treat this concern of the people. When asking about the just actions of God, the people have to discover that God will first come to the temple to investigate the quality of sacrifices brought. The result is that the Levites as the temple staff who held responsibility for overseeing the sacrificial practices will have to endure Yhwh's purifying acts in order to restore proper worship. Yhwh will act as a judge from where he will sit and execute justice to be served in the temple. Then he will also come as a judge to exercise justice on a social level. Various abuses are named: sorcerers, adulterers, perjurers, those who oppress the laborers, widows and orphans, and those who thrust aside the aliens in society. All this culminates in an attitude of disrespect for Yhwh himself. Two of the abuses are transgressions prohibited in the decalogue while the others are dealt with in other legal corpuses of the Torah. It is also interesting that these injustices to fellow human beings are also mentioned in the wisdom literature of the Old Testament.

In 2:13–16 men already married are reprimanded not to divorce "the woman of their youth" but to keep faithful to her. This unit is a testimony to the high regard Yhwh has for marriage. Marriage is more than a mutual contract between a man and a woman; it also has religious and social consequences for the community at large. Furthermore, it is clear from this passage that a man may not simply swop "the woman of his youth" for another one when it is convenient for him to do so. This is what probably happened in society. Judean men divorced their wives to marry women from the surrounding cultures. These women most probably kept on worshipping their (foreign) gods. In this respect Yhwh once again acts as the defender of the rights of the helpless in society. It is also of some significance that it is said that one who divorces covers his garment with violence. Violence is a particularly strong word to use in this regard. In a sense divorce involves an element of violence, leaving the former marriage partners with some emotional and even physical scars caused by the violence of divorce. Although we would be hesitant today to denounce interfaith marriages as contrary to the will of God, the warning of the text is still applicable: interfaith marriages do have the potential of luring one away from one's religion and become unfaithful to God. In this respect one has to consider the religious consequences an interfaith marriage may have upon one's relationship with God.

2. God is the God of the past

God is also known from the past. God has been the God of his people since the time of the ancestors. In particular Jacob is named (1:2; 2:12; 3:6). Jacob is known for his deception of his twin brother, elderly father

Malachi, Prophet Proclaiming the Lord in the Present, Past, and Future

as well as his uncle. The people of Israel have a long history of sin and unfaithfulness against Yhwh, the covenant God. At the same time God has a long history of keeping faithful to the covenant with his people.

The prophet makes extensive use of the Sinai tradition appealing to the covenant and its stipulations to urge the people to be obedient to the covenant with Yhwh (1:6—2:9; 2:10-12). The fact that God is Father and Creator (2:10) is also a reference to the past. That Yhwh is father of Israel means a relationship of origin in the sense that Yhwh "fathered" his people, that is, they owe their existence to Yhwh who brought them into being a people (Deut 32:6). It is significant to note how the idea of Yhwh as Father of Israel is closely linked with Yhwh as Creator. In Malachi this link is found in 2:16. The same idea is found in Deuteronomy 32:6. The origin of Israel is seen as a creative deed of Yhwh in the history of his people, by which he called Israel into being. Also, the strong emphasis on the correct way of bringing sacrifices coupled with the appropriate duties of the priests can be traced back to covenantal stipulations found in the books of Leviticus and Deuteronomy. It is also interesting to note that the term "my altar" (1:7-8) may originate from the former prophets, the term occurs in 1 Samuel 2:28, 33, where the malpractices of the house of Eli are described during the time of Samuel. Perhaps the prophet wanted to indicate a similarity between the malpractices—and their outcome - of a priestly house way back in history and the current situation of the priests.

3. God is the God of the future

From the present time the prophet also takes a look to the future opening up an eschatological vision for believers. The judgment in future will result in righteous worship (3:1-4). The wicked will be judged while there will be joyful deliverance for faithful believers (3:13—4:3[3:13-21]). In view of the eschatological time of deliverance believers are encouraged not to lose faith or become skeptical about God. They are reminded of a book of remembrance written with the names of those who honor his name. These people are the treasured possession of Yhwh himself, recalling once again the age old covenant language so well known to the people. In the end it will be the righteous that will prevail, while the evil people within the society of Israel will suffer total destruction.

There is a movement from the past (Jacob and Esau in 1:2-5) to the future (3:13—4:3[3:13-21]) in the book. Ultimately, it is foreseen that somebody like Elijah will come with a mission to reconcile the disrupted society of Israel. This can only be accomplished when the people adhere to the ordinances already given to Moses (4:4–6[3:22–24]).

To summarize Malachi's message briefly: Live today in obedience to God with a memory of the past (what God did) and may the future inspire you.

Selected Bibliography

Assis, E. "Structure and Meaning in the Book of Malachi." In *Prophecy and Prophets in Ancient Israel*, edited by J. Day, 354–69. London: T. & T. Clark, 2010.

Berquist, J. L. *Judaism in Persia's Shadow: A Social and Historical Approach*. Minneapolis: Fortress, 1995.

Clendenen, E. R. "The Structure of Malachi: A Textlinguistic Study." *Criswell Theological Review* 2 (1987) 3–17.

Floyd, M. H. *Minor Prophets. Part 2*. FOTL XXII. Grand Rapids: Eerdmans, 2000.

Hill, A. E. *Malachi: A New Translation with Introduction and Commentary*. Anchor Bible. New York: Doubleday, 1998.

Meinhold, A. *Maleachi*. BKAT Band XIV/8. Neukirchener: Neukirchen-Vluyn, 2006.

Petersen, D. L. *Zechariah 9–14 and Malachi: A Commentary*. Old Testament Library. Louisville, KY: Westminster John Knox, 1995.

Snyman, S. D. "Rethinking the Demarcation of Malachi 2:17—3:5." *Acta Theologica* 31.1 (2011) 156–68.

———. "Suffering in Post-Exilic Times—Mal 3:13–24 as a Case in Point." *Old Testament Essays* 20.3 (2008) 786–97.

Stuart, D. "Malachi." In *The Minor Prophets. An Exegetical and Expository Commentary* vol. 3, edited by T. E. McComiskey. Grand Rapids: Baker, 1998.

Van der Woude, A. S. *Haggai Maleachi*. Prediking van het Oude Testament. Nijkerk, the Netherlands: Callenbach, 1982.

Verhoef, P. A. *The Books of Haggai and Malachi*. NICOT. Grand Rapids: Eerdmans, 1987.

Weyde, K. W. *Prophecy and Teaching: Prophetic Authority, Form Problems and the Use of Traditions in the Book of Malachi*. BZAW 288. Berlin: de Gruyter, 2000.

Chapter 16

Jonah, Prophet Struggling with Yhwh's Mercy

Historical Setting of the Book

"Jonah, the son of Amittai" (1:1) is no doubt "Jonah, the son of Amittai, the prophet, from Gath Hepher" (2 Kgs 14:25b) in Zebulon of lower Galilee (Jos 19:10, 13). He prophesied that Jeroboam II (782–753) would restore Israel's borders formerly attained by Solomon (2 Kgs 14:25a; cf. 1 Kgs 8:65). This expansion occurred during a period of Assyrian weakness which ended with Tiglath-Pileser III (745–727 BCE), who reestablished Assyrian hegemony over the Levant. Thus, in Jonah's time Israel enjoyed a time of peace and prosperity.

While traditionally the book of Jonah was considered autobiographical, several arguments are advanced as proof that the book was not composed by the prophet himself. For some it seems unlikely that an author would level a scathing criticism against himself. The fact that Jonah does not claim authorship and is referred to in the third person is taken as another indication (Feuillet, 1975: 397). The psalm (Jonah 2) is, however, voiced in the first person as is the discourse in chapter 4. Those scholars who consider the book anonymous, put forward various proposals regarding its dating, ranging from pre- to post-exilic times. If one reasons that "great city" (3:3) refers to Nineveh as the Assyrian capital, it has to be noted that the city achieved that status only during Sennacherib's reign (705–681 BCE), that is well after Jonah's time (Sweeney, 2000: 304). Still, Nineveh was an important Assyrian city long before becoming the chief administrative center (Roux, 1985: 251). That "Nineveh *was* a great city" (3:3) for some implies that it was already destroyed (in 612

BCE) before the book's composition (Magonet, 1992: 940). But, being the narrative backbone, the past tense does not necessarily mean Nineveh was distant from the narrator's memory (cf. Gen 29:17). Thus, the arguments for a late date do not necessarily exclude the possibility that the eighth-century prophet Jonah himself composed the book. In any case, Sirach's mention of the Twelve Prophets (49:10) indicates the *terminus ad quem* of the composition of Jonah, for this evidently implies the book being regarded as Scripture by the beginning of the second century BCE.

Classifying Jonah's literary genre as parable (Allen, 1976: 181), or any other non-historical form (cf. Alexander's list of ten non-historical genres; 1988: 70), would settle the question of its historicity. If one assumes the story of the big fish that swallowed Jonah is fictional (Sweeney, 2000: 304), then Jonah would be a folktale (Sasson, 1990: 16). Whether miracles signal fictionalization or not goes beyond the scope of literary considerations. The same issue can be raised concerning the wilderness wandering narratives, the Elijah and Elisha biographies and the Gospels. Literarily, they attest that miracle stories can be part of historical narratives. Certain expressions are sometimes held to point to Jonah's fictional character, for example the "king of Nineveh" (3:6; Allen, 1976: 186) rather than the "king of Assyria" (cf. 2 Kgs 15:29; 19:36). According to Assyrian inscriptions, however, Assyrian kings who ascend the Babylonian throne are called "king of Babylon." Also, designating a king by his empire's chief city is not foreign to biblical narrative (Deut 1:4 and 2:24; Judg 4:2 and 4:17; 2 Chr 24:23; cf. Stuart, 1987: 441). Ahab, the "king of Israel" (1 Kgs 20:43), is called the "king of Samaria" (1 Kgs 21:1) because the story shifts to that city. In Jonah Nineveh is central, not Assyria. It seems that historical prophetic narrative best qualifies the book's genre.

Content and Structure of the Book

The story of Jonah is artistically composed. The four chapter scenes are symmetrically paired (Landes, 1976: 489):

1. Jonah's flight at sea from the call to go to Nineveh, and the ensuing storm (Jonah 1–2)

2. Jonah's preaching in Nineveh and the aftermath concerning the city (Jonah 3–4)

The paired scenes are then drawn into parallels by recurring narrative formulae:

1. "The word of Yhwh came to Jonah . . . : 'Arise, go to Nineveh the great city and proclaim . . .'" (1:1–2; 3:1–2);
2. "Jonah prayed to Yhwh" (2:1[2]; 4:2).

Paralleled, chapters 1 and 3 find non-Israelites, threatened with divine judgment, saved by Yhwh. Similarly, in chapters 2 and 4 Jonah, in divinely appointed dire circumstances, is delivered by Yhwh. The structure highlights Yhwh's merciful character which is also the point of the book's conclusion (Walton, 2008: 270).

Theology of the Book

Being the fifth of the twelve Minor Prophets, Jonah differs from them and all other prophetical books by its concentration on the prophet's strange experiences rather than his message (Stuart 1987: 431). All that happens to him and to those with whom he has dealings, underscores Yhwh's desire of his gracious character to be praised.

Yhwh orders Jonah to prophesy against Nineveh. In defiance, the prophet boards a ship bound in the opposite direction. Yhwh raises a storm at sea. To save the sailors, Jonah tells them to throw him overboard. They do and the sea calms. Yhwh appoints a fish to swallow Jonah. From the fish he prays for deliverance. Yhwh makes it vomit Jonah on land. Commissioned again by Yhwh, Jonah preaches in Nineveh which repents and is delivered. Jonah bemoans Yhwh's mercy.

1. Yhwh's judgment leads to salvation

The key theological point is: Yhwh compassionately delivers from judgment. Menaced with divine judgment, men are moved to seek Yhwh's saving grace. Prayers and confessions of faith are employed to underscore this theme:

Ch. 1	Jonah and sailors threatened with drowning at sea Captain's call to prayer: "call to your god . . . that we may not perish" (1:6) Jonah's credo: "I fear Yhwh . . . who made the sea [place of judgment] and the dry ground [place of deliverance]" (1:9) Sailors' prayer: "Yhwh, let us not perish" (1:14) They are delivered from drowning.

Ch. 2	Jonah in the depths of the sea
	Jonah's prayer: "I called out to Yhwh from my distress" (2:2[3])
	Jonah's credo: "Salvation belongs to Yhwh" (2:9[10])
	Fish spews him on dry ground.
Ch. 3	Ninevites about to be judged
	King's prayer: "God may ... relent and turn from his fierce anger, so that we may not perish" (3:9)
	Ninevites are delivered from disaster.
Ch. 4	Jonah desired Nineveh's doom
	Jonah's credo: "I knew that you are a gracious God and merciful, slow to anger and abounding in steadfast love, and relenting from disaster" (4:2)
	Yhwh chooses to save Nineveh.

Yhwh's acts of judgment and salvation irrupt into the realm of nature. To accomplish his purposes, he moves the wind and the waves. Even a big fish, a plant, and a tiny worm do his bidding. Nature bears witness to his prerogative to destroy or to deliver (cf. Ps 19:1–4; Rom 1:20). Ancient Near Eastern religious belief held that the gods' existences depended on the material world, some owing their origins to it. It is not so with Yhwh. At the heart of the eloquently structured narrative about the storm at sea (1:4–16; Bergey, 2006: 35–36), Jonah confesses his worship of Yhwh "who made the sea and the dry land" (1:9):

1   Yhwh hurls (טול) wind on the sea (ים);
     Storm (סער) at sea (ים) begins; sailors are afraid (5–4) (ירא)
   2   Sailors cry out (זעק) each to his gods (5) (אל אלהיו)
     3   Sailors hurl (טול) ship's cargo in the sea (ים) to lighten (inf. להקל) it for them (5) (מעליהם)
       4   Captain addresses (אמר) Jonah: "Pray ... perhaps Yhwh will give us thought" (עשת sibilant) (6)
         5   Sailors cast lots to know (ידע) who was drawing this evil; "Tell us" (נגד); they question him (8–7) (מה)
         C   Jonah's credo: "I fear [ירא] Yhwh, *the God of heaven, who made the sea* [ים] *and the dry land*" (9) (יבשה)
         5'   Sailors, fearful, now know (ידע) because Jonah told (נגד) them; they question him (11–10) (מה)
       4'   Jonah addresses (אמר) the sailors: "Hurl me into the sea ... it will quiet down' (שתק sibilant) (12)
     3'   Sailors row hard to return (inf. להשיב) to dry ground (יבשה); storm grows stronger against them (13) (עליהם)
   2'   Sailors cry out (קרא) to Yhwh (14) (אל יהוה)

Jonah, Prophet Struggling with Yhwh's Mercy

1' Sailors pray and hurl (טול) Jonah in the sea (ים); storm's raging (זעף) at sea (ים) ceases; they greatly fear (ירא) Yhwh (15–16)

The framed central element, Jonah's credo, is not the classical confession of Yhwh, creator of the "heavens" and "earth" (e.g., Gen 2:4; Exod 20:11; Neh 9:6). Here he is the maker of the "sea," where his judgment is experienced, and the "dry land" (יבשה), where deliverance from drowning is found. Yhwh who made both can use one to destroy and the other to save. These terms are juxtaposed elsewhere only in passages describing the Egyptians' judgment in the sea and the Israelites' deliverance by their crossing on dry ground (Exod 14:16, 22, 29; 15:19; Neh 9:11; Ps 66:6). Vomited on "dry land" Jonah was delivered from the sea (2:10[11]). The fourfold recurrence of Yhwh's "appointing" (מנה) also highlights this theme: he first appoints two saving objects, the fish and the plant (1:17 [2:1]; 4:6), then two which destroy, the worm and the dry wind (4:7, 8).

2. Yhwh's mercy overcomes judgment

Yhwh can "relent" (נחם) of the disaster, or "evil" (רעה), he said he would do (3:10; 4:2), just as he did as a result of Moses' intercession concerning the golden calf incident (Exod 32:12, 14). It is not that his prophetic word—"Yet forty days, and Nineveh shall be overthrown" (3.4)—failed (cf. Childs, 1979: 420). He can judge evil by threatening "evil" (1:7, 8) in order to graciously deliver those who turn to him from it (3:8, 10a). The prophet Jeremiah uses the very language of this lesson driven home in Jonah to exhort his contemporaries: "if that nation, concerning which I have spoken, turns from its evil, I will relent of the disaster [ונחמתי על הרעה] that I intended to do to it" (18:8).

Yhwh's gracious character is described in a confessional way (4:2b, 11; cf. Exod 34:6–7); its outworking is seen in his saving acts, in particular of non-Israelites. Jonah first fled the call to go to Nineveh because he knew Yhwh would show mercy (4:2a). Yhwh delivered Jonah from the sea and the fish in order to save Nineveh from judgment through the preaching of the prophetic word, the instrument of his grace (1:2; 3:2, 10; 4:11). Moreover, Jonah's confession of faith during the storm at sea (1:9) resulted in the foreign sailors worshiping Yhwh (1:16).

Ironically, Yhwh's deliverance of the Ninevites provokes Jonah's anger (4:1). His unexpected reaction stands in sharp contrast with his thanksgiving for his own deliverance expressed in the psalm (2:2[3],

9[10]). Rather than gratitude for Yhwh's grace shown to others, Jonah ventilates his petty displeasure over the loss of personal comforts (the miraculous vine, 4:6). His self-centeredness is confronted by Yhwh himself in the last verses: "You pity the plant . . . should not I pity Nineveh . . . ?" (4:10, 11). As channels of his compassion for others, Yhwh's question invites all readers to reflect upon their values, priorities, and prejudices.

3. Jonah and the New Testament

Jesus' mysterious mention of "the sign of Jonah" (Matt 12:39; 16:4; Luke 11:29), linking his burial to Jonah's three days and nights in the fish (Matt 12:40; Jonah 1:17[2:1]), draws upon the Ninevites' deliverance through repentance and faith in the word Jonah preached (cf. Matt 12:41; Luke 11:30, 32). "Greater than Jonah," Jesus exhorts his listeners to heed this lesson. As a "wicked and adulterous generation" (Matt. 12:39), they are destined for judgment like the Ninevites of Jonah's day, unless they listen to God's word through Jesus.

The *Mekilta of Rabbi Ishmael* (beginning of the second century CE, but holding many older traditions) views the "death" of Jonah as voluntary and vicarious since he said: "throw me into the sea" (1:12). He is like Moses and David who asked God to take their lives to save Israel (cf. Exod 33:31; Num 11:15; 2 Sam 24:17). This tradition was no doubt familiar to Jesus and his hearers. For Jonah and Jesus, their deliverance from death by being raised up (Jonah 2:6[7]) after three days and nights was miraculous. Like Jonah's reappearance, Jesus' resurrection on the third day affirmed the authenticity of his word and mission.

The story of Jonah illustrates the instrumental role of God's covenant people to bring salvation to the nations. It demonstrates the sovereign outworking of Yhwh's covenant promises that nations, through faith in his word, would be blessed through Abraham's descendants (e.g., Gen 12:1-3; 17:5; Isa 42:1, 6; 49:6-7; 65:1; Acts 3:25; Gal 3:7-9). Such promises laid the foundation for Paul's evangelistic ministry to the Gentiles and all subsequent missions' activity (Rom 10:11-21; 15:9-12, 16; Eph 3:6).

Bibliography

Alexander, T. Desmond, et al. *Obadiah, Jonah and Micah*, TOTC 23. Leicester, UK: InterVarsity, 1988.

Allen, Leslie C. *The Books of Joel, Obadiah, Jonah and Micah*, NICOT. Grand Rapids: Eerdmans, 1976.

Bergey, Ronald. "Le Crédo de Jonas dans le récit de la tempête en mer." In *Texte et historicité, Récit biblique et histoire. Aiguillages théologiques*, edited by Pierre Berthoud and Paul Wells, 29–40. Aix-en-Provence, France: Kerygma, 2006.

Childs, Brevard S. *Introduction to the Old Testament as Scripture*. Philadelphia: Fortress, 1979.

Feuillet, André. "Le Livre de Jonas." In *Etudes d'exégèse et de théologie biblique, Ancien Testament*, 395–433. Paris: Gabalda, 1975.

Landes, George M. "Jonah, Book of." In *Interpreter's Dictionary of the Bible, Supplementary Volume*, edited by Keith R. Crim and George A. Buttrick, 488–91. Nashville, TN: Abingdon, 1976.

Magonet, Jonathan. *Form and Meaning: Studies in Literary Techniques in the Book of Jonah*. Sheffield, UK: Almond, 1983.

———. "Jonah, Book of." In *Anchor Bible Dictionary*, vol. 3, edited by David Noel Freeman, 936–42. New York: Doubleday, 1992.

Roux, Georges. *La Mésopotamie, Essai d'histoire politique, économique et culturelle*. Paris: Seuil, 1985.

Sasson, Jack M. *Jonah*, Anchor Bible 24B. New York: Doubleday, 1990.

Stuart, Douglas. *Hosea-Jonah*. Word Biblical Commentary 31. Waco, TX: Word, 1987.

Sweeney, Marvin A. *The Twelve Prophets 1. Berit Olam. Studies in Hebrew Narrative and Poetry*. Edited by David W. Cotter. Collegeville, PA: Liturgical, 2000.

Trible, Phyllis. *Rhetorical Criticism, Context, Method and the Book of Jonah*. Guides to Biblical Scholarship. Minneapolis: Fortress, 1994.

Walton, John H. "Jonah." In *Theological Interpretation of the Old Testament*, edited by Kevin J. Vanhoozer, 268–75. Grand Rapids: Baker Academic, 2008.

Chapter 17

Joel, Prophet Proclaiming God's Future Judgment

Historical Setting of the Book

UNLIKE SEVERAL PROPHETIC BOOKS in the Old Testament, the title of this book presents no historical information other than that the prophet Joel was a son of Pethuel, a person otherwise unknown. This signifies either of two possibilities: either (1) the prophet Joel was well known to the primary readers of his book so that no other explanation was needed; or (2) knowledge about his time was not essential for the understanding of his message. In fact, if this book was, as has often been argued, "a liturgical text intended for repeated use on occasion of national lament" (Dillard, 2009: 243; cf. Ogden, 1983: 97–106), details about the historical background might not be a help, but rather a hindrance to its purpose. Though it is true that the book is richly concerned with cultic matters (1:9, 13–14; 2:12, 14–15), however, there is no clear evidence to support the claim that it was originally intended as a cultic liturgy (Allen, 1976: 31).

In spite of the uncertainties about the origin of the book, several details in the book make it possible to infer the time when Joel was active. For example, the book contains historical details such as the outbreak of a terrible plague of locusts (1:4), the oppression of the Jews by foreigners and the Jewish Diaspora (3:1–5[4:1–5]), the Philistines and the Phoenicians who sold the Jews into slavery to the Greeks (3:6[4:6]), the priests and the elders being regarded as the leaders of the people (1:13; 2:17), and the presence of the temple and the city wall (1:14; 2:7, 9). Nevertheless, since these historical data can be interpreted in various ways, they may not sufficiently settle the historical issues involved in the interpretation of the book. Even though each of these historical data can be interpreted in various ways, being combined they point to the situation of the post-exilic Jewish community as the background of the book. To be more precise, the late fifth century or the early fourth century, when the priests played a dominant role around the rebuilt temple of Jerusalem (cf. Ezra 7; Neh 11:3; 12:1).

Content and Structure of the Book

The book of Joel is divided in two parts, the first of which deals with a national disaster that already happened and yet will come in the future (1:2—2:17), the second with the restoration of Israel and the judgment of her enemies (2:18—3:17[2:18—4:17]). The fact that the declaration of "the Day of Yhwh" is scattered throughout in both parts (1:15; 2:1b, 2a, 11b; 2:31[3:4]; 3:1, 14, 18a[4:1, 14, 18a]) indicates that the aforementioned disaster/judgment and restoration are somehow related to an eschatological event in a direct or indirect manner. It is often claimed, however, that the "Day of Yhwh" passages in chapters 1 and 2 are secondarily interpolated, because they do not fit the surrounding context (Bewer, 1974: 56). According to this theory, a later eschatologist who wrote 2:28—3:21[3:1—4:21] inserted the "Day of Yhwh" passages into the existing literary piece (1:1—2:27) and combined it with his own writing. As a result, it is argued, the plague of locusts and the famine described in chapters 1 and 2 are also turned into eschatological events (Bewer, 1974: 65; Kaiser, 1984: 293). Since, however, the "Day of Yhwh" passages in chapters 1 and 2 match well with the theme and the style of the whole book, they can hardly be excluded as secondary (Harrison, 1991: 875; cf. Zenger, 2008: 530).

In fact, each part of the book of Joel is well organized as an organic whole, as has already been pointed out by several scholars (cf. Prinsloo, 1985: 4). The locust plague (1:4) and the ensuing call to lament and repentance (1:5-20) structurally correspond to the portrayal of Yhwh's army which will invade Israel on the Day of Yhwh (2:1-11) and the following call to lament and repentance (2:12-17), respectively. Furthermore, the message of restoration in 2:18ff. is tantamount to God's answer to the foregoing lament and repentance. In particular, as the disaster and the call to repentance are twofold, so is the message of restoration: 2:18–27 tells about the rehabilitation of the economic plight caused by the plague of locusts (cf. Treier, 1997: 15) and then 2:28—3:17[3:1—4:17] focuses on the eschatological renewal starting from the outpouring of the Spirit. That 2:28—3:17 deals with the eschatological events distinct from those historical ones in 2:18-27 can be deduced from the fact that it ends with the words "you will know," the same recognition formula that closes the passage in 2:18-27, thereby forming a clear literary parallel to the latter. Lastly, 1:1 and 1:2–3 form the title and the introduction, respectively, whereas 3:18–21[4:18-21] form the conclusion.

The above-mentioned can be illustrated with the following scheme:

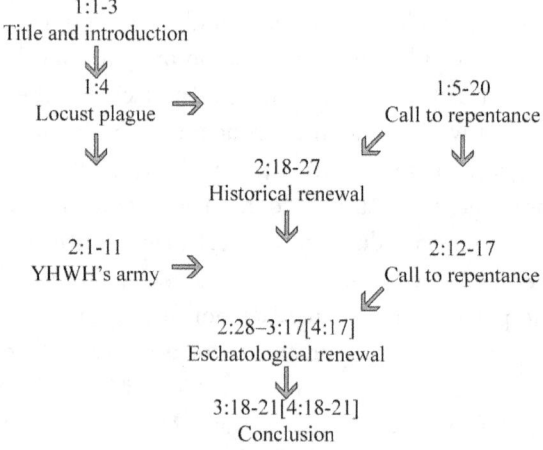

Theology of the Book

The book's structure as delineated above indicates that the prophet Joel interpreted the national catastrophes in his days as the ominous forerunners of the Day of YHWH. According to the prophetic tradition held in ancient Israel, he warned both his contemporaries and later generations that YHWH would once appear on earth, acting in judgment against those hostile to him and his people (Isa 13; Ezek 30:3; Amos 5; Zeph 1; Zech 14:1). So it is obvious that the Day of YHWH stands out as the most prominent theological theme of this book.

Joel, Prophet Proclaiming God's Future Judgment

1. The Day of Yhwh

As was already indicated before, the phrase "the Day of Yhwh" (1:15; 2:1, 11, 31[3:4]; 3:14[4:14]) and similar expressions such as "a day" (2x in 2:2), "the day' (1:15), "that day" (3:18[4:18]) and "those days" (2:29[3:2]; 3:1[4:1]) occur quite often in the book. As W. Kaiser explains aptly, "the Day of Yhwh" refers to "a generic or collective event in which are gathered all the antecedent historical episodes of judgment and salvation along with the future grand finale and climactic event in the whole series" (Kaiser, 1983: 111). This viewpoint can be substantiated from the way in which Joel relates the present locust disaster to the coming eschatological event when Yhwh will visit his people, commanding his great and mighty army at their front (2:11). Although it is often argued that the two calamities described in chapters 1 and 2, whether natural or military, represent the historical events transpired in Joel's time (Stuart, 1987: 231; Bewer, 1974: 52), both the future tense (*yiqtol* verbs) and the apocalyptic tints appearing in 2:1–11 testify that this passage deals with Yhwh's eschatological act as distinct from the historical one described in 1:4–13.

As the prophet Amos compared the Day of Yhwh to darkness and gloom (Amos 5:18–20), Joel does the same thing in 2:2, 10, 31[3:4]. Using phraseology and images associated with the invasion of swarming locusts, Joel warns that on that day the earth will be devastated like areas consumed by fire (2:3–6) and the cities be destroyed by Yhwh's own army (2:7–9). The only way for the people to avoid this complete destruction is to return to Yhwh with fasting, weeping, and mourning (2:12). Some scholars hesitate to associate the prophet's call to return as such with the call to repentance because there is no mention in the book of any specific sin the people might have committed (Ogden, 1983: 105; Simkins, 1993: 446). However, the statement "rend your heart and not your garments" in 2:13 clearly indicates that the people were then alienated from God in their sinfulness, which necessitated a heartrending repentance on their part in order to be reconciled to him.

This being granted, it is curious why the prophet Joel does not spell out the people's wrongdoings, all the more so because other prophets painstakingly do that. According to A. Schart, who emphasizes the importance of reading the twelve minor prophets in their relationship with each other as an organic whole, the lack of information about the people's sin in Joel can be filled out by inferring knowledge from the adjacent books, i.e., Hosea and Amos (Schart, 2007: 142–43). In this case, it may be argued that what the prophet Joel had in mind when he called the people to repentance was their idolatry (i.e., the Baal cult with its fertility rites). Yet, it is too speculative to assume that the Baal fertility cults still posed a threat to the faith community in Joel's time. Another theory attributes Joel's silence about the people's sin to the book's literary character as a liturgy (Dillard, 2009: 243). Indeed, it is undeniable that the book shows a favorable attitude to cult (cf. 1:13; 2:14). To the present writer, however, it seems wiser to assume that the prophet Joel deliberately avoided specifying the people's sin, so that his prophetic message could be effectively appropriated by future generations with their own problems (cf. 1:3).

2. God who is gracious and compassionate

Although, as already pointed out, the book has a high regard for cult, it does not suppose that the cult itself guarantees its participants the divine blessing. Rather, the "who knows" clause in 2:14 highlights Yhwh's freedom to do anything he wants, whether it is to forgive the people and rescue them or to leave them to further disaster (Zenger, 2008: 533). This does not mean, however, that the image of God the prophet Joel envisages is that of a capricious god whose behavior is arbitrary and, therefore, not trustworthy at all. Citing both from Exodus 32:12, 14 and Exodus 34:4, Joel draws his audience's attention to the fact that Yhwh is "gracious and compassionate, slow to anger and abounding in love, and repenting of evil" (2:13). It is the image of this merciful God that Joel had in mind when he urged the people to return to their God, Yhwh (Prinsloo, 1985: 124). Accordingly, the idea that any cultic activity in and of itself would bring the present plight to an end is foreign to the book of Joel.

The prophet Joel anticipates the reversal of the national disaster solely from Yhwh who is zealous for his land and has compassion on his people (2:18). According to Joel, Yhwh in his great compassion will answer the heartrending repentance and prayer of his people (2:19a) and drive out the locust army far away from the land (2:20). Interestingly, the locust army is here designated as הצפוני (*haṣṣĕphônî* "the northerner"), a term reminiscent of the traditional prophetic motif of "the enemy from the north" (Jer 4:6, 7; Ezek 38:15; 39:2). For this reason, not a few commentators understand the locust plague in the book of Joel *figuratively* as symbolizing an Assyrian or Babylonian invasion on Israel (Stuart, 1987:

232–34; Garrett, 1997: 298). However, the use of the designation הצפוני (*haṣṣĕphônî* "the northerner") has to be explained in relation to the book's overall concern about eschatology. That is to say, since the prophet Joel foresees in the present locust plague the eschatological enemy invading the people of God, he applies to the locust army "an eschatological notion colored by both Jeremiah's and Ezekiel's usage" (Allen, 1976: 88–89; cf. Wolff, 1985: 74). Seen in this way, the propitious end of the historical locust plague foretold in 2:18–27 can be appreciated as a pledge of the eschatological restoration to be realized in the Day of Yhwh.

Besides the mention of the destruction of the locust army, it is stated in 2:21–26 that Yhwh will graciously restore the fertility of the land in response to the repentance of the people. It is noteworthy that the three addresses of the threefold call to rejoice in 2:21–23—i.e., land, beasts of the field, and sons of Zion—correspond to those affected by the locust plague and their bitter laments described in 1:5–20 (Wolff, 1985: 75). This again indicates that the return of fertility is promised in answer to the people's lament about their despairing conditions due to the locust plague. As a prophetic spokesman for the Lord, Joel proclaims that Yhwh will repay the people for the years that the various locust swarms have eaten (2:25). Furthermore, it is assured in 2:23 with the *perfectum propheticum* that Yhwh will send them the *autumn rain* as well as the *spring rain*, both covenant blessings mentioned in Deuteronomy 11:13–15, which will result in a rich harvest of grain and an overflowing of the new wine and oil in the vats (2:24). As stated above, the restoration of the fertility as such should be taken as pointing to the ultimate renewal of the earth which will come true in the future (cf. 3:18 [4:18]).

Here it is worth mentioning that in 2:18–27, where God's restorative intervention is highlighted, some specific covenant ideas come to the fore. For instance, those who are given the promise of restoration are called *God's people* in particular, a title imbued with the covenant concept: עמו (*'ammô* "his people") in verse 18, עמי (*'ammî* "my people") in verses 26 and 27. Likewise, Yhwh is entitled אלהיכם (*'ĕlōhêkem* "your God") in vs. 23, 26–27, a designation bringing God's relationship with his people into relief. Moreover, God addresses his people time and again with the personal pronoun "you," stressing his intimate relationship with them. Most of all, the statement at the end of this passage, i.e., that God would be in the midst of Israel and he alone would be their God, is nearly the same as the standard covenant formula. All these instances prove that the promised restoration in 2:18–27 is no other than the covenant blessing sanctioned through the covenant relationship between Yhwh and his people (cf. Deut 28:1–14). If this is true, the locust plague and the drought described in chapters 1 and 2 can be viewed as the covenant curses to be imposed on those who break the covenant (cf. Deut 28: 23–24, 42). Thus, we could say that the book of Joel bears witness to Yhwh's covenant loyalty who eventually restores his people after a short period of discipline (cf. Isa 54:7, 8; Hos 6:1).

3. The outpouring of the Spirit and the final judgment

Having the preceding point clarified, it is necessary to remember once again that God's restoring activities as described in 2:18–27 look forward to the eschatological restoration. The prophet Joel explains in 2:28—3:17 [3:1—4:17] how those final *magnalia Dei* will turn out to be. First of all, he mentions the pouring out of God's Spirit upon כל־בשׂר (*kol-bāsār*: "all flesh") in 2:28–29 [3:1–2]. No doubt, by the words "all flesh" Joel does not refer to all human beings, but to those faithful "remnants" who call upon the name of Yhwh (cf. 2:32[3:5]). Joel promises that these remnants will experience the so-called *democratization* of the Spirit (Stuart, 1987: 229). This means that the selectivity that limits the gift of the Spirit to some individuals, will be abrogated, so that everyone will have a direct access to the presence and revelation of God in the same way as the ancient prophets had: prophesying, dreaming dreams, and seeing visions (2:28[3:1]; cf. Num 11:29). According to the New Testament writers, Joel's prophecy about the Spirit was fulfilled on the day of Pentecost (Acts 2:16–21). Since the gift of the Spirit ensures the people the eschatological fellowship with their God, the Spirit's outpouring on Pentecost can rightly be understood as "'the beginning' of the progression of the Day of the Lord" (VanGemeren, 1988: 97).

Directly connected to the prophecy about the outpouring of the Spirit, the prophet Joel speaks about other eschatological phenomena, mostly gloomy and dreadful in nature: wonders in the heavens and on the earth, namely blood, fire, and columns of smoke (2:30 [3:3]), the sun darkening and the moon becoming blood (2:31 [3:4]). Together with these enigmatic words reminding us of the theophany on Mount Sinai there occurs expressions like "deliverance," "escape," "survivors," and most of all "the great and terrible Day of Yhwh" (2:31–32[3:4–5]). Thus, these verses make clear that the Day of Yhwh also has a negative, destructive side; it will bring judgment upon those who rebel against Yhwh, and oppress and mishandle his people (cf. Treier, 1997: 21).

Indeed, the passage in 3:1–17[4:1–17]) reveals how Yhwh is going to take vengeance on them by "returning their deeds on their head" (3:8 [4:8]). In particular, Joel mentions here the great final combat between Yhwh and his enemies which will take place in the valley of judgment, i.e., the valley of יהושפט (*Yehôšāfāṭ*: "Yhwh has judged"). In this decisive war all the nations threatening God's people will be destroyed just as the grapes being trampled in the winepress (3:13[4:13]; cf. Rev 14:17–20). This will happen because Yhwh, as the mighty divine warrior, will fight on behalf of his people. The latter is most vividly illustrated with the image of a lion roaring in the wilderness (3:16[4:16]; cf. Amos 1:2): "Yhwh will roar from Zion and thunder from Jerusalem."

Joel's Message for Current Believers

Lastly, it is necessary to think in brief concerning the implication the message of the prophet Joel has for us as modern believers. As is explained above, Joel foresaw the approach of the Day of Yhwh in the locust plague of his days and delivered the prophetic message about it. It could be said that Joel's prophecy has been fulfilled through Jesus' earthly ministry culminating in his crucifixion, since the latter brought about the promised salvation while, at the same time, setting the seal on the destructive destiny of unbelievers (John 3:18). The fact that Jesus regarded John the Baptist as the prophet Elijah who had been supposed to come right before "the great and terrible Day of Yhwh" (Mal 4:5) also supports the idea that Joel's prophecy was already fulfilled through Jesus Christ. This is further substantiated by the fact that the outpouring of the Spirit as promised in the book of Joel took place on the day of Pentecost after Jesus' resurrection (Acts 2:16–21).

In spite of all these evidences, however, it is undeniable that we still live in the world where the salvation Jesus achieved through his redemptive work is being constantly threatened by the evil powers of all kinds. It is in this context that the New Testament writers draw our attention to "the Day of the Lord," i.e., Jesus' *parousia*, when the evil powers will be utterly destroyed (1 Thess 5:2; 2 Thess 2:2; 2 Pet 3:10). At that time, the present world will be completely renewed to the blissful Paradise as the prophet Joel anticipated in 3:18[4:18]. It is by no means off the mark, therefore, to say that the various natural disasters sweeping over the entire world in our days function to remind us of the Day of the Lord approaching as the locust plague in Joel's time (cf. Garrett, 1997: 325). Through the book of Joel, as it were, YHWH still speaks to his people as the lion roaring in the wilderness: "Repent of your sinfulness and return to me!"

Bibliography

Allen, L. C. *The Books of Joel, Obadiah, Jonah, and Micah*. New International Commentary on the Old Testament. Grand Rapids: Eerdmans, 1976.

Bewer, J. A. *Obadiah and Joel*. International Critical Commentary. Edinburgh: T. & T. Clark, 1974.

Dillard, R. B. "Joel." In *The Minor Prophets: An Exegetical and Expository Commentary*, edited by Thomas E. McComiskey, 239–313. Grand Rapids: Baker Academic, 2009.

Garrett, D. A. *Hosea, Joel*. New American Commentary. Nashville, TN: Broadman & Holman, 1997.

Harrison, R. K. *Introduction to the Old Testament*. Grand Rapids: Eerdmans, 1991.

Kaiser, O. *Einleitung in das Alte Testament*, 5th ed. Gütersloh: Gütersloher, 1984.

Kaiser, W. "The Promise of God and the Outpouring of the Holy Spirit: Joel 2:28–32 and Acts 2:16–21." In *The Living and Active Word of God: Studies in Honor of Samuel J. Schultz*, edited by M. Inch and R. Youngblood, 109–22. Winona Lake, IN: Eisenbrauns 1983.

Ogden, G. S. "Joel 4 and Prophetic Responses to National Laments." *Journal for the Study of the Old Testament* 26 (1983) 97–106.

Prinsloo, W. S. *The Theology of the Book of Joel*. Beihefte zur Zeitschrift für die alttestamentliche Wissenschaft 163. Berlin: de Gruyter, 1985.

Schart, A. "The First Section of the Book of the Twelve Prophets: Hosea—Joel—Amos." *Interpretation* 61.2 (2007) 138–52.

Simkins, R. A. "God, History, and the Natural World in the Book of Joel." *Catholic Biblical Quarterly* 55 (1993) 435–52.

Treier, D. J. "The Fulfillment of Joel 2:28–32: A Multiple-Lens Approach." *Journal of the Evangelical Theological Society* 40.1 (1997) 13–26.

VanGemeren, W. A. "The Spirit of Restoration." *Westminster Theological Journal* 50 (1988) 81–102.

Wolff, H. W. *Dodekapropheton. Joel und Amos*. Biblischer Kommentar Altes Testament, 3rd ed. Neukirchen-Vluyn: Neukirchener, 1985.

Zenger, E. "Das Zwölfprophetenbuch." In *Einleitung in das Alte Testament*, 7th ed., edited by E. Zenger et al., 517–86. Studienbücher Theologie. Stuttgart: Kohlhammer, 2008.

Chapter 18

Daniel, Prophet of Divine Presence in Absence

Historical Setting of the Book

THE FINAL AUTHORS OR group responsible for the book of Daniel lived during a period of intense persecution for the Jewish people, and thus situated their book in a time of similar suffering. The epoch of the Babylonian exile forms the backdrop to proclaiming a message of hope to Jews living in Palestine in the second century BCE. These authors combined much older and well-known narratives, symbolic language and prophetic forms to suggest an alternative outcome to turmoil facing the faithful inhabitants of Jerusalem at the time.

The sixth-century exile referred to in the book was a time of disorientation for God's people. The biblical documents that were edited during this period provide the vivid details. In scholarly circles, the books dealing with Israel's history are referred to as the Deuteronomistic History (Joshua—2 Kings). The book of Deuteronomy lays a theological foundation for this subsequent telling of the story of Israel. One of the theological thrusts in the book implies that the people's lack of obedience towards their covenant with God will result in punishment. On the other hand, obedience will incur divine blessings (see Deut 28).

The actual story of Israel opens on a splendid note in the book of Joshua. The Israelites conquer the land that God promised to Abraham, their great ancestor (Gen 15:13–16). However, the story ultimately ends in shame when this Promised Land is lost (2 Kgs 25). Also, the everlasting line of kings God promised to King David (2 Sam 7) seemingly came to an end. Last, but surely not least, the temple that for many guaranteed that God was in their midst (Jer 7:4) was looted in 597 BCE and ultimately destroyed in 586 BCE by the Babylonians. A theological conundrum stared the exiled religious leaders in the face: how could God have allowed things to go so wrong?

The book of Daniel introduces the character for whom the book is named as one of the Jewish exiles, probably captured during the deportation in 597 BCE. The historical details given in Daniel 1:1 are not supported by our knowledge of the events referred to. What is clear from the last verse of this chapter, though, is that the author wants to remind the reader about the whole era of exile. Hence both the Babylonian king Nebuchadnezzar II (634–562 BCE) (Dan 1:1), who is responsible for the exile, and the Persian king Cyrus II (576–530 BCE) (Dan 1:21), who is hailed for its end by allowing the Jews in Babylon to return to Palestine, are noted. A similar fate as that of the exile of the sixth century BCE, but even more frightening, faced a later Jewish community in Jerusalem, midway through the first half of the second century BCE.

Most scholars agree that for the Jewish people in the Persian province of Yehud, including Palestine, the roughly two centuries after the exile were mostly peaceful. The books of Ezra and Nehemiah remind us, however, that at the same time periods of internal strife occurred in this part of the Empire. Originally, the first six narratives in the book of Daniel seem to be aimed at Jews living outside Palestine during this time. As is the case in the books of Nehemiah and Esther, the main characters of these narratives in Daniel occupied high positions at the court of foreign rulers; this may suggest that members of a later target audience found themselves in similar circumstances. In Daniel 1–6 the foreign rulers are depicted as having lived in previous and less peaceful epochs, namely the time of Babylonian and Median rule. The narratives in the first part of the book have also been described as illustrating a lifestyle for Jews living in this foreign environment (Humphreys, 1973). Although the narratives depict Jews in influential positions at foreign courts, however, it does not necessarily mean that such people were the only implied audience. Daniel and his friends could also serve as role models for people with no or very little influence in such high circles.

The Achaemenid Period, as the time of Persian ascendency in the ancient world is referred to, came to an end when Alexander the Great (356–323 BCE) conquered the Persian Empire in 334 BCE. When he died merely a decade later, his four most influential generals laid claim to the empire. Initially, Palestine came under the Ptolemaic Empire, but in 198

Daniel, Prophet of Divine Presence in Absence

BCE the Seleucid emperor Antiochus III (241–187 BCE) brought it under his control. The Seleucid animosity towards the Ptolemaic regime in the south continued under the reign of Antiochus' eventual successor and son, Antiochus Ephiphanes IV (215–164 BCE).

During a campaign against Egypt in 168 BCE a rumor reached Jerusalem that Antiochus IV had died. This set in motion a chain of actions that was co-determined by earlier events.

When Antiochus IV came to power in 175 BCE, Onias III, the high priest, held the highest religious office in Jerusalem. However, Onias' brother, Jason, offered Antiochus a large sum of money in order to be named high priest in Onias' stead. The king accepted the offer, but a mere three years later was persuaded by the promise of a higher bid to name Menelaus high priest. Jason fled from Jerusalem; on hearing the rumor of Antiochus' death he returned to the city to claim back the office he had vacated. The subsequent unrest in Jerusalem led to Antiochus cracking down on the Jewish population: he killed thousands and committed sacrilege in the temple in 167 BCE. Only three years later, after an initial Maccabean uprising, the temple was rededicated.

Both the number of copies of sections from the book of Daniel and the fragments related to the book found at Qumran indicate that the ancient stories about Daniel were still popular during the second century BCE. During this time the stories found a new relevance when they were combined with accounts of the visionary experiences of a specific group. This group was opposed to the militant actions of the Maccabees, and instead waited for direct heavenly intervention to solve the crisis on earth.

Content and Structure of the Book

The reader of the twelve chapters of the book of Daniel in their original languages is challenged by the fact that the book is written partly in Aramaic (Dan 2:4b—7:28) and partly in Hebrew (Dan 1:1—2:4a; 8:1—12:17). Furthermore, this language division does not mirror the two broad literary types the book exhibits, i.e., six court tales (Dan 1–6) and four visions (Dan 7–12). Although many explanations for this phenomenon have been suggested it is perhaps best to view the present form of the book as a deliberate attempt on the part of the authors to convey a specific and focused message. This means that we should give serious consideration to the three-part division created by the use of different languages when trying to understand the theology of the book.

The concentric structure of the Aramaic section of the book was discussed at length by Lenglet (1974). Goldingay (1989a: 8) noted a similar structure in the introductory chapter of the book, written in Hebrew. Later Boccaccini (2002: 171–72) suggested that the last part of the book, also written in Hebrew, reflects a similar concentric pattern. From a literary point of view this structure is important. It implies a focus on those parts that form the core of each of the three sections, the Introduction (Dan 1), the Aramaic part (Dan 2–7), and the Hebrew part (Dan 8–12). This unique structure can be presented as follows:

Introduction (Daniel 1)

1:1–2			General setting—beginning of the exile (a)
	1:3–7		Specific setting—beginning of the court training (b)
		1:8–16	*Central narrative—refusing defiling food (c)*
	1:17–20		Specific setting—end of the court training (b')
1:21			General setting—end of the exile (a')

Aramaic section (Daniel 2–7)

2:1–49*			Four world empires and their end (focus on the first) (a)
	3:1–30		Religious persecution—group crisis (b)
		4:1[3:31]—5:30	*Central narratives—human hubris and consequences (c)*
	6:1–29		Religious persecution—individual crisis (b')
7:1–28			Four world empires and their end (focus on the last) (a')

* 2:1–4a is written in Hebrew to bridge the Introduction and the Aramaic section.

Hebrew section (Daniel 8–12)

8:1–27			Concise vision related to second century—duration of tyranny (a)
	9:1–3		Scriptural revelation—duration of repression (b)
		9:4–19	*Central penitential prayer—reason for repression and tyranny (c)*
	9:20–27		Scriptural interpretation—duration of repression (b')
10:1—12:13			Extended vision related to second century—duration of tyranny (a')

Daniel, Prophet of Divine Presence in Absence

Our discussion will follow the suggested structure of the book. While each of the ten units in the book will be discussed, special attention should be paid to Daniel 1:8–16; Daniel 4–5; and Daniel 9.

Theology of the Book

The book of Daniel packs a powerful message in a powerful manner. It reveals how God, depicted as an awe-inspiring universal ruler, acts in unique ways to the benefit of his afflicted servants in a local context.

1. Introduction (Dan 1): the hidden presence of a giving God

Daniel 1 is structured concentrically around a central narrative (vv. 8–16). The narrative tells of a decision by Daniel not to defile himself by eating food presented to the Jewish captives undergoing training at the Babylonian court. Encircling this central episode are two "layers." The outer layer (vv. 1–2; 21) gives a time frame spanning the exilic period. Also, three earthly kings and the heavenly Sovereign are introduced. The opening verses narrate how a Judean king is "given" (נתן) into the hand of the Babylonian king. The alarming addition to this statement makes God the subject of the action (v. 2). The text presupposes some knowledge of the history of Israel as it is known from the historical narratives in the Old Testament. Here, however, no explanation is given for God's harsh hand in these events. The closing verse of the chapter refers to another foreign emperor, Cyrus the Persian king. The rulers mentioned in the opening verses did not prevail, a new empire holds sway.

The inner layer (vv. 3–7; 17–20) surrounding the central story adjusts the scope from the broader context of the Babylonian exile to focus on the Babylonian court. Here the young and handsome male captives undergo three years of specialized training. The selection criteria for getting onto the course involved physical and intellectual attributes (v. 4). These youths become the objects of a series of actions by others: they are "brought" in (vv. 3, 17); "set" a portion of food (v. 5); "given" new names (v. 7); "spoken" to (v. 19) and "found" to be the best (v. 20). But besides being *acted upon* by other human characters, they find that God *acts towards* them favorably when he "gives" (נתן) them the intellectual qualities (cf. v. 4) they need for service at the foreign court (v. 17).

225

A further narrowing of the focus introduces the central episode. For the first time one of the Jewish characters acts, and does so with conviction. Daniel takes a firm stand not to "defile" himself with the food and wine presented to the trainees. He requests of the superior officer not to make him eat the food of the king (v. 8). At this junction the reader is informed about another act of God: just as in the outer and inner layers God is depicted in the central story as the One who "gives" (נתן), Daniel is given "favor and compassion" (NRSV) before the superior officer. However, it is not this officer who is responsible for the eventual favorable outcome. A lower-ranking servant ultimately adheres to Daniel's request and places the four objectors on their requested diet of vegetables and water. The result is that the appearance of these four young men is remarkably better than that of the rest.

This first chapter reveals one of the claims regarding God that the rest of the book will echo: God controls major and minor events. The major event in this case is the changing of the political landscape. God's action of giving over his people and some of the temple utensils to a foreign empire is not explained here—that comes only later in the book (Dan. 9). Although this event had severely negative consequences for the Jewish people, the opening chapter claims that in the last analysis God stands behind such inexplicable events.

God's control extends to minor events, particularly to the lives of individuals. He sometimes hardens the hearts of individuals for the sake of his people (e.g., the Pharaoh in Exod 9–10). But in Daniel 1 God can be said to soften the heart of an official appointed to oversee the training of the youths in Babylon. The text reveals that God gives Daniel favor in the eyes of the official. In the context of the story, God's action seems to reward Daniel for upholding his convictions. The text makes clear that Daniel did not express this inner conviction in a militant or reactionary manner. He expresses his wish not to eat the food in an "aside" to the official (v. 8). Furthermore, the other Jewish youths are not faulted for sticking to the prescribed diet. In a pluralistic context God can act to the benefit of the many by means of his involvement with the few. The diet Daniel and his friends require is not prescribed in any code of law. Their decision, rather, is fuelled by the urge to express their commitment to God in a unique way. Their reward indicates that God favors those who go beyond the mere letter of the law to show their allegiance. Though Daniel's first attempt is not met by immediate success (v. 10) he finds God's favor extending even to the attitude of their guard. Perhaps knowing that the superior officer will turn a blind eye, the guard fulfills the request.

Immediately after the central story the reader encounters God again as giver. He is credited for providing the four youths with all they need for their service, and more (v. 17). Daniel is also given insight into dreams. God does not remove his representatives from foreign contexts. He does not require them to hide near the fringes of such a society. No, he bestows gifts on them, to allow them to be extremely successful in a less than desirable context. In a secular world, believers should take note of this and take heart.

The theological lines drawn in this introductory chapter are reflected in the rest of the book. Despite seemingly bringing about the broader negative circumstances we have discussed (the frightening fate of the Jewish community in second-century BC Palestine; see "Historical setting of the book"), God is also the one who, in a particular context, bestows gifts on those who live out their commitment to him.

2. Aramaic section (Daniel 2–7): God's direct presence decreases

Daniel 2 and 7: a kingdom established without human hands

Daniel 2 and 7 form the outer layers of the concentrically structured Aramaic section. It should be noted that, from a historical perspective, both these chapters exhibit various signs of having been added to and edited. While supplementary to each other, in their final form they present a specific divine revelation.

Daniel 2 introduces more than one issue. On the one hand it is concerned with how to obtain insight into the unknown future (vv. 13–23; 27–30), in this case the untold dream of king Nebuchadnezzar. On the other hand, the chapter is concerned with the meaning of what is eventually revealed about the future through the dream (vv. 1–12; 24–26; 31–45). As was the case in the introductory chapter, the issues reflect both a particular and a general concern. The avenue through which the puzzling revelation comes to the foreign king is also used to let Daniel in on the secrets of the future—following a plea to God, he receives a vision during the night. This special means of revelation addresses the particular situation that Daniel and his friends, but also the rest of the Babylonian wise men (v. 13), find themselves in. Unlike in the first chapter, where testimony to God's action is placed in the mouth of the narrator, here

God's involvement is confirmed through three instances of direct speech: firstly, in Daniel's prayer of praise (v. 20–23); secondly, in his speech before the king (v. 28); and lastly, in Nebuchadnezzar's praise to God (v. 47).

The content and interpretation of the dream reveal a more general concern (i.e., the fate of successive world powers). Here God's actions are revealed as more remote. In the dream the stone that destroys the multi-tiered statue is seen being cut without hands (v. 34). Only in the interpretation he gives of the dream does Daniel say this means that the God of heaven is responsible for setting up (a causative verb) the last and eternal kingdom (v. 44). God's involvement is revealed as a testimony of inner conviction. God saves Daniel and his friends by providing an outcome in a desperate situation. This is done in an indirect manner, i.e., by revealing a dream and its interpretation. In the short term and in a specific crisis, God is experienced as the one who saves. In the broader context, the conviction being revealed is that the same God of heaven who solved the immediate problem will, in the long run and permanently, come to the aid of his people.

Chapter 7 forms the structural balance to chapter 2. In this chapter it is Daniel who is troubled by a vision in the night. He sees four dreadful creatures, the last of which boasts ten horns. Three of them are uprooted by another horn that has human features. Thrones are established; an ancient of days is seated; and the last beast is destroyed while the others lose their dominion. Finally, the authority is given to one in the likeness of a son of man.

Few chapters in the Hebrew Bible have received the detailed treatment given to Daniel 7. The reason is quite obvious: the rich imagery employed in the chapter indeed opens the door to many interpretations. Here, our main concern is what is revealed about God. The first—striking—aspect of note is that there is no direct reference to God in the chapter. It is quite clear, though, that in the ancient Near Eastern context the Ancient of Days (vv. 9–10, 13, 22) is a symbol used to denote the divine. In this vision, although thousands revere the Ancient of Days, he is not said to be involved in any concrete actions. Daniel's immediate distress as to the meaning of the vision is made known not by God but by "one standing" there, who in this context should be interpreted as an angelic figure. The whole vision has a more universal character than that in chapter 2. The judgment of the brutal beasts is mentioned within the framework of the heavenly court headed by the Ancient of Days. The attention is captured by a description of the divine being on a throne

(vv. 9–10). Through the account of the dazzling clothes, luminous hair, and nobility of this figure, a stark contrast is created with the beasts that represent the four foreign earthly rulers. The fiery throne suggests the holiness of the One seated on it, while the stream of fire flowing from him refers to judgment. In contrast with the fear created by the beasts, the enthroned divine being inspires awe and wonder. This is emphasized by the picture of thousands upon thousands serving him.

In this vision the author draws on different ancient concepts related to the majesty of a supreme ruler in the heavenly realm. Widely held ideas pertaining to the divine in the ancient Near East are captured in the image of the Ancient of Days. The figure of the one in the likeness of a man (v. 13) did not concern Daniel as much as it troubled subsequent commentators. The further clarification that Daniel requires after a concise initial interpretation (vv. 17–18) makes no mention of this enigmatic being (vv. 19–22). The eventual outcome of all these events links up with the outcome envisaged in chapter 2. There shall be an end to foreign rule when an eternal kingdom is installed and the "holy ones of the Most High" receive authority over it. As in chapter 2, the striking notion here is that the "holy ones" are particularly passive in this process. Human intervention is superfluous in a context where divine judgment over beastly rulers is the final word.

Daniel 3 and 6: trust in God's presence

This does not mean, however, that earthly rulers do not have an impact on the lives of people living under their rule here and now. The middle layer of the concentric pattern in the Aramaic section (Dan 3, Dan 6) deals with persecution and the possibility of martyrdom. In both stories the Jewish characters are victimized for keeping to their religious commitments. Neither the context of the exile nor the time of Persian rule attests to such persecution on religious grounds. A commitment to Jewish identity would have been the burning issue in those contexts. The fear of persecution only becomes acute in the face of the threat posed by Antiochus Epiphanes IV.

In chapter 3 God protects his servants as they face persecution. However, God's involvement in the fate of the three men thrown into the fire is indirect, in the sense that they are protected by an angelic figure. In the mouth of Nebuchadnezzar, this being is "like a son of the gods."

Even before this intervention, the role a god can, or rather cannot, play in such dire circumstances is questioned by the king (v. 15). In the eyes of the powerful ruler no god can rescue someone from his hand. The three men, in their answer to the king's haughty claim, again show an intrinsic commitment to their God. He is the one who may be able to rescue them from the king's power. Their uncertainty in the wake of death (v. 18) does not open the door to their retracting the decision not to worship the golden statue (or, evidently, Nebuchadnezzar himself). This is a powerful message: ultimately, even if there is nothing in it for them, they will still serve their God for who he is. Religion is about serving God, not securing a reward.

The three men do not speak again—they don't need to since they are living proof of their God's power. In a clumsy way Nebuchadnezzar tries to praise the God of Shadrach, Meshach and Abednego. Yet in his doxology God's indirect action receives only a brief mention: he sends an angel to save his servants (v. 28). The rest of the tribute is aimed at singing the praises of the men for their actions and commitment. Again, the king maneuvers himself into a position of power, when he announces what harm he will bring to anyone who blasphemes the God of the three men (Fewell, 1991). People in positions of power often just do not understand what true religion is all about.

The literary counterpart to Daniel 3 in the Aramaic section is the story of Daniel in the lions' den in chapter 6. In this case the plot involves jealousy towards Daniel from his fellow courtiers. They seek his downfall by deceiving the king—Darius in this instance—to decree it a capital offence to worship anyone but the king. Daniel is seized when he performs his regular religious acts in the privacy of his dwelling. In contrast to Nebuchadnezzar (in Daniel 3), Darius (in Daniel 6) is portrayed as being much less intoxicated with power. Instead of challenging Daniel's God, the king here utters the wish that Daniel be saved by the God he serves.

After the miraculous act by which Daniel is indeed saved, we hear both him and the king professing the power of God (vv. 23, 27–28). Daniel tells of God's indirect mode of intervention in sending an angel to shut the lions' mouths. In this instance the reason for God's action is more explicit than it is in chapter 3: Daniel mentions that God came to his aid because he was not found guilty of any offence. The sometimes arbitrary laws in human societies are overturned by God's justice on behalf of his servants. The narrator gives a further perspective, not mentioned overtly elsewhere in the narrative: that Daniel trusted his God (v. 24). The doxology placed in the mouth of Darius is more clearly focused on God's praiseworthiness than was Nebuchadnezzar's earlier attempt. The decree to tremble and fear before this God is motivated by a list of his attributes. These are his eternal existence and reign; his ability to save; and his performance of miraculous acts in heaven and on earth. God is praised in general both for who he is and what he can do. The act of saving Daniel from the lions is mentioned as a specific example of his ability.

Daniel 4 and 5: human hubris will end

The focal point of the Aramaic part of the book is chapters 4 and 5. These narratives are presented in the literary form of interpretation stories dealing with a dream vision (Dan 4—a huge tree) and a written revelation (Dan 5—a hand writing on a wall). In both instances the king is perplexed by the revelation (4:5; 5:6) and his advisors are unable to tell its meaning (4:7; 5:8). At last Daniel, in whom dwells the spirit of the holy gods (4:8; 5:11), is summoned (4:8; 5:13-14) and the interpretation he gives comes true (4:28; 5:30).

However, the message of the stories goes beyond the ability to interpret strange phenomena. In fact, unlike in chapters 2 and 7 there is no direct or indirect reference to how the meaning is revealed to Daniel. The issue in these instances is that God has limited tolerance for foreign rulers who forget the boundaries of their powers. In both stories the kings are warned: Nebuchadnezzar (Dan 4) through a dream; Belshazzar (Dan 5) through what happened to "his father" and a hand writing on the wall. As they stand in their final written forms these stories remain as reminders and warnings to foreign rulers who do not realize that they rule by the grace of the Most High. Those who realize and accept their subordinate state before God and express it in their words and deeds may remain in power (4:34–37). Those who do not take these written warnings to heart will not be tolerated, and will be removed (5:25–30). Not only the foreign rulers, but also those under their rule should know "that the Most High has sovereignty over the kingdom of mortals, and gives it to whom he will" (Dan 4:25, 32; cf. 5:21—NRSV). To the foreign rulers this acts as a sure warning, while to their subjects it is a reassurance.

3. Hebrew section (Daniel 8–12): God's alternative presence in absence

The revelation in the last part of the book can be likened to turning back to look at the path one has been travelling on—i.e., walking with one's back towards the future. In a manner typical of apocalyptic literature, this section provides a description of historical events that led to a current state of affairs. The author appreciates that while it is humanly impossible to look into the future, by following the contours of history one can find comfort in the fact that the current situation is also a temporary state that fits into a divinely restricted time frame. Such assurance gives comfort and hope, especially in desperate times.

Daniel 8 and Daniel 10–12 form the two panels around the central section of the Hebrew part of the book located in chapter 9. In Daniel 8 the ancient superpowers that seemingly determine history are symbolized by means of two animals: a ram (Persia) and a goat (Greece). These are in stark contrast to the brutal beasts in the previous chapter. In that context, the Ancient of Days was the anti-type of the beasts. In the last visions, God is not symbolized at all. Even the serene though silent Ancient of Days disappears from the scene. This expresses the all-too-human experience that at the peak of a crisis God is seemingly absent. At the same time, however, the imagery used for the foreign powers—the two domesticated animals—suggests that these powers are controllable. Even the additional symbols referred to in the vision (i.e., horns) are not from the realm of fantasy, but true to the character of these animals.

The crisis in chapter 8 involves the goat challenging God by attacking the external elements of service to him. Explicit reference is made to the ending of the daily sacrifice in the temple. Furthermore, this enemy is succeeding in its endeavor (v. 12). The angelic mediator, in his explanation of the vision, acknowledges the opposition to God and the destruction caused, even beyond the religious context (vv. 24–25). There is, however, a temporal limit set for these exploits. The final action does not belong to the goat's last horn. In fact, this will be broken. The text also mentions explicitly that this will not be done through human actions (v. 25; cf. 2:45). Unlike the Maccabees, this community will wait on a non-human actor to break the forces working against God.

The counterpart to chapter 8 in the concentric structure of the Hebrew section is the extended vision contained in chapters 10–12. Again, no action by the heavenly ruler is described. In fact, the detailed description of the actions of foreign kings does not even mention involvement by God! The access the visionary gets to the heavenly realm is limited to an *angelus interpres* coming from that domain to meet him in an earthly milieu (10:4).

God is mentioned only in the context of an individual humbling himself before him (10:12) or a group knowing him (11:32). In a time of abusive measures by the foreign king, this individual (12:4) as well as the group of "the wise" (11:33—מַשְׂכִּילִים) will become the agents of knowledge and insight. They now perform the divine functions that earlier in the book were the prerogative of God (1:17; 2:23) or his heavenly messengers (7:16; 8:16). As a result they will receive divine attributes of eternal life (12:2; cf. 12:7) and heavenly grandeur (12:3; cf. 10:6). The absence of God in the time of crisis is filled by the presence of the wise who know him, as the Aramaic part makes clear, as a God who can and will act. While the time towards this eventual final event is ticking (12:7, 11, 12), solace should be taken from the teaching of the wise and, within the context of the prophets, the wonderful new promise this entails: eternal life.

In the middle of these two visions, in chapter 9, the central section of the last part of the book revisits the theme of when a real change in the current situation of the Jewish people will be realized. While the surrounding visions give an overview of history in a broad scope, with God almost absent, the focal chapter of this part of the book draws the attention back to God's particular action throughout the *Heilsgeschichte*. The current situation is the result of this divine action, as already stated in the introduction (1:2). But in the final analysis it is the people of Judah and Israel who are at fault (9:7–8). God acted according to his law as given to Moses and subsequently repeated by the prophets, but the people did not adhere to this covenant (9:6).

However, it does not mean that the older tradition should be discarded as obsolete. A word of the prophets that is not listened to nevertheless becomes a word proclaiming new hope. The "seventy years" in Jeremiah is reinterpreted to bring a new message in a current situation. God, who was active throughout Israel's history, is at work in that same tradition, to bring comfort in a particular situation (Dan 9). Also, on a universal scale through the teaching of "the wise," God opens up to his people unimaginable new vistas in their religious thoughts about him, as well as about life and death, in Israel and beyond (Dan 12).

Bibliography

Boccaccini, G. *Roots of Rabbinic Judaism: An Intellectual History, from Ezekiel to Daniel.* Grand Rapids: Eerdmans, 2002.

Collins, J. J. *Daniel.* Hermeneia. Minneapolis: Fortress, 1993.

Fewell, D. N. *Circle of Sovereignty. Plotting Politics in the Book of Daniel.* Nashville, TN: Abingdon, 1991.

Goldingay, J. *Daniel.* Word Biblical Commentary. Dallas: Word, 1989a.

———. *Daniel.* Word Biblical Themes. Dallas: Word, 1989b.

———. "Daniel in the Context of Old Testament Theology." In *The Book of Daniel. Composition and Reception. Volume 2,* edited by John J. Collins and Peter W. Flint, 639–60. Leiden: Brill, 2002.

Humphreys, W. L. "A Life-Style for the Diaspora: A Study of the Tales of Esther and Daniel." *Journal of Biblical Literature,* 92.2 (1973) 211–23.

Lenglet, A. "La structure littéraire de Daniel 2–7." *Biblica* 53 (1972) 169–90.

Merrill Willis, A. C. *Dissonance and the Drama of Divine Sovereignty in the Book of Daniel.* London: T. & T. Clark, 2010.

Seow, C. L. *Daniel.* Westminster Bible Companion. Louisville, KY: Westminster John Knox, 2003.

Contributors

G. Begerau (Gunnar, b. 1972): Lecturer of Old Testament at the Biblical-Theological Academy, Wiedenest, Germany, and Research Associate of the Department of Old Testament Studies at the University of Pretoria, South Africa.

R. Bergey (Ron, b. 1948): Professor of Hebrew and Old Testament at the Faculty Jean Calvin, Aix-en-Provence, France.

J. Dekker (Jaap, b. 1966): Old Testament scholar, teaching Biblical Studies at the Theological Seminary of the Dutch Reformed Churches at the Apeldoorn Theological University, the Netherlands.

D. J. Green (Douglas, b. 1953): Professor of Old Testament and Biblical Theology at Westminster Theological Seminary, Philadelphia, USA.

J. S. Kim (Jinsoo, b. 1965): Assistant Professor at Hapdong Theological Seminary, Suwon, South Korea.

H. H. Klement (Herbert, b. 1949): Professor of Old Testament at the State-Independent University of Theology, Basel, Switzerland, and at the Evangelical Theological Faculty, Leuven, Belgium.

H. A. J. Kruger (Hennie, b. 1944): Professor (retired SRA) of Old Testament at the University of KwaZulu-Natal, Durban, South Africa.

G. Kwakkel (Gert, b. 1959): Professor of Old Testament at the Theological University of the Reformed Churches, Kampen, the Netherlands, and at the Faculty Jean Calvin, Aix-en-Provence, France.

Contributors

M. J. Paul (Mart-Jan, b. 1955): Professor of Old Testament at the Evangelical Theological Faculty, Leuven, Belgium, and at the Christelijke Hogeschool Ede, the Netherlands.

H. G. L. Peels (Eric, b. 1956): Professor of Old Testament at the Theological University of the Christian Reformed Churches, Apeldoorn, the Netherlands, and Research Associate of the Department of Old Testament Studies at the University of the Free State, Bloemfontein, South Africa.

W. H. Rose (Wolter, b. 1964): Senior Lecturer in Semitic Languages and Cultures at the Theological University of the Reformed Churches, Kampen, the Netherlands.

S. D. Snyman (Fanie, b. 1954): Professor of Old Testament at the University of the Free State, Bloemfontein, South-Africa.

D. C. Timmer (Dan, b. 1974): Associate Professor of Old Testament at Reformed Theological Seminary, Jackson, Mississippi, USA.

H. J. M. Van Deventer (Hans, b. 1967): Professor of Biblical Studies at the Vaal Triangle Campus of the North-West University, Vanderbijlpark, South Africa.

H. F. Van Rooy (Herrie, b. 1949): Research Professor in Old Testament and Semitic Languages at the Potchefstroom Campus of the North-West University, South Africa.

M. J. Williams (Michael, b. 1956): Professor of Old Testament at Calvin Theological Seminary, Grand Rapids, Michigan, USA.

Index of Scripture References

Genesis
20:7	2

Exodus
15:20	3
18:8	209
34:4	216
34:6–7	109, 209
7:1	2

Numbers
12:6	7

Deuteronomy
18:9–15	8
18:9–22	4
18:15–18	3
18:15–20	90
18:18	103
18:21–22	5
18:22	9
32:6	203

1 Samuel
9:9	1

2 Samuel
7	6

1 Kings
18:19	8
22:14	8

2 Kings
3:11–19	7
23:4–5	92
23:10–13	92

Ezra
4:1	176

Isaiah
1:2–3	49
1:4	48
1:9	52
1:21	54
1:25	52
2	55
2:4	IX
4:2–6	52
5:1–7	49
5:19	60
6	47
6:1–5	163, 164
6:3	60, 63
6:5	56, 60, 163
6:9–10	50
6:13B	51
7	57
7:3	51
7:9	53

Isaiah (continued)

7:17	61
8:14	50
8:16	44
8:17	51
8:18	54
9:1–6	58, 59
10:5	61
10:20–23	51
11:1–10	58
11:10–16	62
12	55
12:6	53
13:2–5	60
14:4–23	62
14:26–27	60
14:32	54
19:1–25	63
22:20–25	59
24:23	56
25:6–8	63
28–31	45
28:16	53, 54
28:29	60
30:1–7	61
30:8	11
30:10	1
31:1–3	61
32:1–8	59
33:22	56
33:24	56
37:35	58
40:1–11	162
40:22	166
44:13	166
45:1	168
46–48	168
46:1–13	168
46:3	172
46:10	170
51:9—52:12	164
54:5	63
57:15	166
60:14	53
61:1–11	168
63:11–14	169
66:1	164, 166

Jeremiah

1:1–2	101
1:7	101
1:9	3, 101
1:10	105, 108
1:12	101
2:1—4:4	113
2:13	104
2:18	105
2:34	110
2:36	105
3	108
3:12	108
4:23–31	104
5:9	113
5:26–28	110
5:29	113
7:4	111, 116
7:6–10	110
8:18—19:9	113
10	104
10:10	105
11–20	112
11:3–5	109
11:3–8	112
11:10	109
13:23	107
15:14	109
15:16	101
16:2–9	111
17:4	109
18:7–10	6
20:9	101
22:30	116, 191
23	117
23:1–6	191
23:9	111
23:9–32	101
23:25–32	7
26–29	101
26:3	114
27:9	8
28	6
30–31	114
30–33	108
31:1–3	11
31:10	109
31:20	114

Index of Scripture References

31:31–34	114–16
33	114
33:15	117
33:17	117
34:6–7	115
36	10, 107
36:3	114
36:7	114
42:7	6
46–51	106

Ezekiel

1	131
1–3	137
1:28	133
2–3	131
2:3–4	139
2:5	132
2:7	132
5:13	145
6:7	135
7:1–4	137
10	133
11:16–17	147
11:16–20	133
11:17	139
12	132, 138
12:25	146
14:6	141
16	139
17	140
17:24	145
18	142, 143
18:30–32	141
20	5, 136, 139, 147
20:34	147
20:39	136
29	140
33	132, 142
34	138, 144
34:27	136
36:20–23	137
37	138, 144
40–48	134, 144
43:1–5	134

Daniel

1	225–27
1:1	222
2	227, 228
3	229, 230
4	231
5	231
6	229, 230
7	228
8	232
9	11
10–12	232

Hosea

1	34
1:1	27
1:7	36
1:11	37
2	32
2:2–23	29
2:15	30
2:19–20	36
2:20	31
3:5	37
4	33
4:1	31
4:2	31
4:6	31
4:13–14	32
5:4	34
6:6	31
6:7	30, 31
6:8–9	31
6:11	36
8:1	30
9:15	35
10:1–2	33
10:4	33
10:5–6	33
10:9	34
10:13	33
11:8–9	35
11:9	47
11:10–11	35
13:4	30
14:4	36

239

Joel

1:3	216
1:13	216
2:13	215
2:14	216
2:18–27	217, 218
2:18	216
2:21–26	217
2:28	7
3:1–17	219

Amos

1–2	19
1:1	17, 23
1:2	X, 19
2:4	21
3:1–8	18, 19
3:2	21
3:7	7
3:9	21
3:10	20
4:1–3	20
4:6–11	24
4:13	22
5:8–9	22
5:14–15	5
5:18–20	22
5:26	22
6:1–7	20
6:2	22
7:3	24
7:6	24
7:10–17	19
7:14	4
9:5–6	22
9:7	22
9:11–15	18

Obadiah

10	154
12	154
13	152
15–21	152
15	151, 154
17	152
19–21	153
21	153

Jonah

1:9	208
3:3	205
3:4	6
4:2	209
4:11	209

Micah

1:2–5	70–73
2:12	72
2:13	72
4:1–5	71, 74
4:3	IX
4:13	70
5:1	72
5:14	71
7:16–20	70
7:18–20	73

Nahum

1:2	81, 85
1:7	84
1:11	82
1:12	80
2:2	84
3:18–19	85

Habakkuk

1:2–11	121
2:2–20	122
2:2	10
3:2–15	122
3:17–19	122–24

Zephaniah

1:2–3	90
1:4–6	91, 92
1:4	88
1:7	90
1:13	91
1:14	90
1:15	91

Index of Scripture References

1:17–18	91	4	187
2:1–3	92	4:14	187
2:4–15	93	6:5	187
3:8	92	6:12–15	191
3:9–10	94	6:13	191
3:14–20	94	7–8	191
		8:20–23	190
		9–14	193

Haggai

		9:9–10	192
1:3–11	179	9:9–17	189
1:13	180	9:9	192
1:5	180	12:6	189
2:4	180	12:8	192
2:15	180	12:10–14	189
2:7	181	14:12–13	190
2:22	181	14:17	190

Zechariah

Malachi

1:1–6	190	1:2–4	199
1:7–8	190	1:6	200
1:10–11	186	1:11	199
1:16	188	2:10	203
2:1–13	190	2:13–16	202
2:4–5	188	2:17—13:7	201
2:10	192	3:1–4	203
3:8	191	3:7–12	200, 201

www.ingramcontent.com/pod-product-compliance
Lightning Source LLC
Chambersburg PA
CBHW050852230426
43667CB00012B/2249